WEST ACADEMIC PUBLISHING'S LAW SCHOOL ADVISORY BOARD

JESSE H. CHOPER
Professor of Law and Dean Emeritus,
University of California, Berkeley

JOSHUA DRESSLER
Distinguished University Professor, Frank R. Strong Chair in Law
Michael E. Moritz College of Law, The Ohio State University

YALE KAMISAR
Professor of Law Emeritus, University of San Diego
Professor of Law Emeritus, University of Michigan

MARY KAY KANE
Professor of Law, Chancellor and Dean Emeritus,
University of California, Hastings College of the Law

LARRY D. KRAMER
President, William and Flora Hewlett Foundation

JONATHAN R. MACEY
Professor of Law, Yale Law School

ARTHUR R. MILLER
University Professor, New York University
Formerly Bruce Bromley Professor of Law, Harvard University

GRANT S. NELSON
Professor of Law, Pepperdine University
Professor of Law Emeritus, University of California, Los Angeles

A. BENJAMIN SPENCER
Earle K. Shawe Professor of Law,
University of Virginia School of Law

JAMES J. WHITE
Robert A. Sullivan Professor of Law Emeritus,
University of Michigan

TRADEMARK AND UNFAIR COMPETITION
IN A NUTSHELL®

SECOND EDITION

MARK D. JANIS
Robert A. Lucas Chair of Law
Indiana University Maurer School of Law

The publisher is not engaged in rendering legal or other professional advice, and this publication is not a substitute for the advice of an attorney. If you require legal or other expert advice, you should seek the services of a competent attorney or other professional.

Nutshell Series, In a Nutshell and the Nutshell Logo are trademarks registered in the U.S. Patent and Trademark Office.

© 2013 LEG, Inc. d/b/a West Academic Publishing
© 2017 LEG, Inc. d/b/a West Academic
    444 Cedar Street, Suite 700
    St. Paul, MN 55101
    1-877-888-1330

West, West Academic Publishing, and West Academic are trademarks of West Publishing Corporation, used under license.

Printed in the United States of America

ISBN: 978-1-63460-906-7

PREFACE

There's a rumor that trademark and unfair competition law is easier to comprehend than any other branch of intellectual property law. Don't place too much stock in it. It's true that trademark cases feature more accessible fact patterns than, say, patent cases, and it's true that the trademark statute isn't as dense as some parts of the patent or copyright statutes.

Nonetheless, trademark law presents some subtle difficulties that have tripped up unsuspecting students over the years. One such difficulty is that trademark law encompasses a dual system of registered and unregistered rights—not the norm in U.S. intellectual property law. A second is that trademark law rests heavily on evidence of consumer perceptions, and consumers are notoriously fickle. A third is that trademark law is only beginning to grapple with the challenges presented by online advertising practices and global commerce. And there are others.

This Nutshell addresses the major doctrines of U.S. trademark and unfair competition law, with a small section devoted to state right of publicity law. It is designed for use in conjunction with trademarks and unfair competition law courses, or with the trademark law unit of intellectual property survey courses. The book may be used alongside any trademark law casebook, although the organizational structure tracks that of the casebook

Trademarks and Unfair Competition: Law and Policy by Graeme B. Dinwoodie and Mark D. Janis.

The book attempts to present trademark law in a straightforward, concise way. It summarizes the leading cases and attempts to show the ways in which those cases fit together coherently. It addresses the policy debates that underlie these cases. It also explains the technical analyses that students tend to find most difficult, such as the analysis of priority and use.

There's another rumor about trademark and unfair competition law: it's more fun to study than any other branch of intellectual property law. This, of course, is true.

MARK D. JANIS
Bloomington, Indiana

August 2017

ACKNOWLEDGMENTS

I'm grateful for help from many excellent research assistants on this book, including Leslie Prill and Emily Pence (on the First Edition) and Ryan McDonnell (on the Second Edition). Allison Hess and Casey Nemecek provided outstanding administrative support, as usual. I'm especially indebted to Graeme Dinwoodie, who has taught me much trademark law in the course of our collaborations over many years.

OUTLINE

PREFACE III
ACKNOWLEDGMENTS V
TABLE OF CASES XV

Chapter 1. Introduction to Trademark and Unfair Competition 1
A. Nature of Trademarks 1
B. Nature of Unfair Competition; Relationship with Trademarks 6
C. Overview of the U.S. Trademark System 9
    1. Purposes of the Trademark System 9
    2. Sources of Law; Institutions 11
    3. Introduction to the Major Lanham Act Causes of Action 14
D. Overview of This Text 16

Chapter 2. Distinctiveness 19
A. The Distinctiveness Spectrum 21
B. Descriptiveness; Secondary Meaning 26
C. Genericness 30
    1. Two-Part Test: Relevant Class of Goods/Services + Primary Significance ... 31
        a. Identifying a Relevant Class of Goods/Services 31
        b. Proving Primary Significance 32
    2. Time Frame of the Genericness Inquiry 36
    3. Remedies in Genericness Cases 37
D. Distinctiveness of Non- Verbal Identifiers 39
    1. Logos 40

	2.	Color 42
	3.	Trade Dress.. 43
	4.	Exotic Source Identifiers............................ 49
E.	The Trademark/Copyright Interface................ 50

Chapter 3. Functionality.. 57
A. Categories of Functionality................................ 59
    1. Utilitarian Functionality 59
    2. Aesthetic Functionality.............................. 60
B. The Modern Supreme Court Analysis for Functionality 61
    1. Predecessors to the Modern Supreme Court Analysis 61
    2. Modern Supreme Court Analysis: *TrafFix* Devices.. 65
C. Applying the Modern Supreme Court Functionality Analysis After *TrafFix*.............. 71
    1. Evidence from Utility Patents 71
    2. Evidence of Alternative Designs.............. 74
    3. Examples: Applying the Utilitarian Functionality Test 78
    4. Examples: Applying the Aesthetic Functionality Test 80

Chapter 4. Use 87
A. Use as a Jurisdictional Prerequisite 87
B. Use as a Prerequisite for Establishing Rights.. 89
    1. Actual Use.. 90
    2. Constructive Use 99
    3. Specialized Doctrines for Assessing Priority of Use.. 103

		4.	Identifying the User; Use for the Benefit of Another 110
C.	Non-Use and the Failure to Control Uses 115		
		1.	Non-Use 116
		2.	Failure to Control Uses 119

Chapter 5. Registration 129

A. Procedural Aspects of Registration 130
    1. Application: Bases for Registration 130
    2. Examination; Fraudulent Procurement 134
    3. Appeal 137
    4. Publication; Opposition 138
    5. Post-Registration Process: Renewal; Cancellation; Incontestability 139

B. Substantive Aspects of Registration: Section 2 Bars 145
    1. Section 2(a) Scandalous/ Disparaging Marks 146
    2. Section 2(a) Deceptiveness 149
    3. Sections 2(a) and 2(e): Geographic Indications and Geographic Marks 150
    4. Sections 2(c); 2(a); 2(e)(4): Name Marks 158
    5. Section 2(d) Confusion Bar 163
    6. Section 2(e) Descriptiveness Bar 165
    7. Other Section 2 Bars 165

Chapter 6. Geographic Limits on Trademark Rights 167

A. Geographic Limits on Common Law Rights: *Tea Rose* Doctrine 168

- B. Geographic Limits and Registered Rights 176
  1. The *Dawn Donut* Rule 176
  2. Junior Registrant vs. Senior User 180
  3. Senior Registrant vs. "Intermediate" Junior User: Lanham Act Section 33(b)(5) 182
  4. Registrant vs. Registrant: Concurrent Use Registrations; Limited Area Defense 183
- C. The Territorial Nature of U.S. Trademark Rights 185
  1. Territoriality and the Rule from *Person's* 185
  2. Well-Known Marks 190
- D. The Extraterritorial Enforcement of U.S. Trademark Rights 201

Chapter 7. Confusion-Based Trademark Liability Theories 209
- A. Introduction 209
- B. Actionable Use 213
- C. The Factors Analysis 220
  1. Overview; Introduction to the Factors Analysis 220
  2. Applying the Factors Analysis: Rules of Thumb 230
     a. Similarity of Marks 231
     b. Mark Strength 237
     c. Actual Confusion 239
     d. Relatedness of Goods 243
     e. Other Factors: Intent; Reasonably Prudent Purchaser 245

D.	Confusion Away from the Point of Sale 247	
	1. Initial Interest Confusion 248	
	2. Post-Sale Confusion 255	
E.	Reverse Confusion 259	
F.	Indirect and Vicarious Theories of Liability 264	

Chapter 8. Non-Confusion-Based Claims: Dilution, Cybersquatting, and Counterfeiting **273**

A. Dilution 273
    1. Origins and Evolution of the Dilution Theory 274
    2. Dilution Under the Lanham Act 275
    3. Dilution in the Registration Context 292
B. Cybersquatting 293
    1. Anticybersquatting Consumer Protection Act (ACPA): Lanham Act Section 43(d) 294
    2. ICANN Uniform Domain Name Dispute Resolution Policy (UDRP) 299
    3. The Relationship Between the UDRP and ACPA 301
C. Counterfeiting 302
    1. Civil Liability for Counterfeiting 302
    2. Criminal Liability for Counterfeiting 306
    3. Protection Against Counterfeit Imports 309

Chapter 9. Permissible Uses of Another's Trademark **311**

A. Fair Use of Another's Trademark 311
    1. Descriptive ("Classic") Fair Use 313

	2.	Nominative Fair Use 322
	3.	Fair Use Defenses to Dilution 328
B.	Use of Another's Trademark on Genuine Goods 332
C.	Use of Another's Trademark in Parody, Art, or Speech 344

Chapter 10. False Advertising 353
A. The Evolution of Section 43(a) False Advertising Claims 353
   1. Predecessors to the Modern Section 43(a) False Advertising Claim 353
   2. Post-1988 Section 43(a)(1)(B) 355
B. Threshold Issues in Section 43(a)(1)(B) False Advertising Claims 356
   1. Standing 357
   2. "Commercial Advertising or Promotion" 360
C. Elements of the Section 43(a)(1)(B) False Advertising Claim 362
   1. Falsity and Deception 363
   2. Materiality 368
   3. Causation and Injury 369
D. Remedies 371

Chapter 11. Endorsement, Attribution, and the Right of Publicity 375
A. Section 43(a) False Affiliation Theories 376
   1. False Over-Attribution 377
   2. False Under-Attribution ("Reverse Passing Off") 379

B.	The Right of Publicity 383	
	1.	Origins; Justifications; Relationship with Right of Privacy 384
	2.	Overview of Elements; In-Gross Property Right; Relationship with Copyright and Trademark 387
	3.	Protectable Aspects of Identity 389
	4.	Commercial Purposes; Limitations 392
	5.	Jurisdiction; Choice of Law 398
	6.	Remedies; Duration 399

Chapter 12. Remedies 401
A. Equitable Remedies and Limitations: Injunctive Relief; Laches 401
    1. Preliminary Injunctions 402
    2. Permanent Injunctions 405
    3. Laches 408
B. Monetary Relief 412

INDEX 419

TABLE OF CASES

References are to Pages

A & H Sportswear, Inc. v. Victoria's Secret Stores, Inc., 220, 261
A. Bourjois & Co., Inc. v. Katzel, 340
A.J. Canfield Co. v. Honickman, 32
Abdul-Jabbar v. General Motors Corp., 377
Abercrombie & Fitch Co. v. Hunting World, Inc., 22
Abercrombie & Fitch Co. v. Moose Creek, Inc., 246
Abercrombie & Fitch Stores, Inc. v. American Eagle Outfitters, 80
Able Time, United States v., 309
Academy of Motion Picture Arts & Sciences v. Creative House Promotions, Inc., 255
Adair, In re, 95
Advertise.com, Inc. v. AOL Advertising, Inc., 34
Airs Aromatics, LLS v. Opinion Victoria's Secret Stores Brand Mgmt., Inc., 141
Allard Enters., Inc. v. Advanced Programming Res., Inc., 96
Already, LLC v. Nike, Inc., 20
Amazing Spaces, Inc. v. Metro Mini Storage, 40, 41
American Circuit Breaker Corp. v. Oregon Breakers Inc., 340
American Express Co. v. Goetz, 107
American Greetings Corp. v. Dan-Dee Imports, Inc., 403
American Thermos Prods. Co. v. Aladdin Indus., Inc., 36
American Waltham Watch Co. v. United States Watch Co., 319
Ancient Egyptian Arabic Order v. Michaux, 409
Anheuser-Busch, Inc. v. Balducci Publications, 345
Anti-Monopoly, Inc. v. General Mills Fun Group, Inc., 31
Apotex Inc. v. Acorda Therapeutics, Inc., 368
Apple Inc. v. Samsung Elecs. Co., Ltd., 75
Arlington Specialties, Inc. v. Urban Aid, Inc., 77
Arnold v. ABC, Inc., 317
Attrezzi LLC v. Maytag Corp., 262
Aunt Jemima Mills Co. v. Rigney & Co., 243

TABLE OF CASES

Australian Gold, Inc. v. Hatfield, 248
Au-Tomotive Gold, Inc. v. Volkswagen of America, Inc., 84, 408
Aycock Engineering, Inc. v. Airflite, Inc., 95
B&B Hardware, Inc. v. Hargis Indus., Inc., 228, 229
Baker v. DeShong, 416
Banjo Buddies, Inc. v. Renosky, 413
Barcamerica Int'l USA Trust v. Tyfield Importers Inc., 122
Barcelona.com v. Excelentisimo Ayuntamiento de Barcelona, 301
BASF Corp. v. Old World Trading Co., 370
Bayer, AG, In re, 26
Becton, Dickinson & Co., In re, 73, 75
Bell v. Streetwise Records, Ltd., 113
Belmora, LLC v. Bayer Consumer Care AG, 199
Big O Tire Dealers v. Goodyear Tire and Rubber Co., 260
Blinded Veterans Assn. v. Blinded American Veterans Found., 39
Board of Supervisors of LSU v. Smack Apparel, 48
Bolger v. Youngs Drug Prods. Corp., 348
Borden Ice Cream Co. v. Borden's Condensed Milk Co., 210
Bose Corp., In re, 135
Boston Professional Hockey Association, Inc. v. Dallas Cap & Emblem Mfg., Inc., 221
Bourdeau Bros., Inc. v. I.T.C., 338
Bretford Mfg. Inc. v. Smith Sys. Mfg. Corp., 381
Bridgestone Americas Tire Operations, LLC v. Federal Corp., 238
Bridgestone/Firestone Research Inc. v. Automobile Club de l'Ouest de la France, 410
Bright Beginnings v. Care Comm., 172
Brilliance Audio, Inc. v. Haights Cross Comm'ns, Inc., 333
Brookfield Communications, Inc. v. West Coast Ent. Corp., 105, 106, 250
Brother Records, Inc. v. Jardine, 324
Brunswick Corp. v. British Seagull Ltd., 65
Budge Mfg. Co., Inc., In re, 149
Buffett v. Chi-Chi's, Inc., 160
Burke-Parsons-Bowlby Corp. v. Appalachian Log Homes, Inc., 152

TABLE OF CASES XVII

C.B.C. Distrib. & Mktg., Inc. v. Major League Baseball Advanced Media, 397
C.P. Interests, Inc. v. California Pools, Inc., 171
Cairns v. Franklin Mint Co., 314, 323
California Innovations, Inc., In re, 155
Callaway Golf Co. v. Slazenger, 364
Camel Hair & Cashmere Inst., Inc. v. Associated Dry Goods Corp., 359
Campbell v. Acuff-Rose Music, Inc., 345
Cardtoons, L.C. v. Major League Baseball Players Ass'n, 392
Car-Freshner Corp. v. S.C. Johnson & Son, Inc., 312, 317, 322
Carson v. Here's Johnny Portable Toilets, Inc., 390
Cashmere & Camel Hair Mfrs. Inst. v. Saks Fifth Avenue, 370
Castrol, Inc. v. Pennzoil Co., 363
Cedar Point, Inc., In re, 95
Central Hudson Gas & Elec. Corp. v. Public Serv. Comm'n of N.Y., 372
Central Mfg., Inc. v. Brett, 92
Century 21 Real Estate Corp. v. Lendingtree, Inc., 323
Chamberlain v. Columbia Pictures Corp., 354
Champion Spark Plug Co. v. Sanders, 335
Champions Golf Club, Inc. v. The Champions Golf Club, Inc., 183
Chance v. Pac-Tel Teletrac, Inc., 98
Chatam Int'l, Inc., In re, 235
Cheatham v. Paisano, Pubs., 385, 390
Checkpoint Sys., Inc. v. Check Point Software Technologies, Inc., 210
Chippendales USA, Inc., In re, 25, 48
Chong Lam, United States v., 307
Christian Faith Fellowship Church v. adidas AG, 89
Christian Louboutin S.A. v. Yves Saint Laurent America Holding, Inc., 82
Citigroup Inc. v. Capital City Bank Group, 233
Clark & Freeman Corp. v. Heartland Co. Ltd., 125
Clarke, In re, 49
Cleary v. News Corp., 380
Clorox Co. Puerto Rico v. Proctor & Gamble Comm. Co., 365

Coach Services, Inc. v. Triumph Learning LLC, 239, 245, 279

Coastal Abstract Serv., Inc. v. First Am. Tit. Ins. Co., 360

Coca-Cola Co. v. Busch, 114

Coca-Cola Co. v. Purdy, 297

Comedy III Productions, Inc. v. New Line Cinema, 51

Comedy III Productions, Inc. v. Saderup, 395

Community of Christ Copyright Corp. v. Devon Park Restoration Branch of Jesus Christ's Church, 116

Computer Food Stores, Inc. v. Corner Store Franchises, Inc., 107

Conopco, Inc. v. May Dept. Stores, 242

Conte Bros. Automotive, Inc. v. Quaker State-Slick 50, Inc., 358

Cordua Restaurants, Inc., In re, 26

Cosmetically Sealed Industries, Inc. v. Chesebrough-Pond's USA Co., 317, 321

Couture v. Playdom, Inc., 96

Covertech Fabricating, Inc. v. TVM Building Prods., Inc., 111

CreAgri, Inc. v. USANA Health Sciences, Inc., 108

Crocker Nat'l Bank v. Canadian Imperial Bank of Commerce, 108, 132

Cuisinarts, Inc. v. Robot-Coupe Int'l Corp., 365

Custom Vehicles, Inc. v. Forest River, Inc., 92, 94

DaimlerChrysler AG v. Bloom, 215

Dastar Corp. v. Twentieth Century Fox Film Corp., 8, 52, 376, 380

David Sherman Corp. v. Heublein, Inc., 232

Davidoff & CIE, SA v. PLD Int'l Corp., 335

Davis v. Electronic Arts Inc., 396

Davis v. Walt Disney Co., 349

Dawn Donut Co., Inc. v. Hart's Food Stores, Inc., 111, 120, 176

Delaware & Hudson Canal Co. v. Clark, 312

Designer Skin LLC v. S & L Vitamins Inc., 253

Diallo, United States v., 308

Dippin' Dots, Inc. v. Frosty Bites Distrib., 79

Doe v. TCI Cablevision, 396

Dorpan S.L. v. Hotel Melia, Inc., 181

Downing v. Abercrombie & Fitch, 377

Dryer v. National Football League, 388

DSPT Int'l, Inc. v. Nahum, 296, 297
Duty Free Americas, Inc. v. Estee Lauder Cos., Inc., 363
E.I. DuPont de Nemours & Co. v. Yoshida Int'l, Inc., 35
E.S.S. Ent. 2000, Inc. v. Rock Star Videos, Inc., 350
E.T. Browne Drug Co. v. Cococare Prods., Inc., 30
East Iowa Plastics, Inc. v. PI, Inc., 137
eBay Inc. v. MercExchange, L.L.C., 371, 402
Eco Mfg. LLC v. Honeywell Int'l Inc., 79
Elliot v. Google, Inc., 34
Elvis Presley Enterprises Inc. v. Capece, 244, 348
Emergency One v. American FireEagle, 116, 117
EMI Catalogue P'ship v. Hill, Holiday, Connors, 321
Empresa Cubana Del Tabaco v. Culbro Corp., 199
Enesco v. Price/Costco Inc., 335
Eppendorf-Netheler-Hinz GmbH v. Ritter GmbH, 76
ERBE Elektromedizin Gmbh v. Canady Technology LLC, 82
ETW Corp. v. Jireh Publ'g, Inc., 351, 378, 396
Eva's Bridal Ltd. v. Halanick Enterprises, Inc., 120, 121
Exxon Corp. v. Humble Exploration Co., Inc., 117
Facenda v. NFL Films, Inc., 377, 389
Fair Isaac Corp. v. Experian Information Solutions, Inc., 137
Fair Wind Sailing, Inc. v. Dempster, 416
Fashion Boutique of Short Hills, Inc. v. Fendi USA, Inc., 361
Federal Treasury Enterprise Sojuzplodoimport v. Spirits Int'l N.V., 144
Ferrari S.p.A. Esercizio Fabbriche Automobili E Corse v. McBurnie, 118
Ferrari S.p.A. v. Roberts, 256
Fifty-Six Hope Road Music, Ltd. v. A.V.E.L.A., Inc., 378, 414
Filipino Yellow Pages, Inc. v. Asian Journal Pubs., Inc., 34
First Draft, Inc., In re, 52
First Health Group Corp. v. BCE Emergis Corp., 360
First Niagara Ins. Brokers Inc. v. First Niagara Financial Group, Inc., 190
Fleischmann Distilling Corp. v. Maier Brewing Co., 212, 245
FN Herstal SA v. Clyde Armory Inc., 98
Foote, United States v., 307

TABLE OF CASES

Forney Indus., Inc. v. Daco of Missouri, 42
Forschner Group v. Arrow Trading Co., 152
Fortune Dynamic, Inc. v. Victoria's Secret Stores Brand Mgmt., Inc., 315, 318
FreecycleSunnyvale v. Freecycle Network, 121
Gabbanelli Accordions & Imports, LLC v. Ditta Gabbanelli Ubaldo di Elio Gabbanelli, 305
Gamut Trading Co. v. U.S.I.T.C., 342, 344
General Motors Corp. v. Keystone Automotive Indus., Inc., 256
General Motors Corp. v. Lanard Toys, Inc., 80
General Motors Corp. v. Urban Gorilla, LLC, 259
Genesee Brewing Company, Inc. v. Stroh Brewing Co., 32
Gensler v. Strabala, 54
George Basch Co., Inc. v. Blue Coral, Inc., 415
Gibson Guitar Corp. v. Paul Reed Smith Guitars, LP, 254
Global Tech v. SEB, 267, 271
GoPets Ltd. v. Hise, 295
Gordon & Breach Science Publishers, S.A. v. American Inst. of Physics, 360
GoTo.com, Inc. v. Walt Disney Co., 226, 403
Grocery Outlet Inc. v. Albertson's Inc., 123
Groeneveld Transport Efficiency, Inc. v. Lubcore Int'l, Inc., 78
Groupe SEB USA, Inc. v. Euro-Pro Operating LLC, 368, 372
Grupo Gigante v. Dallo & Co., Inc., 192
Guthrie Healthcare System v. Contextmedia, Inc., 179
H. Marvin Ginn Corp. v. Int'l Ass'n of Fire Chiefs, Inc., 31
Haelan Labs., Inc. v. Topps Chewing Gum, Inc., 384
Hamilton-Brown Shoe Co. v. Wolf Bros. & Co., 151
Hana Financial, Inc. v. Hana Bank, 106
Hancock v. American Steel & Wire Co., 232
Hanover Star Milling Co. v. Metcalf, 2, 3, 6, 168
Hard Rock Cafe Licensing Corp. v. Concession Servs., Inc., 271
Harley-Davidson v. Grottanelli, 37
Harper House, Inc. v. Thomas Nelson, Inc., 373
Harrods Ltd. v. Sixty Internet Domain Names, 299
Haughton Elevator Co. v. Seeberger, 35
Herb Reed Enters., LLC v. Fla. Entm't Mgmt., Inc., 404
Hermes Int. v. Lederer de Paris Fifth Ave., 258

Hoefflin, In re, 159
Holiday Inns, Inc. v. 800 Reservation, Inc., 214
Hugunin v. Land O' Lakes, Inc., 282
Hyson USA, Inc. v. Hyson 2U, Ltd., 411
I.P. Lund Trading ApS v. Kohler Co., 278
Illinois High School Ass'n v. GTE Vantage Inc., 114
Institute for Scientific Info., Inc. v. Gordon & Breach, Science Publishers, Inc., 321
Intermed Commc'ns, Inc. v. Chaney, 95
International Bancorp LLC v. Societe des Bains de Mer et du Cercle des Etrangers a Monaco, 188
International Information Systems Security Certification Consortium, Inc. v. Security University, LLC, 326
International Kennel Club of Chicago, Inc. v. Mighty Star, Inc., 29
International News Service v. Associated Press, 7
International Stamp Art, Inc. v. United States Postal Service, 321
Internet Specialties West v. Milon-Digiorgio Enters., Inc., 409
Interstellar Starship Services, Ltd. v. Epix, Inc., 252
Investacorp, Inc. v. Arabian Investment Banking Corp. E.C., 27
Inwood Labs., Inc. v. Ives Labs., Inc., 66, 265
ITC Ltd. v. Punchgini, Inc., 118, 195, 198, 199
J & J Snack Foods Corp. v. McDonald's Corp., 236
Jack Russell Terrier Network of Northern California v. American Kennel Club, Inc., 379
Jada Toys, Inc. v. Mattel, Inc., 237
Jay Franco & Sons, Inc. v. Franek, 71, 81
Jet, Inc. v. Sewage Aeration Systems, 229
John Allan Co. v. Craig Allen Co., 407
Johnny Blastoff, Inc. v. L.A. Rams Football Co., 97
Johnson & Johnson v. Carter-Wallace, Inc., 354
Joint-Stock Co. "Baik", In re, 152
Jordan v. Jewel Food Stores, Inc., 394
Jules Jordan Video, Inc. v. 144942 Canada Inc., 388
K Mart Corp. v. Cartier, Inc., 342
Karl Storz Endoscopy-America, Inc. v. Surgical Technologies, Inc., 337
Kehoe Component Sales, Inc. v. Best Lighting Prods., Inc., 382

Kelly Services, Inc. v. Creative Harbor, LLC, 100
Kentucky Fried Chicken Corp. v. Diversified Packaging Corp., 123
King v. Innovation Books, 379
King-Seeley Thermos Co. v. Aladdin Indus., Inc., 39
King-Size, Inc. v. Frank's King Size Clothes, Inc., 312
KP Permanent Make-Up, Inc. v. Lasting Impression I, Inc., 312, 314, 318
Kraft Foods Group Brands LLC v. Cracker Barrel Old Country Store, Inc., 241
L & J.G. Stickley, Inc. v. Canal Dover Furniture Co., Inc., 119
L.D. Kichler Co. v. Davoil, Inc., 135
L.E. Waterman Co. v. Modern Pen Co., 320
L'Aiglon Apparel v. Lana Lobell, Inc., 354
La Quinta Worldwide LLC v. Q.R.T.M., S.A., 405
Lacoste Alligator S.A. v. Everlast World's Boxing Headquarters, 231
Lahoti v. VeriCheck, Inc., 297
Lamparello v. Falwell, 252, 296
Larami Corp. v. Talk to Me Programs, Inc., 102
Larry Harmon Pictures Corp. v. Williams Restaurant Corp., 88
Laws v. Sony Music Entertainment, Inc., 388
Leelanau Wine Cellars Ltd. v. Black & Red Inc., 319
Les Halles de Paris, J.V., In re, 154, 157
Lever Brothers Co. v. United States of America, 342
Levi Strauss & Co. v. Abercrombie & Fitch Trading Co., 284
Levitt Corp. v. Levitt, 320
Lexmark International, Inc. v. Static Control Components, Inc., 200, 357
Libman Co. v. Vining Indus., Inc., 232, 240
Lindy Pen Co., Inc. v. Bic Pen Corp., 414
Lockheed Martin Corp. v. Network Solutions, Inc., 267
Loew's Theatres, Inc., In re, 153
Louis Vuitton Malletier v. Dooney & Bourke, 232
Louis Vuitton Malletier, S.A. v. Akanoc Solutions, Inc., 269, 305
Louis Vuitton Malletier, S.A. v. Haute Diggity Dog, LLC, 285, 289, 290, 329, 345
Louis Vuitton Malletier, S.A. v. LY USA, Inc., 305

Louis Vuitton Malletier, S.A. v. My Other Bag, Inc., 330
Lugosi v. Universal Pictures, 392
Lyons Partnership v. Giannoulas, 349
M.Z. Berger & Co., Inc. v. Swatch AG, 100
M2 Software Inc. v. M2 Communications Inc., 235
Majestic Distilling Co., In re, 240
Malletier v. Burlington Coat Factory Warehouse, Corp., 231
Maloney v. T3 Media, 388
Marriott Corp., In re, 92
Marshak v. Treadwell, 410
Martin v. Carter Hawley Hale Stores, Inc., 159
Martin's Herend Imports, Inc. v. Diamond & Gem Trading USA, Co., 343
Mastercrafters Clock & Radio Co. v. Vacheron & Constantin-Le Coultre Watches, Inc., 255
Matal v. Tam, 147
Mattel, Inc. v. MCA Records, 350
Mattel, Inc. v. Walking Mountain, Prods., 350
May Dept. Stores Co. v. Prince, 111
Mayer/Berkshire Corp. v. Berkshire Fashions, Inc., 229
McAirlaids, Inc. v. Kimberly-Clark Corp., 73, 76
McBee v. Delica Co., 204
McDermott v. San Francisco Women's Motorcycle Contingent, 139
McDonald's Corp. v. Druck and Gerner, D.D, 236
McFarland v. Miller, 392, 399
McLean v. Fleming, 409
McNeil Nutritionals v. Heartland Sweeteners, 242
Mead Data Cent., Inc. v. Toyota Motor Sales U.S.A., Inc., 275, 282
Medinol Ltd. v. Neuro Vasx, Inc., 135
Merck Eprova AG v. Gnosis S.p.A., 366, 414
Metro Traffic Control, Inc. v. Shadow Network, Inc., 135
Metro-Goldwyn-Mayer Studios Inc. v. Grokster, 267
Midler v. Ford Motor Co., 391
Millennium Laboratories, Inc. v. Ameritox, Ltd., 75
Mil-Mar Shoe Co., Inc. v. Shonac Corp., 33
Mishawaka Rubber & Woolen Mfg. Co. v. S.S. Kresge Co., 2
Mobil Oil Corp. v. Pegasus Petroleum Corp., 249
Montana v. San Jose Mercury News, Inc., 393

XXIV   *TABLE OF CASES*

Morgan Brown, In re, 108
Morton-Norwich Prods., Inc., In re, 61
Moseley v. V Secret Catalogue, Inc., 277
Mother's Restaurants, Inc. v. Mother's Other Kitchen, Inc., 192
Motschenbacher v. R.J. Reynolds Tobacco Co., 390
MPC Franchise, LLC v. Tarntino, 136
Multi Time Machine, Inc. v. Amazon.com, Inc., 253
Murphy Door Bed Co. v. Interior Sleep Sys., Inc., 35, 39
Nantucket, Inc., In re, 153
National Ass'n for Healthcare Communications, Inc. v. Central Arkansas Area Agency on Aging, Inc., 171, 173
National Basketball Ass'n v. Motorola, Inc., 369
National Business Forms & Printing, Inc. v. Ford Motor Co., 281
Natural Answers Inc. v. SmithKline Beecham Corp., 117
Network Automation, Inc. v. Advanced Systems Concepts, Inc., 219, 225, 226, 251
New England Duplicating Co. v. Mendes, 93
New Kids on the Block v. News Am. Publ'g Inc., 323
New West Corp. v. NYM Co. of Cal., Inc., 93, 98
Newbridge Cutlery Co., In re the, 151
Newport News Holdings Corp. v. Virtual City Vision, Inc., 296
Nextel Comm., Inc. v. Motorola, Inc., 50
Nike, Inc. v. Maher, 287
Nissan Motor Co. v. Nissan Computer Corp., 279
Nitro Leisure Prods., L.L.C. v. Acushnet Co., 337
Nora Beverages, Inc. v. Perrier Group of America, Inc., 37, 234
Northern Light Tech., Inc. v. Northern Lights Club, 297
Novartis Consumer Health, Inc. v. Johnson & Johnson-Merck Consumer Pharm. Co., 364, 367
Octane Fitness, LLC v. Icon Health & Fitness, Inc., 415
Oliveira v. Frito-Lay, Inc., 51
One Indus., LLC v. Jim O'Neal Dist., Inc., 105
Oppedahl & Larson, LLP, In re, 25
Oriental Financial Group, Inc. v. Cooperativa de Ahorro y Credito Oriental, 405
Original Appalachian Artworks v. Granada Electronics, 343
PACCAR Inc. v. Telescan Techs., L.L.C., 326

TABLE OF CASES　　　　　　　　XXV

Packard Press, Inc. v. Hewlett-Packard Co., 235
Packman v. Chicago Tribune Co., 321
Pagliero v. Wallace China Co., 63
Panavision Int'l v. Toeppen, 293
Paramount Pictures Corp. v. White, 94
Park 'n Fly, Inc. v. Dollar Park and Fly, Inc., 143
Parks v. LaFace Records, 351
Patsy's Italian Restaurant, Inc. v. Banas, 176
PBM Prods., LLC v. Mead Johnson & Co., 371
Peaceable Planet, Inc. v. Ty, Inc., 162
PepsiCo, Inc. v. Grapette Co., 126
Pernod Ricard USA, LLC v. Bacardi U.S.A., Inc., 366
Person's Co. Ltd. v. Christman, 185
Petrella v. Metro-Goldwyn-Mayer, Inc., 412
Petroliam Nasional Berhad v. GoDaddy.com, Inc., 298
Phoenix Ent. Partners, LLC v. Rumsey, 55
Pizza Hut, Inc. v. Papa John's Int'l, Inc., 366, 367, 369
Planetary Motion, Inc. v. Techsplosion, Inc., 96
Playboy Enters., Inc. v. Netscape Communications Corp., 250
Playboy Enters., Inc. v. Welles, 324
Polaroid Corp. v. Polarad Electronics Corp., 223
Pom Wonderful LLC v. Coca-Cola Co., 356
Porous Media Corp. v. Pall Corp., 369
PPX Enterprises, Inc. v. Audiofidelity Enterprises, Inc., 412
Prestonettes, Inc. v. Coty, 3, 333
Princeton Vanguard, LLC v. Frito-Lay N. Am., Inc., 31
PRL USA Holdings, Inc. v. United States Polo Ass'n Inc., 407
Pro-Football, Inc. v. Harjo, 411
Progressive Dist. Services, Inc. v. United Parcel Service, Inc., 227
Pyro-Spectaculars, Inc., In re, 163
Qualitex Co. v. Jacobson Prods. Co., Inc., 42, 58, 66
Quick Techs., Inc. v. Sage Group PLC, 413, 414
Quik-Print Copy Shops, Inc., In re, 27
Quiksilver, Inc. v. Kymsta Corp., 183
Radiance Foundation, Inc. v. National Assoc. for the Advancement of Colored People, 330, 347
Rath, In re, 109, 132
Raxton Corp. v. Anania Assocs., 175

XXVI TABLE OF CASES

Rearden LLC v. Rearden Commerce, Inc., 99
Recot, Inc. v. Becton, 239
Red Baron-Franklin Park, Inc. v. Taito Corp., 344
Rescuecom Corp. v. Google Inc., 216
Research in Motion, Ltd. v. Defining Presence Marketing Group, Inc., 332
Ritchie v. Simpson, 139
Robi v. Reed, 113
Rogers v. Grimaldi, 349
Rolex Watch, U.S.A., Inc. v. AFP Imaging Corp., 284, 287, 292
Rolex Watch, U.S.A., Inc. v. Canner, 256
Rolex Watch, U.S.A., Inc. v. Michel, 337
Rose Art Indus. v. Swanson, 236
Rosetta Stone Ltd. v. Google, Inc., 225, 270, 280, 281, 331
Ross Cosmetics Dist. Ctr. v. United States, 310
Samson Crane Corp. v. Union Nat'l Sales, Inc., 369
San Francisco Arts & Athletics, Inc. v. United States Olympic Committee, 352
Sands, Taylor & Wood Co. v. Quaker Oats Co., 260
Sauer, In re, 160
Save Venice New York, Inc., In re, 153
Saxlehner v. Wagner, 327
SCA Hygiene Prods. Aktiebolag v. First Quality Baby Prods., LLC, 412
Scandia Down Corp. v. Euroquilt, Inc., 406
Scarves by Vera, Inc. v. Todo Imports Ltd., 244
Schwan's IP, LLC v. Kraft Pizza Co., 37
Seabrook Foods v. Bar-Well Foods, 40
Secular Organizations for Sobriety, Inc. v. Ullrich, 112
Serbin v. Ziebart Int'l Corp., 359
Seven-Up Co. v. Coca-Cola Co., 360
Shalom Children's Wear Inc. v. In-Wear A/S, 107
Shaw v. Lindheim, 379
Shell Oil Co. v. Commercial Petroleum, Inc., 334
Shell Oil Co., In re, 138, 264
Shniberg, In re, 150
ShutEmDown Sports, Inc. v. Lacy, 135
Sierra On-Line, Inc. v. Phoenix Software, Inc., 321
Silverman v. CBS Inc., 117
Singer Mfg. Co. v. Briley, 37
SKF USA Inc. v. I.T.C., 343

TABLE OF CASES XXVII

Skil Corp. v. Rockwell Int'l Corp., 355
Skydive Arizona, Inc. v. Quattrocchi, 369
Slep-Tone Entertainment Corp. v. Wired for Sound Karaoke and DJ Services, LLC, 55
Slokevage, In re, 46
Smith v. Chanel, Inc., 327
Sony Corp. of America v. Universal City Studios, Inc., 268
Southland Sod Farms v. Stover Seed Co., 362, 367
Sovereign Military Hospitaller Order of Saint John of Jerusalem of Rhodes & of Malta v. Fla. Priory of Knights Hospitallers of Sovereign Order of Saint John of Jerusalem, Knights of Malta, the Ecumenical Order, 136
Specht v. Google Inc., 118
Specialized Seating, Inc. v. Greenwich Industries, L.P., 73, 77
Spirits Int'l N.V., In re, 156
Sports Unlimited, Inc. v. Lankford Enter., Inc., 360
Sporty's Farm L.L.C. v. Sportsman's Market, Inc., 296
SquirtCo. v. Seven-Up Co., 223
Stanfield v. Osborne Indus., Inc., 120
Star Indus., Inc. v. Bacardi & Co., Ltd., 41
Starbucks Corp. v. Wolfe's Borough Coffee, Inc., 284, 286, 287, 289
Starbucks U.S. Brands LLC v. Ruben, 241
Steele v. Bulova Watch Co., 202
Sterling Drug, Inc. v. Bayer AG, 204
Streamline Production Sys., Inc. v. Streamline Mfg., Inc., 240
Sugar Busters v. Brennan, 125
Sullivan v. CBS Corp., 224
SunAmerica Corp. v. Sun Life Assurance Co., 411
SunEarth, Inc. v. Sun Earth Solar Power Co., Ltd., 416
Sunmark, Inc. v. Ocean Spray Cranberries, Inc., 313
Swatch AG v. Beehive Wholesale, LLC, 138
Sweetarts v. Sunline, Inc., 172
Synergistic Int'l LLC v. Korman, 413, 414
Syngenta Seeds v. Delta Cotton Co-operative, Inc., 382
T.A.B. Sys. v. Pactel Teletrac, 107
Talk to Me Products, Inc. v. Larami Corp., 102
Tally-Ho, Inc. v. Coast Community College Dist., 174
Tana v. Dan Tanna's, 225

XXVIII TABLE OF CASES

Tandy Corp. v. Malone & Hyde, 408
Taubman Co. v. Webfeats, 406
TCPIP Holding Co., Inc. v. Haar Comm., Inc., 278
Telstra Corp. Ltd. v. Nuclear Marshmallows, 300
TE-TA-MA Truth Foundation—Family of URI, Inc. v. World Church of the Creator, 33
Thane Int'l, Inc. v. Trek Bicycle Corp., 280
Therasense v. Becton Dickinson & Co., 136
Tiffany (NJ) Inc. v. eBay Inc., 267
Timberlane Lumber Co. v. Bank of America National Trust & Savings Ass'n, 206
Time Warner Cable, Inc. v. DIRECTV, Inc., 365
Tobinick v. Novella, 362
Tom Doherty Assocs. v. Saban Entm't, 405
Toney v. L'Oreal USA, Inc., 389
Top Tobacco, L.P. v. North Atlantic Operating Co., Inc., 237, 280
Toro Co. v. ToroHead Inc., 279
Toyota Motor Sales U.S.A., Inc. v. Tabari, 324
Toys "R" Us, Inc. v. Akkaoui, 288
Trademark Cases, 1, 11, 87
Trader Joe's Co. v. Hallatt, 205
TrafficSchool.com, Inc. v. Edriver, Inc., 372, 373
TrafFix Devices, Inc. v. Marketing Displays, Inc., 61, 66
Trans Continental Records, Inc., In re, 153
Tumblebus Inc. v. Cranmer, 123, 175
Two Pesos, Inc. v. Taco Cabana, Inc., 43
Union Carbide Corp. v. Ever-Ready, Inc., 28, 241
United Distillers, PLC, In re, 161
United Drug Co. v. Theodore Rectanus Co., 168
United Foods, Inc., United States v., 348
United Indus. Corp. v. Clorox Co., 363, 364
United States Jaycees v. Philadelphia Jaycees, 111
University Book Store v. University of Wisconsin Board of Regents, 124
University of Alabama Bd. of Trustees v. New Life Art, Inc., 351
V Secret Catalogue, Inc. v. Moseley, 288
Vail Associates, Inc. v. Vend-Tel-Co., Ltd., 239
Valu Engineering, Inc. v. Rexnord Corp., 74
Van Dyne-Crotty, Inc. v. Wear-Guard Corp., 105
Vanity Fair Mills, Inc. v. T. Eaton Co., Ltd., 203

TABLE OF CASES

Vaudable v. Montmartre, Inc., 191
Verisign, Inc. v. XYZ.COM LLC, 370
Vertex Group LLC, In re, 50
Virgin Enterprises Ltd. v. Nawab, 224
Visa Int'l Service Assoc. v. JSL Corp., 283, 285, 286
Viterra Inc., In re, 234
Voice of the Arab World v. MDTV Medical News Now, Inc., 402
Vornado Air Circulation Sys., Inc. v. Duracraft Corp., 70
Waits v. Frito-Lay, Inc., 377
Wallace Int'l Silversmiths, Inc. v. Godinger Silver Art Co., Inc., 64
Wal-Mart Stores, Inc. v. Samara Brothers, Inc., 44
Warner Bros. Ent., Inc. v. X One X, Prods., 54
WarnerVision Entertainment Inc. v. Empire of Carolina, Inc., 103
Web Printing Controls Co. v. Oxy-Dry Corp., 239
Weiner King, Inc. v. The Wiener King Corp., 184
West Florida Seafood, Inc. v. Jet Restaurants, Inc., 97
White v. Samsung Electronics America, Inc., 391
White, In re, 160
William R. Warner & Co. v. Eli Lilly & Co., 265, 314
Winter v. DC Comics, 396
Winter v. Natural Resources Defense Council, Inc., 404
Wolfard Glassblowing Co. v. Vanbragt, 407
Wonder Labs, Inc. v. Procter & Gamble Co., 312, 316
Wreal, LLC v. Amazon.com, Inc., 404
Wyatt Earp Enters., Inc. v. Sackman, Inc., 163
Yale Electric Corp. v. Robertson, 2, 243
Yankee Candle v. Bridgewater Candle, 46
Zacchini v. Scripps-Howard Broadcasting Co., 385, 392
Zatarains, Inc. v. Oak Grove Smokehouse, Inc., 26, 29
Zazu Designs v. L'Oreal, S.A., 98
Zirco Corp. v. American Tel. & Tel. Co., 102
Zobmondo Entertainment, LLC v. Falls Media, 27
Zyla v. Wadsworth, 381

TRADEMARK AND UNFAIR COMPETITION
IN A NUTSHELL®

SECOND EDITION

CHAPTER 1

INTRODUCTION TO TRADEMARK AND UNFAIR COMPETITION

This chapter provides an introduction to the field of trademark and unfair competition law. It begins with a discussion of the nature and definition of trademarks (Section A). It then turns to a discussion of the relationship between unfair competition actions and trademark infringement actions (Section B). Next, it presents an overview of the U.S. trademark system (Section C). Finally, it concludes with a brief introduction to the contents of this text (Section D), explaining how the text is laid out and what each chapter covers.

A. NATURE OF TRADEMARKS

In modern U.S. law, trademarks are classified as intellectual property, along with copyrights and patents, among others. Trademarks do share some similarities with other types of intellectual property, but trademarks are also different in a number of ways. The Supreme Court detailed some of the differences in an early decision known as *The Trademark Cases*, 100 U.S. 82 (1879). Utility patent rights are rights in inventions, and are granted only for inventions that are new and non-obvious. 35 U.S.C. §§ 101–103. Copyrights are rights in original, creative expression. 17 U.S.C. § 102. By contrast, as the Supreme Court pointed out in *The Trademark Cases*, "neither originality, invention, discovery, science, nor art is in any way essential" to the creation of trademark rights. Instead, the trademark "may be, and generally is, the adoption of something already in existence as the distinctive symbol of the party using it." Such a symbol may be "plain, simple, old, or well-known," but may still serve as the basis for a claim of trademark rights. For example, the term APPLE used in connection with computers and other electronic devices is a widely-known and valuable trademark of Apple Inc., but the term by itself is not a proper subject of copyright—it is neither original to Apple Inc., nor minimally creative. Although popular press accounts of intellectual property rights often treat trademarks and copyrights interchangeably, the law differentiates between the two types of rights.

All intellectual property is intangible. In cases involving trademark rights, courts have characterized the relevant intangible in various ways. In the early twentieth century, courts began to speak of trademarks as rights in the "goodwill" associated with the goods or services of a particular business. *See, e.g.*, *Hanover Star Milling Co. v. Metcalf*, 240 U.S. 403 (1916). Other courts referred to rights in a producer's commercial "reputation," *Yale Electric Corp. v. Robertson*, 26 F.2d 972 (2d Cir. 1928), or rights to the "commercial magnetism" of a symbol used for certain goods or services. *Mishawaka Rubber & Woolen Mfg. Co. v. S.S. Kresge Co.*, 316 U.S. 203 (1942). Accordingly, when we speak of APPLE as a trademark for electronic devices, we are in effect saying that the word "apple" has come to operate as a symbol of the "goodwill" associated with particular devices manufactured by Apple, Inc. These constituents—the word, the products, and the goodwill—define the traditional trademark right when considered collectively.

The interconnection among these constituents also explains why courts have spoken of trademark rights as "limited" property rights as opposed to in gross property rights. *See, e.g.*, *Hanover Star Milling Co. v. Metcalf*, 240 U.S. 403 (1916) (referring to trademark rights as property rights, but only "appurtenant to an established business or trade in connection with which the mark is used"). As Justice Holmes put it in *Prestonettes, Inc. v. Coty*, 264 U.S. 359 (1924), a trademark "does not confer a right to prohibit the use of [a] word or words. It is not a copyright . . . ." Instead, a trademark right, as traditionally understood, only gives a right to prohibit others from using a word or symbol in connection with goods or services in such a way as to usurp the right holder's goodwill. Thus, Apple, Inc., does not gain absolute dominion over the term "apple" by owning trademark rights in APPLE for electronic devices under the traditional formulation.

The definition of "trademark" in the U.S. trademark statute (the Lanham Act, introduced below in Section C.2), reflects and restates these principles:

> The term "trademark" includes any word, name, symbol, or device, or any combination thereof . . . used by a person . . . to identify and distinguish his or her goods, including a unique product, from those manufactured or sold by others and

to indicate the source of the goods, even if that source is unknown.

15 U.S.C. § 1127 (Lanham Act § 45). This definition reveals two critical points about the nature of trademarks. First, virtually any symbol that can be perceived can potentially operate as a trademark—the definition encompasses "any word, name, symbol, or device, or any combination thereof . . . ." Second, rather than expressly referring to "goodwill" or "reputation," the definition sets out a pair of related functional requirements: to be a trademark, a word (or other type of subject matter) must function to "identify and distinguish" a producer's goods from those of others, and it must function to "indicate the source of the goods." We refer to those two functions together as the *source identification functions.* Source identification is a central concept driving the doctrine of trademark distinctiveness, which we discuss in Chapter 2.

The Lanham Act definitions distinguish between several types of marks. The definition of "trademark" cited above is restricted to terms or other symbols used in connection with *goods*. Separately, the Lanham Act defines a "service mark" as a term or other symbol used in connection with *services* (FEDERAL EXPRESS for delivery services, for example). *See* 15 U.S.C. § 1127 (Lanham Act § 45) (requiring that a service mark "identify and distinguish" the services of one person from those of another, and "indicate the source of the services"). The Lanham Act also defines "certification mark" and "collective mark." A *certification mark* is a word, name, symbol, or device, or any combination thereof, which is used "to certify regional or other origin, material, mode of manufacture, quality, accuracy, or other characteristics" of a person's goods or services "or that the work or labor on the goods or services was performed by members of a union or other organization." *Id.* An example is the "heart healthy check" logo appearing on food that meets certification requirements of the American Heart Association. A *collective mark* is a trademark or service mark that is used by members of a collective group or organization to distinguish goods or services of the organization from those of others, or to indicate membership in the organization. *Id.* Examples include AAA (for the American Automobile Association) and the FTD logo (for an organization of florists—Florists' Transworld Delivery). In this text, we follow conventional practice in using the terms "trademark" or "mark" as umbrella terms to refer to all of these classes of marks, unless we specifically indicate otherwise.

The Lanham Act also distinguishes all of these types of marks from "trade names." The Act defines "trade name" (and "commercial name") as "any name used by a person to identify his or her business or vocation." 15 U.S.C. § 1127. Marks, by contrast, are used to identify particular products or services. The differences are not always sharp. For example, MCDONALD'S is a service mark for fast food restaurant services, but it also may be considered a trade name when used in reference to the fast food franchisor's entire business. In any event, trade names have little legal significance for our purposes; the law focuses primarily on marks.

B. NATURE OF UNFAIR COMPETITION; RELATIONSHIP WITH TRADEMARKS

The law of trademarks in the U.S. is usually referred to today as trademark *and unfair competition* law. The reference to unfair competition law has both historical and modern significance.

Today's "trademark and unfair competition" law originated in the U.S. in the early nineteenth century, or arguably earlier, as unfair competition law. The concept of limited property rights in trademarks described in the preceding section developed later. Even into the early twentieth century, many courts viewed trademark law as "but a part of the broader law of unfair competition." *Hanover Star Milling Co. v. Metcalf*, 240 U.S. 403 (1916).

The early unfair competition cases frequently involved simple tort claims of "passing off" (or "palming off"). A typical claim of passing off arose when a defendant attempted to pass off its goods in the marketplace as those of the plaintiff, presumably to take advantage of the plaintiff's goodwill and to divert sales away from the plaintiff. A defendant might engage in passing off by marking its goods with a mark that resembled the plaintiff's and then selling those goods as if they emanated from the plaintiff. The passing off claim rested on the tortious nature of the defendant's conduct (and the resulting injury to the plaintiff's business and to competition more generally). This was arguably broader, and perhaps different from, a pure property-based cause of action such as trademark infringement, which would rest on the existence of valid trademark rights in a mark and evidence that those trademark rights were violated.

In the famous case *International News Service v. Associated Press*, 248 U.S. 215 (1918), the Supreme Court seemed to endorse a leading role for the unfair competition claim in intellectual property cases, but the case has been read narrowly. International News Service (INS) had copied information from Associated Press (AP) reports and had republished the information as if it had originated from INS, without crediting AP. The information was valuable and time-sensitive; typically, it constituted news on war events from the battlefront in Europe. In some instances, INS gathered the information from AP reports published in East Coast newspapers and relayed it to INS member newspapers on the West Coast, who sometimes published it before the competing AP member newspapers did. The Supreme Court recognized that INS's conduct did not amount to traditional passing off, because INS was not putting the AP mark on an INS product and passing it off as AP's. (Indeed, INS's conduct was "reverse" passing off: taking *AP*'s product and selling it as if it originated from *INS*.) However, the Court concluded that unfair competition was not limited to cases of passing off. A court could entertain an equitable claim for an injunction against unfair competition in circumstances where a party acquired something "fairly at substantial cost" and a competitor misappropriated it for the purpose of garnering his own profits and disadvantaging the other party. Such conduct would be an attempt by the competitor "to reap where it has not sown." It would interfere with the normal operation of a legitimate business "precisely at the point where the profit is to be reaped," and hence should be characterized as unfair competition.

The core insight that unfair competition claims encompass more than just passing off remains true in theory. In practice, however, courts have tended to consign unfair competition to a relatively limited role, primarily as a reference to actions for infringement of unregistered trademarks under Lanham Act § 43(a), discussed below in Section C.2. In *Dastar Corp. v. Twentieth Century Fox Film Corp.*, 539 U.S. 23 (2003), the Court endorsed the proposition that "unfair competition" under Lanham Act § 43(a) could apply only to "certain unfair trade practices" spelled out by Section 43(a)'s "inherently limited wording."

Thus, under the modern U.S. framework, the law of trademarks predominates, with the law of unfair competition usually playing a modest supplemental role. The next section explains the goals of the modern trademark system and introduces the primary sources of law, institutions, and causes of action.

C. OVERVIEW OF THE U.S. TRADEMARK SYSTEM

1. PURPOSES OF THE TRADEMARK SYSTEM

Trademark systems ordinarily aspire to serve the interests of all participants in the market economy: producers of goods and services; their marketplace rivals; and consumers. There is no universally-accepted theoretical basis for the grant of trademark rights, although some of the justifications below are well-established.

Traditional justification. A passage from the legislative history of the Lanham Act recites both producer- and consumer-protection justifications for the trademark system. The trademark system is said to protect producers by ensuring that "where the owner of a trademark has spent energy, time and money in presenting to the public the product, he is protected in his investment from its appropriation by pirates and cheats." S. Rep. No. 1333, 79th Cong., 2d Sess. 3 (1946). In addition, the system is said to protect the consuming public "so that it may be confident that, in purchasing a product bearing a particular trademark which it favorably knows, it will get the product which it asks for and which it wants to get." *Id.* These may be referred to as the traditional justifications for the trademark system.

Economic justification. Contemporary scholars have restated the traditional justifications in economic terms. Trademarks are said to benefit consumers by reducing consumers' "search costs," which, in this context, refers to the costs that consumers incur when searching for products or services. Trademarks benefit producers by encouraging producers to invest in consistent product quality. The economic efficiency of the competitive marketplace is thought to be promoted where consumers experience search cost savings and have the assurance of consistent product quality.

Modern marketing justification. The traditional and economic justifications, at least stated simply as above, may not fully capture the communicative and cultural significance of trademarks. Trademarks may serve as the focal point for an overall social experience that may extend well beyond the actual attributes of the goods or services with which the trademarks are used. HARLEY-DAVIDSON for motorcycles may be an example; "Tiffany blue" for boxes used for elegant TIFFANY jewelry may be another. The psychological impact of marks may be difficult to translate into traditional or economic terms, but it may be unfair to ignore that impact— unfair to consumers who assign value to the social meaning with which the mark is imbued, and unfair to producers who have attempted to generate that value. On the other hand, if marks serve an important social communicative function, awarding exclusive rights in marks might chill communication in contexts in which robust communication is vital— such as in the political arena, for example. Accordingly, this "modern marketing" justification, as we will call it, recognizes substantial new value in trademarks but does not necessarily hold that brand owners should capture the entirety of that value.

2. SOURCES OF LAW; INSTITUTIONS

Sources of law. In the U.S., trademark rights originate from the common law. Congress' power to enact a federal trademark registration system derives from the Commerce Clause, Art I. Sec. 8 Cl. 3. The authority granted to Congress in the intellectual property clause, Art. I Sec. 8 Cl. 8, to create copyright and patent systems, does not authorize Congress to create a federal trademark system, because trademark rights are distinct from copyrights and patents, as discussed above in Section A. *The Trademark Cases*, 100 U.S. 82 (1879).

The Trademark Act of 1946, 15 U.S.C. §§ 1051–1141n (the "Lanham Act"), is the statutory authority for the federal trademark system. Practitioners frequently refer to individual statutory provisions by their Lanham Act designations (§§ 1–74). For example, the statute's trademark infringement provision, found at 15 U.S.C. § 1114, is Lanham Act § 32. We will adopt that practice in this text. The Lanham Act includes Subchapters I–IV:

Subchapter I: provisions relating to the registration of marks on the Principal Register

Subchapter II: provisions relating to the registration of marks on the Supplemental Register

Subchapter III: provisions relating to the enforcement of rights in registered and unregistered marks, and related matters

Subchapter IV: provisions relating to applications for registration under the procedures of the Madrid Protocol

The most important provisions for a general study of trademark law as presented in this text are found in Subchapters I and III.

Congress has amended the Lanham Act several times, most recently in 2006. Important amendments include:

- 1962: amendments to Section 32 to eliminate the requirement that confusion had to be of "purchasers" and relate to "the source of origin of . . . goods and services"

- 1988: Trademark Law Revision Act of 1988, introducing an "intent-to-use" system and making various amendments to Section 43(a), including amendments relating to the false advertising cause of action

- 1995: Federal Trademark Dilution Act of 1995, introducing a dilution cause of action, Section 43(c)

- 1999: Anticybersquatting Consumer Protection Act of 1999, introducing a cause of action for domain name cybersquatting, Section 43(d)

- 2003: amendments to implement the Madrid Protocol

- 2006: Trademark Dilution Revision Act of 2006, making amendments to the Section 43(c) anti-dilution cause of action

Institutions. The U.S. Patent and Trademark Office (PTO) and the federal courts are the primary institutions in the U.S. trademark system. The PTO, a federal administrative entity, is responsible for examining applications for federal trademark registration. Applications are assigned to individual trademark examiners for an initial registrability decision. Dissatisfied applicants can appeal the examiner's decision to the Trademark Trial and Appeal Board (TTAB), an administrative board within the PTO staffed by administrative law judges who sit in panels. Lanham Act § 20. Decisions of the TTAB are reviewable in court. Applicants may appeal directly to the U.S. Court of Appeals for the Federal Circuit, typically the preferred route. Alternatively, applicants can institute a civil suit against the PTO in federal district court on a de novo record, with appeal to the appropriate regional appellate court. Lanham Act § 21.

Lawsuits to enforce federal trademark rights under the Lanham Act—whether registered or unregistered rights—are brought in federal district court. Lanham Act § 39. Appeal is to the appropriate regional circuit court, not to the Court of Appeals for the Federal Circuit. Thus, while the Federal Circuit has a significant role in reviewing PTO rejections of applications for registration, that court does not have as large a role in shaping the law of trademark enforcement. Decisions of the appellate courts in trademark cases are reviewable in the Supreme Court by certiorari jurisdiction.

3. INTRODUCTION TO THE MAJOR LANHAM ACT CAUSES OF ACTION

A typical trademark dispute may be expected to include: (1) a "trademark infringement" allegation under Lanham Act § 32(1)(a), assuming that the dispute involves a registered mark; (2) an alternative and often largely duplicate claim that may be denominated "unfair competition" or "false designation of origin" under Lanham Act § 43(a)(1)(A), which is used to enforce rights in unregistered marks; and (3) a claim for trademark dilution under Lanham Act § 43(c). The Lanham Act also includes several other important causes of action including: (1) false advertising claims (Lanham Act § 43(a)(1)(B)); and (2) cybersquatting claims (Lanham Act § 43(d)).

The Lanham Act includes no dedicated cause of action for violations of the right of publicity. However, many states recognize a right of publicity, either by statute or by common law.

A detailed discussion of these claims appears in later chapters (Chapter 7—trademark infringement and false designation of origin; Chapter 8—dilution and cybersquatting; Chapter 10—false advertising; Chapter 11—right of publicity). A brief overview of the major elements of the trademark infringement, false designation of origin, and anti-dilution actions is provided below, because it is useful for placing the intervening chapters of this book (Chapters 2–6) into context.

Consider a hypothetical trademark dispute involving the mark COCA-COLA for soft drinks. Suppose that a new market entrant seeks to market a soft drink under the name KOKA-COLA. It is likely that Coca-Cola, Inc., owner of the COCA-COLA mark, would bring an action claiming trademark infringement, false designation of origin, and (quite possibly) trademark dilution. The elements necessary to make out a prima facie case under each of these claims may be summarized as follows:

(1) Trademark Infringement—Section 32(1)(a)

    a. unauthorized use (by defendant)

    b. of the plaintiff's valid, registered mark

    c. giving rise to a likelihood of confusion

(2) False Designation of Origin ("Unfair Competition")—Section 43(a)(1)(A)

    a. unauthorized use (by defendant)

    b. of the plaintiff's valid mark

    c. giving rise to a likelihood of confusion

(3) Trademark Dilution—Section 43(c)

    a. unauthorized use (by defendant)

    b. of the plaintiff's valid, famous mark

    c. giving rise to a likelihood of dilution

D. OVERVIEW OF THIS TEXT

The remainder of this text is organized in two main sections. The first section, comprised of Chapters 2–5, deals with the conditions for establishing trademark rights—that is, the conditions for demonstrating trademark validity (listed as part of element (b) in each of the causes of action in the preceding section). There are three principal conditions for establishing trademark rights at common law: (1) distinctiveness (Chapter 2); (2) non-functionality (Chapter 3); and (3) adoption and use (Chapter 4). These three conditions also apply for establishing registered rights, except that the prerequisite of adoption and use applies differently for registered rights, due to the option of applying for registered rights based on a bona fide intent to use. In addition, there are other substantive and procedural prerequisites for establishing registered rights, as discussed in Chapter 5.

The second major section of this text, comprised of Chapters 6–12, covers the rules for enforcing registered and unregistered trademark rights, along with the rules governing related causes of action. Chapter 6 covers the territorial scope of trademark rights. Chapter 7 deals with confusion-based causes of action under Lanham Act Sections 32(1)(a) and 43(a)(1)(A), covering the "unauthorized use" element (element (a) listed in the previous subsection of this text) and likelihood of confusion (element (c) listed in the previous subsection). Chapter 8 covers non-confusion-based causes of action, such as anti-dilution actions under Lanham Act § 43(c) and cybersquatting actions under § 43(d). Chapter 9 covers permissible uses of marks. Chapters 10 and 11 deal with other causes of action: false advertising under Lanham Act § 43(a)(1)(B) (Chapter 10) and the right of publicity under state law (Chapter 11). Chapter 12 explains remedies available under the Lanham Act.

CHAPTER 2
DISTINCTIVENESS

There are three principal requirements for establishing valid trademark rights: distinctiveness; non-functionality; and adoption and use. In this Chapter, we cover distinctiveness. *See* Chapter 3 for a discussion of non-functionality, and Chapter 4 for a discussion of adoption and use. We discuss the basic distinctiveness spectrum (Section A), the concepts of descriptiveness and secondary meaning (Section B), genericness (Section C), and distinctiveness of non-verbal identifiers (Section D). We conclude with a discussion of the trademark/copyright interface (Section E).

Distinctiveness issues may arise in four different settings:

First, when a mark owner files an application to register a mark with the U.S. Patent and Trademark Office (PTO), the trademark examiner must analyze whether the mark is distinctive.

Second, the PTO may be called upon to assess distinctiveness if an interested party opposes the issuance of a registration (in an "opposition" proceeding) or petitions to cancel an issued registration (in a "cancellation" proceeding). The PTO's determinations are reviewable in court, as discussed in Chapter 1.

Third, if the mark owner sues in federal district court for infringement of a registered mark, the alleged infringer may assert that the registered mark is not distinctive as a defense to infringement, and the court will determine whether the registered mark is distinctive, except where the rules of incontestability precludes a distinctiveness challenge. *See* Chapter 5, discussing incontestability; Lanham Act § 33(b). In *Already, LLC v. Nike, Inc.*, 133 S.Ct. 721 (2013), Nike had asserted that two of Already's shoe designs violated Nike's registered marks, and Already had counterclaimed that Nike's marks were invalid. Subsequently, Nike covenanted not to assert the marks against any of Already's existing shoe designs or any future colorable imitations of those designs. The Supreme Court determined that in view of the covenant, Already could not proceed with its counterclaim. The covenant's broad language reaching all of Already's existing designs and colorable imitations of them, coupled with the fact that Already had no concrete plans to create designs that would not be covered by the covenant, mooted the case.

When a court reviews a registered mark for distinctiveness, the court must treat the registration as *prima facie* evidence that the mark is distinctive, and the alleged infringer must overcome this presumption. If the court decides that the registered mark is not distinctive, the court may order the PTO to cancel the registration. Lanham Act § 37.

Fourth, if the owner of an unregistered mark sues in federal district court under Lanham Act § 43(a)(1)(A), the mark owner must establish that the mark is distinctive, and if the mark owner fails to do so, the court will dismiss the claim absent special circumstances, as discussed in Section C.5.

Although distinctiveness issues may arise in any of the different procedural contexts discussed above, the substantive rules of distinctiveness discussed in the remainder of this chapter are the same in all contexts.

A. THE DISTINCTIVENESS SPECTRUM

A central requirement for the award of trademark rights is that the mark be distinctive. Without distinctiveness, there is no mark. The requirement was developed primarily through case law, which remains the main source of distinctiveness rules. The Lanham Act incorporates the concept of distinctiveness in Section 45's definition of trademark (stating that a trademark is something that is used "to identify and distinguish" goods from those manufactured by others, and to "indicate the source of the goods") and Section 2 (stating that an applicant may register a mark "by which the goods of the applicant may be distinguished from the goods of others" unless specified circumstances exist).

Distinctiveness in trademark law is not a synonym for novelty. The word APPLE is not new, but may be distinctive under trademark law when used in connection with computers. Likewise, distinctiveness is not simply an assessment of creativity. The phrase FROSTED FLAKES for a frosting-coated corn flake cereal may not be especially creative, but, after a period of use in the marketplace, may well be recognized as distinguishing the maker's goods and identifying source, and thus may be deemed distinctive. The conditions for protecting trademarks differ from those for protecting patents or copyrights. Through its reliance on distinctiveness as a condition for protection, the trademark regime differs from the patent and copyright regimes, which rely on conditions such as novelty and originality, respectively.

The law recognizes two classes of distinctive marks: "inherently" distinctive marks and marks that have acquired distinctiveness. A mark that is inherently distinctive is one that is likely to be perceived as distinguishing goods or identifying source merely because of the nature of the mark or the context of its use. A mark that has acquired distinctiveness is one that comes to be perceived as distinguishing goods or identifying source as a result of its use in the marketplace. RESTATEMENT (3D) OF UNFAIR COMPETITION § 13 (1995). If a mark is inherently distinctive, no evidence of its actual reception in the marketplace is needed in order to adjudge the mark distinctive. If a mark fails to qualify as inherently distinctive, the mark owner must produce evidence of use in the marketplace in order to establish distinctiveness.

Modern courts analyze distinctiveness by analyzing where a mark should fall on the spectrum of distinctiveness set forth in *Abercrombie & Fitch Co. v. Hunting World, Inc.*, 537 F.2d 4 (2d Cir. 1976). On the *Abercrombie* spectrum, marks are categorized as either (1) arbitrary/fanciful; (2) suggestive; (3) merely descriptive; or (4) generic. Fanciful marks are coined words or phrases that have been created solely for use as marks—for example, XEROX for photocopiers. Arbitrary marks are standard English words that have no apparent connection to the underlying goods—such as APPLE for computers. Suggestive marks are those that may evoke the qualities of the goods or services but still require the consumer to employ his or her imagination to reach a conclusion about the goods. COPPERTONE for sun-tan lotion is an example. Merely descriptive terms are those that simply identify qualities or characteristics of the underlying goods—as in SOFT used for soft pillows. Generic terms restate the class to which the goods belong—such as BEER for beer.

Arbitrary/fanciful marks lie at one end of the *Abercrombie* spectrum; they are inherently distinctive marks having the highest degree of distinctiveness. Suggestive marks are deemed to have a slightly lesser degree of distinctiveness, but still qualify as inherently distinctive. Merely descriptive marks cannot qualify as inherently distinctive, but may acquire distinctiveness as a result of being used in the marketplace. Generic marks cannot qualify as distinctive. The chart below summarizes these concepts:

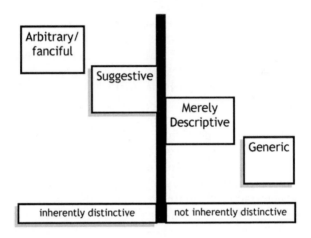

Prior to the passage of the Lanham Act in 1946, a different set of labels prevailed in distinctiveness analysis. Pre-1946 terminology distinguished between technical trademarks (what we now would call inherently distinctive marks) and trade names. Only technical trademarks could be registered under trademark law. Descriptive marks might be protected upon a showing of secondary meaning, but only under unfair competition principles. In addition, prior to 1988, the statute did not refer to "generic" marks, but instead used the label "common descriptive names."

To categorize a mark on the *Abercrombie* spectrum, one must necessarily consider the relationship between the mark and the underlying goods. The term SPICY may be merely descriptive for pepper sauce, but may be arbitrary for shoes. In *Abercrombie*, the court concluded that SAFARI was generic for various types of clothing (such as a safari hat), but could be merely descriptive or even suggestive for boots and shoes.

A distinctiveness inquiry under *Abercrombie* should also take account of other considerations. These include: (1) changes in the term's meaning over time, (2) the "anti-dissection" principle (which provides that the meaning of a composite phrase should be formulated based on the phrase as a whole, not based on dissecting it into its constituent parts), and (3) whether the mark is a word mark or one of a variety of types of non-verbal marks (*see* Part D below). The distinctiveness inquiry under the *Abercrombie* spectrum is treated as a question of fact, *In re Oppedahl & Larson, LLP*, 373 F.3d 1171 (Fed. Cir. 2004), and frequently is said to involve a case-by-case analysis. Courts tend to resist per se rules in distinctiveness analysis. For example, in *Oppedahl & Larson*, the Federal Circuit ruled that the mark PATENTS.COM for patent-tracking software was merely descriptive, but it refused to adopt a bright-line rule that adding ".com" to a descriptive term always resulted in a merely descriptive mark.

In the registration context, the Federal Circuit has stated that distinctiveness should be measured as of the time of registration, not the time of first use. *In re Chippendales USA, Inc.*, 622 F.3d 1346 (Fed. Cir. 2010). However, the court may still find that evidence from other time periods is still probative of probable consumer perceptions as of the time of registration.

In the United States, distinctiveness is to be analyzed on the basis of a U.S. consumer's perception. However, evidence from overseas might still be probative if there is some reason to think that it reflects the probable commercial impression conveyed to U.S. consumers. *In re Bayer AG*, 488 F.3d 960 (Fed. Cir. 2007). Relatedly, under the "doctrine of foreign equivalents," if the words comprising the mark are in a foreign language, they are translated into English for purposes of analyzing distinctiveness. In re Cordua Restaurants, Inc., 823 F.3d 594, 602–03 (Fed. Cir. 2016).

B. DESCRIPTIVENESS; SECONDARY MEANING

Under the *Abercrombie* spectrum, "suggestive" marks must be distinguished from "merely descriptive" marks. This line can be difficult to draw, but it is important, because marks falling on the suggestive side of the line are protected without secondary meaning. In *Zatarains, Inc. v. Oak Grove Smokehouse, Inc.*, 698 F.2d 786 (5th Cir. 1983), the court listed four tests for distinguishing between suggestive and merely descriptive marks:

- **"dictionary" test:** Here, the court examines the ordinary dictionary definition of the term and considers whether the definition refers to qualities or characteristics of the goods at issue. If so, this is evidence that the mark is merely descriptive of the goods.

- **"imagination" test:** Under this test, the court considers whether the consumer perceiving the term must make a leap of imagination to understand the term's relationship to the goods. If so, the mark is more likely suggestive than merely descriptive. If the mark immediately conveys to the consumer information about the qualities of the goods, this favors the conclusion that the mark is merely descriptive. *See In re Quik-Print Copy Shops, Inc.*, 616 F.2d 523 (CCPA 1980) (QUIK-PRINT for printing and publication services is merely descriptive); *see also Investacorp, Inc. v. Arabian Investment Banking Corp. E.C.*, 931 F.2d 1519 (11th Cir. 1991) (INVESTACORP for financial services brokerage is merely descriptive). The imagination test is described by some courts as the primary criterion for distinguishing between suggestive and merely descriptive marks. *Zobmondo Entertainment, LLC v. Falls Media*, 602 F.3d 1108 (9th Cir. 2010).

- **"competitors' need" test:** If competitors who market similar goods are likely to need access to the term in order to describe the qualities of their goods, the term is likely to be merely descriptive.

- **"third party's actual use" test:** If other producers have actually used the term to describe the qualities of similar products, the term is likely to be merely descriptive.

If a term is deemed merely descriptive when used for particular goods, the term may still qualify as distinctive (through acquired distinctiveness) in accord with the *Abercrombie* spectrum if secondary meaning can be shown. *See, e.g.,* Union Carbide Corp. v. Ever-Ready, Inc., 531 F.2d 366 (7th Cir. 1976) (even if EVEREADY for batteries is merely descriptive, it is protectable given abundant evidence of secondary meaning). Secondary meaning is an inquiry into the consumer's perception of the term as actually used in the marketplace in connection with the goods. The notion is that a term may come to have more than one connotation over time. A term such as "soft" for pillows describes a quality of the pillows, and that may always be the term's primary connotation. However, it is conceivable that consistent advertising practices or other efforts on the part of the pillow manufacturer may cause consumers to perceive the term "soft" to refer to the products of a particular pillow manufacturer in addition to referring to a quality of the pillows—that is, to have a secondary connotation in addition to the primary connotation. If this secondary connotation— "secondary meaning"—is shown to exist, the mark is distinctive. The secondary meaning inquiry is designated a question of fact.

The Lanham Act incorporates both the descriptiveness and secondary meaning concepts. In particular, Lanham Act Section 2(e)(1) provides that a mark that is merely descriptive of the underlying goods is barred from registration, but Section 2(f) specifies that the bar can be overcome if the applicant can show that the mark "has become distinctive of the applicant's goods in commerce." Section 2(f) also allows the PTO to presume secondary meaning where the mark has been in use for five years.

Secondary meaning may be proven by direct or circumstantial evidence. Direct evidence may be in the form of consumer testimony or, more frequently, a survey of prospective consumers. Circumstantial evidence from which secondary meaning may be inferred includes the amount and manner of the mark owner's advertising, volume of sales of products bearing the mark, length of time during which the mark has been used, and manner of use. *Zatarains, Inc. v. Oak Grove Smokehouse, Inc.*, 698 F.2d 786 (5th Cir. 1983); RESTATEMENT (3D) OF UNFAIR COMPETITION § 13 cmt. E (1995). Evidence that the mark owner spent large sums on advertising or sold a large volume of product should not by itself suffice to create an inference of secondary meaning. The question is whether it is reasonable to infer that the advertising or sales affected consumer perceptions of the mark in dispute.

The *International Kennel* case illustrates these points. The mark owner succeeded (on preliminary injunction) in showing that the mark INTERNATIONAL KENNEL CLUB for services relating to dog shows had secondary meaning, despite the absence of survey evidence. The court relied on the amount and manner of advertising and the mark owner's fifty years' use to conclude that the mark owner had a better than negligible chance of succeeding on a showing of secondary meaning. *International Kennel Club of Chicago, Inc. v. Mighty Star, Inc.*, 846 F.2d 1079 (7th Cir. 1988).

The context and manner of use of the mark may be quite important in coloring consumer perception, and should be taken into account in a secondary meaning inquiry. For example, where a mark owner sought to establish secondary meaning for COCOA BUTTER FORMULA used on beauty products, but could offer circumstantial evidence showing only that the mark was always presented to consumers as PALMER'S COCOA BUTTER FORMULA, the court found the evidence insufficient to create an inference of secondary meaning in COCOA BUTTER FORMULA standing alone. *E.T. Browne Drug Co. v. Cococare Prods., Inc.*, 538 F.3d 185 (3d Cir. 2008).

Mark owners sometimes argue that evidence of an alleged infringer's intentional copying of the mark is circumstantial evidence that the mark must have secondary meaning. But courts recognize that there may be other legitimate reasons for copying a mark that negate the inference of secondary meaning. For example, the mark might be a commonplace descriptive term.

C. GENERICNESS

Under the *Abercrombie* spectrum, generic terms marks cannot qualify as distinctive. This is the longstanding rule from common law. It is also adopted in the Lanham Act, which provides that generic terms cannot be registered, and that a registration can be cancelled at any time on the ground that the registered mark is generic. Lanham Act § 14(3). Prior to 1988, the statute and cases referred to "common descriptive" terms rather than to "generic" terms, but this caused confusion, so Congress shifted to the label "generic."

1. TWO-PART TEST: RELEVANT CLASS OF GOODS/SERVICES + PRIMARY SIGNIFICANCE

Courts have developed a number of tests for genericness. The Federal Circuit has adopted a two-part test. In the first part, one must specify the genus of the products at issue. In the second part, one asks whether the mark's "primary significance" to the relevant public is as a reference to that genus. *Princeton Vanguard, LLC v. Frito-Lay N. Am., Inc.*, 786 F.3d 960, 965 (Fed. Cir. 2015). (The test is sometimes referred to as the *Ginn* test, after *H. Marvin Ginn Corp. v. Int'l Ass'n of Fire Chiefs, Inc.*, 782 F.2d 987, 989 (Fed.Cir.1986)). The Lanham Act likewise requires that the primary significance test be used, and rejects tests based on "purchaser motivation." Lanham Act § 14(3). This language overruled *Anti-Monopoly, Inc. v. General Mills Fun Group, Inc.*, 684 F.2d 1316 (9th Cir. 1982), a dubious decision which had found the mark MONOPOLY for a board game generic because a survey had shown that most purchasers were motivated to purchase the game because of the game's attributes, not because of the identity of the manufacturer.

a. Identifying a Relevant Class of Goods/Services

The exercise of identifying the relevant class of goods/services in a genericness analysis is a fact-bound question to be evaluated on a case-by-case basis. In a number of cases, the relevant class of goods/services will be self-evident and not disputed. In some cases, however, the analysis will be difficult.

This is particularly true in "new product category" cases. A producer might introduce a new product that differs from established product classes in some characteristic and then might assert trademark rights in the use of that characteristic in connection with the new product. If there is evidence that the characteristic has come to serve as the label for the new product category, then trademark rights in the use of that characteristic may be denied for genericness. For example, the brewer Genesee introduced a new ale called HONEY BROWN ALE and sought to prevent its competitor Stroh's from introducing ales under the designation "honey brown." The Third Circuit concluded that the designation was generic. *Genesee Brewing Company, Inc. v. Stroh Brewing Co.*, 124 F.3d 137 (2d Cir. 1997). Under the Third Circuit's approach, a new product should be "considered its own genus" in cases where the producer introduces a new product "that differs from an established product class in a particular characteristic, and uses a common descriptive term of that characteristic as the name of the product." *A.J. Canfield Co. v. Honickman*, 808 F.2d 291 (3d Cir. 1986) (finding generic the mark DIET CHOCOLATE FUDGE SODA for a chocolate-flavored soft drink).

b. Proving Primary Significance

To assess primary significance, courts should begin by identifying the relevant purchaser universe for the goods or services at issue. In cases involving ordinary consumer goods such as groceries or hotel services, it is reasonable to assume that the relevant purchaser for purposes of the analysis is the general consuming public. Other cases may involve specialized products—for example, engineering equipment or surgical devices—and here, the primary significance of the term at issue must be measured by reference to the appropriate sub-group of the consuming public.

Once the relevant purchaser universe has been identified, the inquiry into primary significance can proceed. Many types of evidence may be used to prove primary significance:

- **dictionary definitions/part-of-speech designations:** dictionary evidence may be relevant to the extent that it equates the mark with the genus of the goods. In *Mil-Mar Shoe Co., Inc. v. Shonac Corp.*, 75 F.3d 1153 (7th Cir. 1996), which involved the mark SHOE WAREHOUSE for retail shoe stores, the court held that a dictionary definition of "warehouse" could be probative of primary significance even if the relevant definition (defining "warehouse" as a retail store) was not the first listed definition. In *TE-TA-MA Truth Foundation—Family of URI, Inc. v. World Church of the Creator*, 297 F.3d 662 (7th Cir. 2002), the court declined to find CHURCH OF THE CREATOR generic for use in connection with a religious organization. Dictionary definitions of the individual terms did not reveal how consumers used the composite phrase in contemporary culture. CHURCH OF THE CREATOR did not restate the class of all monotheistic religions. In addition, where a dictionary definition (or other evidence) suggests that a term is generic, adding ".com" as a top-level domain indicator generally will not upgrade the status of the mark from generic to merely descriptive. *Advertise.com, Inc. v. AOL Advertising, Inc.*, 616 F.3d 974 (9th Cir. 2010).

Relatedly, it is sometimes said that if a mark is used as an adjective, it is more likely to be source-identifying than if it is used as a noun or a verb. In *Elliot v. Google, Inc.*, 860 F.3d 1151 (9th Cir. 2017), Elliot invoked the "part-of-speech" test to support an assertion that the mark GOOGLE for online search services was generic, citing evidence that "Google" is commonly used as a verb to refer to online searching. A Ninth Circuit panel rejected this argument. Verb use does not necessarily indicate generic use, the court pointed out. A person who refers to "googling" might be using the word in an indiscriminate sense (to refer to the class of online search services), which could constitute evidence of genericness, but the person might just as well be using the word in a discriminate sense (to refer to searches carried out through the Google site), which would not be indicative of genericness.

- **third-party uses:** if third parties routinely use the mark to refer to the genus of goods, this is evidence that the primary significance of the mark is generic. *Filipino Yellow Pages,*

Inc. v. Asian Journal Pubs., Inc., 198 F.3d 1143 (9th Cir. 1999) (widespread uses of "Filipino Yellow Pages" to refer to any telephone directory organized by product or service and catering to Filipinos); *Murphy Door Bed Co. v. Interior Sleep Sys., Inc.*, 874 F.2d 95 (2d Cir. 1989) (media usages of "Murphy bed" in reference to any bed that folded into a wall closet).

- **mark owner's uses:** the mark owner's own use of the mark in a generic sense can be a powerful admission of genericness. The mark owner's frequent references to "Otis escalators" suggested that the mark owner (Otis) itself perceived "escalator" to refer to the genus of moving stairways. *Haughton Elevator Co. v. Seeberger*, 85 U.S.P.Q. 80 (Comm'r Pat. 1950).

- **surveys:** survey evidence may also be offered to prove or disprove genericness. Two types of genericness surveys are common. One type, the "Teflon" survey, provides respondents with a list of terms, including the mark at issue, and asks respondents to characterize the terms as "brand names" or "common names." A survey of this general type was used in *E.I. DuPont de Nemours & Co. v. Yoshida Int'l, Inc.*, 393 F. Supp. 502 (E.D.N.Y. 1975), in which the mark TEFLON for non-stick cooking surfaces was found not to be generic. Another common type of genericness survey, the "Thermos" survey, seeks to determine how respondents would ask for the product at issue and whether respondents use the alleged mark as the label for the category of goods. In a case involving the mark THERMOS for vacuum-insulated bottles, *American Thermos Prods. Co. v. Aladdin Indus., Inc.*, 207 F. Supp. 9 (D. Conn. 1962), respondents were requested to say what they would ask for if they entered a store to purchase a container to keep liquids hot or cold. If respondents said that they would ask for a "Thermos," this was evidence of generic usage. If they said that they would ask for a "vacuum bottle" or the like, this was evidence cutting against genericness.

2. TIME FRAME OF THE GENERICNESS INQUIRY

The outcome of a distinctiveness inquiry may depend upon the time frame of the inquiry. For example, a term might be merely descriptive of underlying goods when first adopted, but may develop secondary meaning over time.

The time frame also may be important in genericness analysis. Perhaps the most common pattern in the cases is this: a term is distinctive when adopted, but, over time, becomes generic (a phenomenon sometimes called "genericide"). ASPIRIN for acetylsalicylic acid tablets is one famous example. Frequently, the reason that a mark becomes generic over time is that the mark owner has succeeded so thoroughly in identifying the mark with the underlying goods that the public comes to equate the mark with the entire class of goods, not merely the mark owner's goods. Consistent with this notion that a mark may become generic over time, courts appear to take the view that genericness is not measured as of the time the mark owner adopted the mark. Instead, in litigation, genericness is to be determined as of the date when the alleged infringer entered the market using the accused infringing mark. *See, e.g., Nora Beverages, Inc. v. Perrier Group of America, Inc.*, 164 F.3d 736 (2d Cir. 1998).

A question not definitively resolved in the cases is whether a term that was generic when adopted, or was later deemed generic, may become distinctive again, although one court expressed skepticism in a case involving the mark HOG for large motorcycles. *Harley-Davidson v. Grottanelli*, 164 F.3d 806 (2d Cir. 1999); *but cf. Singer Mfg. Co. v. Briley*, 207 F.2d 519 (5th Cir. 1953) (SINGER for sewing machines is not generic; although it had previously lost its source—indicating significance for a time). In *Schwan's IP, LLC v. Kraft Pizza Co.*, 460 F.3d 971 (8th Cir. 2006), the court held that if a term is generic when adopted, no amount of survey evidence will overcome that determination.

3. REMEDIES IN GENERICNESS CASES

Suppose that a mark owner sues a competitor for infringement and seeks an injunction, and the competitor persuades the court that the mark at issue has become generic. Ordinarily, the court would deny the mark owner a remedy; after all, the effect of a determination of genericness is that the mark owner can claim no valid trademark rights in the mark. If a court were to pursue this approach in every case, without regard for the factual nuances, at least two concerns would arise. First, even in a case in which the evidence of genericness is overwhelming, there still are likely to be a few consumers who perceive the mark as source-identifying, and for those consumers, the competitor's use of the mark might well cause confusion. Evidence that an otherwise generic mark has some residual source-indicating significance is sometimes referred to as evidence of "de facto" secondary meaning. Relatedly, a mark has become generic among one segment of the populace but remains source-indicating among another segment is sometimes discussed as a "dual usage" mark for which there may be the prospect of some Lanham Act remedy. Second, the equities in any given genericness case may not be tilted entirely away from the mark owner, especially in cases of genericide—that is, where the mark owner's own efforts to promote the mark may have succeeded so thoroughly over time that consumers may have come to equate the mark with the underlying goods or services.

In light of these concerns, some courts in genericness cases have awarded mark owners some limited injunctive relief against infringers even when finding that the mark at issue is generic. For example, even though the court found that MURPHY BED was generic for a bed that folds into a wall closet, the court precluded the mark owner's competitor from advertising its product as the "original" or "genuine" Murphy Bed. *Murphy Door Bed Co. v. Interior Sleep Sys., Inc.*, 874 F.2d 95 (2d Cir. 1989). In the THERMOS case, the court required that when the competitor used the term "thermos," it also used its house mark (ALADDIN'S). *King-Seeley Thermos Co. v. Aladdin Indus., Inc.*, 321 F.2d 577 (2d Cir. 1963). Courts have justified these awards of relief by permitting the mark owner to assert a claim for unfair competition under 15 U.S.C. § 1125(a). *See, e.g., Blinded Veterans Assn. v. Blinded American Veterans Found.*, 872 F.2d 1035 (D.C. Cir. 1989). Necessarily this is a variety of unfair competition theory that does not depend upon the existence of still valid trademark rights.

D. DISTINCTIVENESS OF NON-VERBAL IDENTIFIERS

The *Abercrombie* spectrum for distinctiveness applies most readily to word marks, but a wide range of other, non-verbal signifiers (such as logos, product packaging and product designs, colors, sounds, and scents) might also qualify as the type of subject matter for which trademark rights may be granted. Courts (and the PTO) apply the *Abercrombie* spectrum only in part to assess the distinctiveness of these non-verbal marks. Non-verbal marks may qualify as merely descriptive (and may be shown to be distinctive with evidence of secondary meaning) and may qualify as generic. For example, a drawing of an apple used on a bottle of apple juice (or on an apple) is surely either merely descriptive or (more likely) generic. The rules discussed above in Parts B and C apply here just as they do for word marks.

However, some courts have concluded that the *Abercrombie* spectrum does not apply well to assess the inherent distinctiveness of non-verbal marks. *See Amazing Spaces, Inc. v. Metro Mini Storage*, 608 F.3d 225 (5th Cir. 2010) (observing that the *Abercrombie* test was not likely to provide much insight into whether a non-verbal mark intrinsically indicated source). Accordingly, courts have crafted tests for *inherent* distinctiveness that vary depending upon the type of non-verbal mark. Generally, it is more difficult to show inherent distinctiveness under these tests than under the *Abercrombie* test.

1. LOGOS

Perhaps the simplest type of non-verbal mark is the logo or "design" mark. An example is the "three-stripe" pattern on adidas shoes. Consumers probably consider the stripes to be decorative, but consumers also probably rely on the stripes to identify the shoes as originating from adidas. In such a circumstance, the stripes are likely to be functioning as trademarks, even if they are also incidentally decorative. *See* TRADEMARK MANUAL OF EXAMINING PROCEDURE ("TMEP") § 1202.03.

In *Seabrook Foods v. Bar-Well Foods*, 568 F.2d 1342 (CCPA 1977), the court set forth a test for inherent distinctiveness that is now widely used to analyze the inherent distinctiveness of logos, even though the *Seabrook* case itself involved the appearance of product packaging. Under the *Seabrook* test for inherent distinctiveness, the following factors are considered:

(1) Whether [the logo] was a "common" basic shape or design;

(2) Whether it was unique or unusual in a particular field;

(3) Whether it was a mere refinement of a commonly adopted and well-known form of ornamentation for the goods; or

(4) Whether it was capable of creating a commercial impression distinct from the accompanying words.

A Second Circuit panel applied the *Seabrook* test to assess the distinctiveness of a vodka producer's stylized and colored letter "O" used in connection with orange-flavored vodka. *Star Indus., Inc. v. Bacardi & Co., Ltd.*, 412 F.3d 373 (2d Cir. 2005). The court concluded that the stylized O "had sufficient shape and color stylization" to qualify it as inherently distinctive under the *Seabrook* test, even though a linear representation of the letter "O" might well fail the first prong of the *Seabrook* test as a common basic shape. However, the court declined to find confusion liability in the case.

The Fifth Circuit refined this analysis in *Amazing Spaces, Inc. v. Metro Mini Storage*, 608 F.3d 225 (5th Cir. 2010). The court characterized the *Seabrook* factors as "variations on a theme rather than discrete inquiries," in that the factors were primarily directed towards determining whether the logo at issue was commonplace, and hence not inherently distinctive. Amazing Spaces' "star symbol" at issue was, in fact, commonplace, according to the court. Even though it was arguably stylized (it was shaded and set within a circle), the stylized aspects of the design were not likely to differentiate the logo from other star logos, the court determined. The court contrasted other stylized star logos: the star used in connection with the Dallas Cowboys NFL franchise included a white border; the star used in connection with Wal-Mart stores included the words "Wal" and "Mart" around the star. These features did distinguish the respective logos from other star logos, the court asserted.

Courts sometimes decline to consider the fourth *Seabrook* inquiry in the course of an inherent distinctiveness analysis. *See, e.g., Forney Indus., Inc. v. Daco of Missouri*, 835 F.3d 1238 (10th Cir. 2016). The reasoning is that the fourth inquiry relates to whether the logo mark is registrable separately of any accompanying words, not whether the logo mark itself is inherently distinctive.

2. COLOR

In *Qualitex Co. v. Jacobson Prods. Co., Inc.*, 514 U.S. 159 (1995), the Court held that the color of a product alone could serve as a source indicator and thus could be the subject of trademark rights if it met the requirements for trademark validity. In its opinion, the Court discussed both the distinctiveness and non-functionality elements of trademark validity. (*See* Chapter 3 for a more detailed discussion of the *Qualitex* case and its bearing on the non-functionality requirement.) Regarding distinctiveness, the Court appeared to say that color alone could qualify as distinctive if there was evidence that the color indicated source. Thus, the Court appeared to reject the principle that there could be a blanket exclusion of subject matter from protectability, but appeared to adopt the principle that some categories of marks could be subjected to a blanket secondary meaning requirement—that is, they could be deemed incapable of satisfying the requirements for inherent distinctiveness as a matter of law. In *Forney,* a panel of the Tenth Circuit held that color used in product packaging could be inherently distinctive "only if specific colors are used in combination with a well-defined shape, pattern, or other distinctive design." *Forney,* 835 F.3d at 1248.

3. TRADE DRESS

Trade dress refers to the overall commercial impression associated with a product or service. It may include elements of a product's packaging, a product's shape, visual or other elements of a retail store or restaurant, or other symbols that may indicate source. Some courts also use "trade dress" informally in other cases involving non-verbal marks, such as color. Courts have experienced difficulty fashioning rules of distinctiveness for trade dress.

The Two Pesos *analysis.* In *Two Pesos, Inc. v. Taco Cabana, Inc.*, 505 U.S. 763 (1992), Taco Cabana claimed unregistered trade dress in the interior and exterior décor of its Mexican restaurants and brought an action under Lanham Act § 43(a) to restrain a competitor from using the trade dress. A jury had found the asserted trade dress to be inherently distinctive, and the Fifth Circuit affirmed. The Supreme Court granted certiorari to address whether, as a matter of law, trade dress was capable of qualifying as inherently distinctive. The Court pointed out that neither Section 43(a) nor Section 2 of the Lanham Act imposed a secondary meaning requirement on plaintiffs seeking to establish protectable trade dress. It also asserted that a blanket secondary meaning requirement for trade dress would conflict with the goals of the Lanham Act: by delaying the establishment of trade dress rights until secondary meaning was established, such a rule might make it more difficult for businesses (especially small businesses) to recoup investments in goodwill, and ultimately might hinder some businesses from entering new markets at all.

The Court did not express a clear view about the precise test to be used for determining whether trade dress was inherently distinctive. Instead, it merely observed that the lower court had been "quite right" to apply the *Abercrombie* factors.

The Wal-Mart *analysis.* After the *Two Pesos* decision, the circuit courts developed a variety of conflicting tests for assessing inherent distinctiveness of trade dress, especially product design trade dress. It was widely expected that the Supreme Court would intervene again to resolve the circuit split, and, in *Wal-Mart Stores, Inc. v. Samara Brothers, Inc.*, 529 U.S. 205 (2000), the Court did, albeit in a surprising fashion. In *Wal-Mart,* plaintiff Samara Bros. asserted unregistered trade dress in girls' dress patterns. The Court characterized the dress patterns as "product design" trade dress, as distinguished from "product packaging" trade dress, and ruled that unregistered product design trade dress could not qualify as inherently distinctive, as a matter of law; it could only qualify as distinctive upon a showing of secondary meaning. The Court reasoned that nothing in Section 43(a) or Section 2 mandated the conclusion that every category of mark could potentially qualify as inherently distinctive. The Court also invoked its *Qualitex* decision for the proposition that at least one category of marks—color marks—could never be inherently distinctive. In addition, the Court offered three policy rationales for its decision: (1) that consumers do not tend to rely on product design to identify source; (2) that an uncertain rule of inherent distinctiveness for product design trade dress would harm competition by making it too easy for trade dress claimants to file dubious lawsuits against potential market entrants and withstand summary judgment; and (3) that product design could "ordinarily" be protected under other intellectual property regimes, such as copyright or design patent.

The Court attempted to distinguish *Two Pesos*. *Two Pesos* was "inapposite" because the restaurant décor at issue there was not product design, but was either product packaging "or else some tertium quid that is akin to product packaging . . . ." Thus, while *Two Pesos* had established the general principle that trade dress could be inherently distinctive, it did not compel a ruling that product design trade dress could be inherently distinctive.

The Court recognized that drawing the line between product design and product packaging (or some other tertium quid) might be difficult, so it counseled courts to classify ambiguous trade dress as product design. Accordingly, in close cases, courts are to err on the side of requiring evidence of secondary meaning.

The Court in *Wal-Mart* did not identify a governing test for inherent distinctiveness of product packaging or tertium quid trade dress. It appears from subsequent decisions that courts are likely to apply either the *Abercrombie* factors or the *Seabrook* test to assess inherent distinctiveness of these categories of trade dress.

The Federal Circuit invoked this rule to support its conclusions in *In re Slokevage*, 441 F.3d 957 (Fed. Cir. 2006). The applicant sought trade dress protection for V-shaped cut-out areas and accompanying closure flaps for clothing. The court determined that design features incorporated into a clothing product should be classified as product design, rejecting the applicant's argument that design referred only to an article's overall impression or shape. The court did not consider the case to be close, but noted that if it had, the *Wal-Mart* opinion would counsel in favor of designating the trade dress as design in any event. The court also ruled that the classification of trade dress as product design or product packaging (or other) was a question of fact.

The First Circuit's decision in *Yankee Candle v. Bridgewater Candle*, 259 F.3d 25 (1st Cir. 2001) is also instructive on the product design/product packaging distinction, and on approaches to proving secondary meaning for trade dress after *Wal-Mart*. In the court's view, Yankee Candle had claimed two types of trade dress: a "combination" claim (to trade dress in the appearance of its candles, its catalogue, and its vertical display system used in retail stores) and a claim to the features of the labels on its candle products. As to the combination claim, the court reasoned that if product design included only features "inherent [in] the actual physical product," then the combination claim would not constitute product design, but neither would it fit clearly into the product packaging or even the "tertium quid" categories. Accordingly, the court invoked the *Wal-Mart* rule for close cases and found the combination trade dress to constitute product design.

As to the label claim, the court asserted that detachable labels were "a classic case of product packaging," such that Yankee Candle could attempt to establish inherent distinctiveness. However, because the labels simply combined a number of common features, they could not qualify as inherently distinctive under the *Abercrombie* or *Seabrook* tests.

Proceeding to its analysis of secondary meaning, the court agreed with the lower court that Yankee Candle had failed to prove secondary meaning for either the combination trade dress or the label trade dress. Yankee Candle had (1) failed to introduce any survey evidence; (2) failed to show that its sales and advertising evidence was directed to the specific trade dress at issue (because even if the advertising had featured the trade dress, it was not "look-for" advertising that specifically directed consumers to the trade dress features); and (3) failed to persuade the court that alleged copying of some elements by the defendant gave rise to an inference of secondary meaning. The court called for a "vigorous evidentiary showing" of secondary meaning, which Yankee Candle had not provided, in the court's view.

The Fifth Circuit reached a contrary conclusion on the secondary meaning point in *Board of Supervisors of LSU v. Smack Apparel*, 550 F.3d 465 (5th Cir. 2008), involving a claim to trade dress in collegiate color combinations on apparel. Despite the lack of survey evidence, the court found secondary meaning based on circumstantial evidence that arguably indicated consumers' desire to associate with a particular university and its sports teams. The apparel at issue did include some "other indicia" in addition to the color combination—such as references to game scores and a football championship.

The Federal Circuit decided that the "Cuff and Collars" costume worn by Chippendales dancers (in connection with male exotic dancing) constituted product packaging trade dress and applied the *Seabrook* factors to assess whether the trade dress was inherently distinctive. The court concluded that the costume failed the inherent distinctiveness test; it was a "mere refinement" of a commonly-adopted form of ornamentation, as evidenced by the fact that Playboy had popularized a similar costume for adult entertainment. *In re Chippendales USA, Inc.*, 622

F.3d 1346 (Fed. Cir. 2010). The issue of secondary meaning was not adjudicated in the case.

4. EXOTIC SOURCE IDENTIFIERS

The TTAB has held that the scent of a product is capable of performing the trademark function of identifying and distinguishing the product. *In re Clarke*, 17 U.S.P.Q.2d 1238 (TTAB 1990). Clarke sought to register "a high impact, fresh, floral fragrance reminiscent of Plumeria blossoms," used in connection with sewing threads and yarns. The TTAB concluded that Clarke had established prima facie distinctiveness by showing that "customers, dealers and distributors of her scented yarns and threads have come to recognize [Clarke] as the source of these goods." The TTAB's remark may indicate that the TTAB was finding distinctiveness on the basis of a showing of secondary meaning. The opinion is silent as to whether the TTAB would have given Clarke the opportunity to attempt to establish inherent distinctiveness. However, the *Clarke* decision predates both *Qualitex* and *Wal-Mart*. In light of those cases, it seems likely that scent marks would be deemed incapable of inherent distinctiveness as a matter of law, such that distinctiveness could only be established via a showing of secondary meaning.

In more recent decisions, the TTAB has attempted to apply *Qualitex* and *Wal-Mart* to sound marks. The TTAB has held sound marks used in connection with goods that make sound in their normal operation cannot be inherently distinctive; secondary meaning must be shown. *In re Vertex Group LLC*, 89 U.S.P.Q.2d 1694 (TTAB 2009); *Nextel Comm., Inc. v. Motorola, Inc.*, 91 U.S.P.Q.2d 1393 (TTAB 2009).

E. THE TRADEMARK/COPYRIGHT INTERFACE

The cases discussed in this final section do not, strictly speaking, involve distinctiveness analysis. However, like distinctiveness cases, these cases deal with a fundamental question about the protectability of marks, and they test the resiliency of the apparent decision in *Qualitex* that there can be no blanket exclusion of subject matter from protection. The common thread in these cases is a concern that permitting trademark protection for selected types of subject matter would upset the balance struck under the *copyright* statute. This might occur, the argument goes, if subject matter that is excluded from copyright protection (or subject matter for which the copyright term has expired) could be protected anyway under trademark law, for a potentially indefinite duration.

The law of the trademark/copyright interface includes a few basic rules, but otherwise is unclear. On the copyright side, the regulations of the Copyright Office attempt to set up an absolute prohibition, barring from copyright protection "[w]ords and short phrases such as names, titles, and slogans; familiar symbols or designs; mere variations of typographic ornamentation, lettering or coloring . . . ." 37 CFR § 202.1. The more difficult issue, however, is the extent to which trademark protection is available for subject matter that has been or could be the subject of copyright protection.

In *Oliveira v. Frito-Lay, Inc.*, 251 F.3d 56 (2d Cir. 2001), the court dealt with a claim of trademark rights in a recorded performance of a musical composition. The composition was "The Girl from Ipanema," and recording artist Astrud Oliviera claimed that the recorded performance was her signature song and essentially served as a source identifier for her persona. The court ruled that a recorded musical composition could conceivably serve as source identifier under some instances—such as a snippet of a recording of "Sweet Georgia Brown" played in connection with performances of the Harlem Globetrotters basketball team. However, the court ruled against Oliveira, holding that a recorded performance of a composition cannot function as a trademark identifying the performer. That is, a performing artist cannot acquire trademark rights in a recording of her own performance. Extending trademark protection to recordings in such circumstances would disrupt marketplace expectations, and such an extension would be a matter for Congress.

By contrast to the case-specific approach seemingly endorsed in *Oliviera*, the Ninth Circuit in *Comedy III Productions, Inc. v. New Line Cinema*, 200 F.3d 593 (9th Cir. 2000) seemed to be determined to establish an absolute rule. Analyzing a claim of trademark rights in a short video clip depicting a Three Stooges performance, the court focused on the fact that copyright protection in the video clip had expired. The court ruled that "[i]f material covered by copyright law has passed into the public domain, it cannot then be protected by the Lanham Act without rendering the Copyright Act a nullity."

Concerns about the trademark/copyright interface also animate the TTAB's rules about whether to permit the author of a book to claim that his or her name serves as a mark when used in connection with the book. According to the TTAB, a writer's name cannot be registered as the trademark for a novel, because allowing a trademark registration could "perpetuate the [copyright] monopoly," in particular by creating a potential obstacle for those who wished to copy and market the novel after its copyright had expired (because the corresponding trademark rights in the author's name used in connection with the novel could endure indefinitely). *In re First Draft, Inc.*, 76 U.S.P.Q.2d 1183 (TTAB 2005). However, the TTAB also takes the view that copyright law presents no barrier to registering a writer's name when used in connection with a *series* of written works. This aspect of the rule seems to have little to do with considerations of copyright policy and more to do with ensuring that the author's name in fact is serving as a source indicator.

The critical case on the trademark/copyright interface is *Dastar Corp. v. Twentieth Century Fox Film Corp.*, 539 U.S. 23 (2003). General Dwight Eisenhower had written a book about his war experiences called "Crusade in Europe." Under a copyright license, Fox had developed a television series based on the book. Fox had held the copyright in the television series, but had failed to renew the copyright. Dastar then took tapes of the Fox television series, edited them lightly, and repackaged and sold them as a videotape set without indicating that the videotapes were derived from the Fox television show (or from the Eisenhower book).

Fox sued Dastar under the Lanham Act, asserting that the omission of proper credit to Fox was a false representation about the Dastar product, and thus was a violation of Section 43(a)(1). Such an allegation is referred to as an allegation of "reverse passing off," because the defendant (Dastar) was selling the plaintiff's goods without the plaintiff's mark. (Regular or forward passing off occurs when the defendant is selling the defendant's goods under the plaintiff's mark, thus passing the goods off as originating from plaintiff.)

The Court rejected Fox's claim of reverse passing off, reasoning that Section 43(a)(1)'s prohibition against false designations of "origin" extended only to representations about the origin of the tangible goods at issue, not the authorship of the creative content of those goods. The Court also rested its ruling on policy grounds—specifically the policy of avoiding a conflict with copyright law. The Court ruled that where copyright in a work has expired, a Lanham Act action for omitting to credit author on the work will be disallowed, to avoid creating a "mutant species of copyright." Otherwise, parties such as Dastar who attempt to copy and market public domain works would face a dilemma: if they credited the author, they would risk suit for a false representation that the author endorsed Dastar's product; but if they omitted credit to the author, they would risk suit for a false representation about authorship.

The *Dastar* case has been applied in numerous cases to strike down claims about authorship credit or other similar representations about who was responsible for the creative content of manufactured goods. *Dastar* demonstrates that the Court will react against trademark claims when those claims are perceived to spring from a desire to circumvent the limitations of the copyright law.

In *Gensler v. Strabala*, 764 F.3d 735 (7th Cir. 2014), the court held that *Dastar* did not necessarily preclude a Section 43(a) claim that was based on Gensler's allegation that Strabala had made misrepresentations calculated to deceive consumers about whether an individual architect had been responsible for "designing" several major architectural projects. As the court saw it, Gensler could be understood to be alleging that Strabala had made a false claim as to the origin of services. Because the allegation did not rest on Strabala's making of copies, the allegation was not an attempt to use the Lanham Act to circumvent copyright law. The court vacated the Rule 12(b)(6) dismissal and remanded. And in *Warner Bros. Ent., Inc. v. X One X Prods.*, 840 F.3d 971 (8th Cir. 2016), the court held that *Dastar* did not preclude a Lanham Act allegation by Warner against a firm that extracted images from movie publicity materials and licensed the images for use on numerous consumer products.

But in another important case, the Seventh Circuit held that *Dastar* precluded a Section 43(a) claim involving unauthorized copies of karaoke accompaniment tracks. *Phoenix Ent. Partners, LLC v. Rumsey*, 829 F.3d 817 (7th Cir. 2016). Plaintiff Slep-Tone and its successor Phoenix produced the tracks under the SOUND CHOICE trademark and associated trade dress. But Slep-Tone did not own the copyrights in the tracks, so when its customers (owners of bars and restaurants) allegedly began making unauthorized copies of Slep-Tone discs containing the tracks (and containing Slep-Tone's trademarks and trade dress), Slep-Tone sued under Section 43(a). Slep-Tone argued that when bar patrons heard the unauthorized tracks played (and saw the accompanying trademarks and trade dress displayed) they would believe that the track was an authorized Slep-Tone product. The court disagreed, reasoning that *Dastar* informed the analysis in two ways: first, as a general caution against Lanham Act claims that seemed to be substitutes for copyright claims; and, second, for the understanding that "origin" in Section 43(a) meant the manufacturing origin of the tangible goods sold in the marketplace. The court concluded that any confusion on the part of bar patrons was not about the source of the tangible goods, because the patrons only saw the creative content of the tracks, not the particular medium from which the tracks were played. The Ninth Circuit reached the same result on the same reasoning in *Slep-Tone Entertainment Corp. v. Wired for Sound Karaoke and DJ Services, LLC*, 845 F.3d 1246 (9th Cir. 2017).

We discuss *Dastar* further in Chapter 11, which considers claims for false attribution.

CHAPTER 3
FUNCTIONALITY

This chapter deals with the doctrine of functionality. Non-functionality is one of three primary prerequisites for trademark protection, the other two being distinctiveness (Chapter 2) and adoption and use (Chapter 4). Functionality concerns usually arise in cases involving non-verbal marks, especially product design trade dress. Section A of this chapter explains the two categories of functionality. Section B details the modern Supreme Court analysis for functionality, and Section C analyzes cases that apply the modern framework.

Non-functionality is a condition of protection for both registered and unregistered marks. Subject matter that, as a whole, is functional, is barred from registration under Lanham Act Section 2(e)(5). In that context, the examiner has the initial burden of establishing that the subject matter sought to be registered is functional. A registered mark can be challenged for functionality even if the registration has attained incontestable status. Lanham Act § 33(b)(8). (*See* Chapter 5 for a discussion of the concept of incontestability). When unregistered trade dress is asserted in a Lanham Act Section 43(a) action, it also must be shown to be non-functional, but the person who asserts the trade dress protection must prove that the trade dress is non-functional. Lanham Act § 43(a)(3).

The trademark law concept of functionality must be distinguished from the concept of functionality that is used in the common lexicon. When people describe a design as being "functional," the term may simply refer to the fact that the underlying product, or features of the product, have some use. A product design that is functional in the trademark sense is one that is so important to competing in the market for the product that even if the design is distinctive, trademark protection must be denied. To emphasize the distinction between functionality in its trademark law sense and functionality in its colloquial sense, some courts refer to the trademark law concept as "de jure functionality" and the colloquial concept as mere "de facto functionality."

The functionality doctrine may play a particularly important role in ensuring that product design trade dress protection under the Lanham Act is compatible with the protection of inventions under utility patent law. Lanham Act protection may extend indefinitely; utility patent protection subsists only for twenty years from the utility patent application filing date. If the trademark system permitted protection for functional subject matter, then a mark owner might enjoy intellectual property protection akin to a perpetual patent. At least, this is one of the primary concerns underlying the functionality doctrine, as many of the functionality cases reflect. For example, in *Qualitex Co. v. Jacobson Prods. Co.*, 514 U.S. 159 (1995), the Supreme Court explained that "the functionality doctrine prevents trademark law, which seeks to promote competition by protecting a firm's reputation, from instead inhibiting legitimate competition by allowing a producer to control a useful product feature." The Court said that it was the province of utility patent law, not trademark law, to encourage invention through the grant of exclusive rights in new product designs. The concerns about competition that are sometimes invoked to explain why functionality doctrine precludes trademark protection for useful product features have also been invoked in other contexts where competition concerns arise, resulting in doctrines such as aesthetic functionality.

A. CATEGORIES OF FUNCTIONALITY

Modern U.S. courts recognize two types of functionality. The first may be referred to as "utilitarian" or "mechanical" functionality, although courts sometimes omit the modifier, or use alternatives such as "traditional" functionality. The second is called "aesthetic" functionality. We supply some definitions and examples below.

1. UTILITARIAN FUNCTIONALITY

Industrial designers typically develop products having design features that accomplish something while also lending visual appeal to the product. The sleek appearance of a sports car chassis may provide aerodynamic benefits, while also providing an appearance that sports car buyers find to be appealing. If it were shown that only by adopting this particular shape could car makers achieve the aerodynamic benefits, or even if it were shown that this particular shape is so superior to others that rivals could not effectively compete without adopting it, then the shape might well be deemed functional in the trademark sense. We would consider this an example of "utilitarian" functionality in that the functionality derives from the mechanical advantages of the product's design. Most cases on functionality are of this type.

2. AESTHETIC FUNCTIONALITY

Courts have recognized a second variety of functionality termed "aesthetic" functionality. One way to understand the differences between mechanical functionality and aesthetic functionality is to distinguish between a product design whose primary purpose is to make a product useful in the traditional sense and a product design whose primary purpose is to contribute to the product's aesthetic appeal. For example, whereas the primary purpose of a car chassis design may be to confer aerodynamic advantages (as discussed above), the primary purpose of an engraved pattern on the rim of a dinner plate may be to make the dinner plate pleasing in appearance—and, importantly, to match with other dishes in the set. Some courts have concluded that even when a design does not make a product more useful in the narrow sense of the word, it might nonetheless contribute such value that rivals would need access to it in order to compete. A classic hypothetical concerns the heart-shaped box for Valentine's Day candy. The heart shape does not make the box structurally more stable, nor easier to stack, nor does it necessarily provide optimal carrying capacity. These would all be classic mechanical advantages. Instead, the heart shape functions (of course) as such a powerful symbol of the season that rivals would be unable to compete effectively using alternative shapes. While it would not be strictly necessary to speak of "aesthetic" functionality in referring to this situation ("functionality" would seem to serve just as well), courts have drawn the distinction and arguably have adopted slightly different tests for the respective forms of functionality, as we explain in Part B below.

B. THE MODERN SUPREME COURT ANALYSIS FOR FUNCTIONALITY

Under current U.S. law, the leading trademark case on functionality is *TrafFix Devices, Inc. v. Marketing Displays, Inc.*, 532 U.S. 23 (2001). To understand the functionality analysis articulated in *TrafFix Devices* and applied in subsequent cases, it is useful to turn first to a few important cases that preceded *TrafFix*. We do so in B.1 below, followed in B.2 by an analysis of *TrafFix*.

1. PREDECESSORS TO THE MODERN SUPREME COURT ANALYSIS

Morton-Norwich *factors*. The Court of Customs and Patent Appeals (CCPA) (predecessor to the Court of Appeals for the Federal Circuit) sets out an influential test for mechanical functionality in *In re Morton-Norwich Prods., Inc.*, 671 F.2d 1332 (CCPA 1982). The applicant sought to register the shape of a spray bottle used for various household cleaners and similar products. The CCPA suggested that there were four factors that could aid the court in determining whether designs should be deemed functional in a trademark case:

(1) Existence of expired utility patent disclosing utilitarian advantages of the design;

(2) Advertising/promotion touting utilitarian advantages of the design;

(3) Existence of alternative designs which perform the function equally well; and

(4) Whether or not the design results from a comparatively simple, cheap, or superior method of manufacturing the article.

It is relatively simple to connect these factors with the core purposes of the functionality doctrine. Factors (1) and (2)—to the extent that they refer to the mark owner's own patent and advertising documents—recognize that a mark owner's statements about utilitarian advantages of the design should be taken as highly credible. The evidentiary value of a mark owner's statements in a patent document should be valuable whether or not the patent is expired. However, if the design appears in an expired patent, the concern over separating the respective domains of utility patent and trademark subject matter may be implicated, because there may be a concern that the mark owner is seeking the equivalent of extended, or even perpetual, patent protection through the trademark system.

Morton-Norwich factors (3) and (4) would seem to go to the heart of the concerns that motivate the functionality doctrine. If a rival can adopt no alternative design that performs the function equally well (factor 3), then there would seem to be good reason to deny trademark protection and permit protection, if at all, through the patent system lest competition be adversely affected. Similarly, if alternative designs theoretically exist, but practical considerations (such as cost) render them non-viable (factor 4), then this, too, should cut against the grant of trademark protection.

Applying this test, the CCPA reversed the PTO's functionality rejection. There was evidence that competitors had adopted a multiplicity of different shapes for spray bottles, and these bottles apparently all capably operated as spray bottles. This alone seemed to persuade the CCPA that the design at issue was not functional. The *Morton-Norwich* factors became a prominent test for mechanical functionality prior to the *TrafFix Devices* decision. Courts are divided over the current viability of the *Morton-Norwich* test, as we explain in B.3 below.

Pagliero *and restatement standards for aesthetic functionality.* In another line of cases preceding *TrafFix Devices*, some courts endorsed and applied the concept of aesthetic functionality. In an important early Ninth Circuit decision, *Pagliero v. Wallace China Co.*, 198 F.2d 339 (9th Cir. 1952), the court ruled that a design that was "an important ingredient in the commercial success" of a product was *de jure* functional, and thus unprotectable, even if the design contributed to the product's success by providing aesthetic appeal rather than mechanical benefits. The case involved china patterns. The defendant argued that it needed to replicate the plaintiff's china patterns in order to compete in the market for replacement china, since purchasers of the replacement china would naturally insist that the pattern on the replacement match the original. The court agreed with this position, characterizing the pattern as an "essential selling feature" of the product.

The *Pagliero* standard was rejected as unpersuasive in *Wallace Int'l Silversmiths, Inc. v. Godinger Silver Art Co., Inc.*, 916 F.2d 76 (2d Cir. 1990). The *Wallace* court objected to *Pagliero* because under that standard, "the commercial success of an aesthetic feature automatically destroys all of the originator's trademark interest in it," even if there is no evidence that competitors would be foreclosed from developing equally desirable alternative designs. On the other hand, the *Wallace* court did not reject the concept of aesthetic functionality altogether; it merely insisted that there be evidence that no viable alternative designs would be available to competitors. A similar aesthetic functionality standard appeared in the Restatement (3d) of Unfair Competition, Section 17(c), and the standard bears a close resemblance to *Morton-Norwich* factor (3), which had traditionally been used in utilitarian functionality cases, as noted above.

In *Wallace*, the mark owner (Wallace) had appealed from the denial of a preliminary injunction motion. Wallace claimed trade dress in a design for a line of silverware; defendant Godinger produced a much less expensive line of silver-plated products. Both the Wallace and Godinger silverware included elements that the court described as "typical baroque elements," such as "scrolls, curls, and flowers." Both the trial and appellate courts concluded that allowing Wallace to claim trademark protection would hinder competition in the silverware market, or at least in the market for baroque silverware. The court struggled with Wallace's apparent effort to claim basic baroque elements, as opposed to claiming the precise expression of those elements in a particular design.

In another aesthetic functionality case, *Brunswick Corp. v. British Seagull Ltd.*, 35 F.3d 1527 (Fed. Cir. 1994), the Federal Circuit applied the *Morton-Norwich* factors to find aesthetic functionality. Brunswick claimed trademark protection in the color black used on outboard boat motors. British Seagull opposed registration on the ground of aesthetic functionality. The color black did not enhance the mechanical function of the boat motor. Rather, the color black matched with boats of all colors and caused the motor to appear small in size relative to the boat, two traits that were highly desirable to consumers. The Federal Circuit upheld a finding of aesthetic functionality based on these arguments.

2. MODERN SUPREME COURT ANALYSIS: *TRAFFIX DEVICES*

The Supreme Court addressed the functionality standard in a few cases prior to *TrafFix Devices*. In *Inwood*, a case dealing primarily with contributory infringement (*see* Chapter 7), the Supreme Court commented in a footnote that the functionality doctrine would operate to deny protection for an article's trade dress where the asserted trade dress was "essential to the use or purpose of the article" or where the trade dress "affect[ed] cost or quality" of the article. *Inwood Labs., Inc. v. Ives Labs., Inc.*, 456 U.S. 844 (1982). The Court reiterated this statement of the functionality doctrine in *Qualitex*, another case that did not turn primarily on functionality. *Qualitex Co. v. Jacobson Prods. Co., Inc.*, 514 U.S. 159 (1995). According to the Court in *Qualitex*, a product feature is functional " 'if it is essential to the use or purpose of the article or if it affects the cost or quality of the article,' that is, if exclusive use of the feature would put competitors at a significant non-reputation-related disadvantage."

The Court elevated the *Inwood/Qualitex* dicta into a general test for functionality in *TrafFix Devices, Inc. v. Marketing Displays, Inc.*, 532 U.S. 23 (2001). The Court noted that in *Inwood* and *Qualitex*, product design had been found to be functional if the design was essential to the use or purpose of the product, or if it affected the cost or quality of the product. The Court said that it had "[e]xpand[ed] upon the meaning of the phrase" to find that a design was functional if the exclusive use of it would put competitors at a significant non-reputation-related disadvantage, again quoting from *Qualitex*.

The Court then added important and somewhat perplexing gloss to its *Inwood/Qualitex* rule. Although the lower court (and, indeed, many others) had interpreted the functionality standard to call for an analysis of the competitive need for access to the design at issue, the Supreme Court found that competitive need was "incorrect as a comprehensive definition" of functionality. Apparently this was so because under the Court's standard, a design that was not strictly competitively necessary could nonetheless "affect the cost or quality of the product" and thus could be deemed functional. The Court declared that "[w]here the design is functional under the *Inwood* formulation"—that is, the essential to the use or purpose/affects the cost or quality standard—there is "no need to proceed further to consider if there is a competitive necessity" for the design. This comment seemed to call into question the use of alternative designs evidence to assess utilitarian functionality.

The Court also appeared to separate the analysis of utilitarian functionality from that of aesthetic functionality. The inquiry into "substantial non-reputation-related disadvantage" was proper only in cases of aesthetic functionality, the Court claimed. The Court also seemed to be saying that alternative designs evidence could be used in the aesthetic functionality inquiry.

Although the Court's pronouncements on the general standard of functionality are probably the most important aspect of the *TrafFix* case for the future of functionality analysis, the *TrafFix* case presented a much narrower functionality issue. Marketing Displays (MDI) had held utility patents directed to dual-spring sign stands that helped keep outdoor signs upright in windy conditions. After the utility patents expired, TrafFix introduced sign stands that were apparently copies of MDI products. MDI asserted a trade dress claim under Lanham Act Section 43(a). The trial court granted summary judgment that the asserted trade dress was functional, ruling that MDI had failed to produce sufficient evidence of non-functionality to raise a triable issue of fact. The Sixth Circuit reversed, reasoning that the trial court should have considered evidence of alternative designs (a hidden spring mechanism, for example) that would have performed the function equally well without copying the appearance of MDI's products. The Sixth Circuit had also apparently suggested that there was confusion among the circuits as to whether the existence of an expired utility patent foreclosed a claim of trade dress on the part of the patent owner. It was this last issue that impelled the Supreme Court to grant *certiorari*.

On this issue, the Court ruled that the existence of an expired utility patent is "strong evidence that the features claimed therein are functional." To the extent that a trade dress owner was asserting trade dress under Section 43(a) of the Lanham Act, such that the trade dress was presumed functional unless the trade dress owner satisfied the burden of showing non-functionality (Section 43(a)(3)), the existence of an expired utility patent added "great weight" to that statutory presumption. In such circumstances, the trade dress owner bore the "heavy burden" of showing non-functionality. To discharge the burden, a trade dress owner would need to show, for example, that the design of the product was merely "ornamental, incidental, or arbitrary . . . ."

Applying this rule, the Court decided that the existence of the expired patents alone barred the trade dress claim. The Court determined that the "central advance" claimed in the MDI patents was a dual-spring design. The actual claims of the patents specified that the springs be "spaced apart," and the products at issue used springs that were close together, but this did not matter, according to the Court, because MDI had argued in previous patent litigation that a product with springs close together infringed the claims under patent law's doctrine of equivalents, even if the product did not infringe the claims literally. The written description of the patents also supported the determination of functionality, according to the Court, because the dual-spring was described as serving the purpose of keeping the sign upright in heavy wind, and provided an "operational advantage" over single-spring designs (namely, minimizing twisting). In addition, statements in the patents' prosecution histories (the written records of negotiations between the patent applicant and the patent examiner) suggested functionality—for example, by touting the lower cost of a two-spring design compared to designs with larger numbers of spring.

The Court's analysis of the effect of patent protection on trade dress claims differs in some important ways from analyses in certain pre-*TrafFix* appellate decisions. In *Morton-Norwich*, the CCPA treated the existence of expired utility patent protection as a factor in the functionality analysis, but not as virtually dispositive. In a decision that some would regard as aberrational, *Vornado Air Circulation Sys., Inc. v. Duracraft Corp.*, 58 F.3d 1498 (10th Cir. 1995), the Tenth Circuit had adopted yet a different approach. The *Vornado* court decided that functionality doctrine was insufficient by itself to police the boundary between utility patent law and trademark law. Accordingly, the court ruled that where a product design was "part of a claim in a utility patent" and was "a described, significant inventive aspect of the invention . . . so that without it the invention could not fairly be said to be the same invention," then patent law principles should forbid the protection of the subject matter as trade dress, even if the trade dress were deemed non-functional.

It is significant that the Court in *TrafFix* did not adopt the *Vornado* approach. The concept of a "described, significant inventive aspect" has no solid grounding in utility patent law, and would have proven deeply troublesome to apply.

Having reached the conclusion that the existence of MDI's expired utility patents barred MDI's trade dress claim, the *TrafFix* Court emphasized that there was no need to engage in "speculation about other design possibilities, such as using three or four springs which might serve the same purpose," or using a box or framework that would hide the springs from view. In this regard, the emphasis in *TrafFix* departs quite substantially from that in *Morton-Norwich*, where CCPA placed considerable weight on the evidence of alternative designs.

Wrapping up its analysis, the Court in *TrafFix* added comments that inject considerable confusion into the functionality jurisprudence. According to the Court, if MDI had been claiming trade dress in "arbitrary curves in the [product's] legs or an ornamental pattern printed on the springs," the functionality analysis might produce a different outcome, because those designs might be shown to serve no purpose within the terms of the utility patent. As we have detailed in this chapter, it was well-established before *TrafFix* that trade dress in the design of a useful article is not destroyed merely because the design accomplishes some purpose. That is mere *de facto* functionality, possessed by virtually any industrial design.

C. APPLYING THE MODERN SUPREME COURT FUNCTIONALITY ANALYSIS AFTER *TRAFFIX*

The *TrafFix Devices* opinion has proven to be enigmatic on many points. Two points of particular controversy warrant special mention: (1) how to use evidence from utility patents in a functionality analysis; and (2) the continuing role of evidence of alternative designs. After discussing these points, we offer a series of examples of post-*TrafFix* cases dealing with mechanical functionality and aesthetic functionality, respectively.

1. EVIDENCE FROM UTILITY PATENTS

In *Jay Franco & Sons, Inc. v. Franek*, 615 F.3d 855 (7th Cir. 2010), Judge Easterbrook demonstrated how significantly evidence of utility patent protection may bear on the functionality analysis, and commented that although the Supreme Court's rule in *TrafFix* referred to expired utility patents, the logic of the rule extended also to utility patents still in force. Indeed, Judge Easterbrook asserted that evidence from newer utility patents might be more powerful because technological change might affect the determination of functionality.

Franek's predecessor had registered "the configuration of a round beach towel." However, various round towel designs were disclosed in certain utility patents. One such patent disclosed a round towel having drawstrings that could be pulled to turn the towel into a bag. Claim 1 of the patent recited a "towel-bag construction" including a non-rectangular towel having a casing along its perimeter with a cord threaded through the casing, and claim 2 specified that the non-rectangular towel was circular, in order to enable the user to change positions towards the changing angle of the sun without moving the towel. Under the rules of patent infringement, a mere round towel would not infringe the patent's claims; it would have to include both the casing and the cord, or equivalents. However, according to Judge Easterbrook, proof of infringement is not necessary. The mere mention of the circular towel in the claim was apparently enough "to signal that a round-towel design is useful for sunbathers," and in turn to trigger the *TrafFix* presumption of functionality. Likewise, the fact that the utility patent was probably invalid did not matter; only where the utility patent was invalid for lack of utility would invalidity cut against the presumption of functionality. According to Judge Easterbrook, it was important to weigh the utility patent evidence so heavily because otherwise it might be too easy for a firm to establish trade dress protection and use it to block others from developing innovative improvements. Exclusive power of this type is supposed to be the domain of utility patents, not trademarks, and utility patents have a limited duration. *See also Specialized Seating, Inc. v. Greenwich Industries, L.P.*, 616 F.3d 722 (7th Cir. 2010) (relying on utility patent evidence, and asserting that a goal of the functionality doctrine is "to separate the spheres of patent and trademark law").

The Federal Circuit relied on the existence of a utility patent in upholding the functionality rejection of the trade dress at issue in *In re Becton, Dickinson & Co.*, 675 F.3d 1368 (Fed. Cir. 2012). The fact that the utility patent merely disclosed the features at issue was sufficient; it was not necessary that the features be claimed in the utility patent, according to the majority. Judge Linn, dissenting, explicitly rejected this proposition. The use of utility patent evidence in post-*TrafFix* functionality determinations remains problematic, even at the Court of Appeals for the Federal Circuit, the court presumptively most familiar with utility patent documents.

In *McAirlaids, Inc. v. Kimberly-Clark Corp.*, 756 F.3d 307 (4th Cir. 2014), the claimed trade dress was a repeating pattern of embossed dots on "airlaid"—a cellulose fiber material used in packaging. McAirlaids had utility patent protection on its airlaid manufacturing process and on the resulting product, but the court ruled that the particular dot pattern claimed as trade dress was not the "central advance" in those patents, even though the airlaid bearing the dot pattern had been made using the patented process. The patent drawings depicted hexagonal shapes, rather than dots, and the description in the patents referred to a variety of different potential shapes for the embossing studs used in the process. The patents therefore did not provide "strong evidence" of functionality, unlike the patent in *TrafFix*.

2. EVIDENCE OF ALTERNATIVE DESIGNS

In *Valu Engineering, Inc. v. Rexnord Corp.*, 278 F.3d 1268 (Fed. Cir. 2002), the Federal Circuit insisted that in analyzing mechanical functionality, it remained proper to consider alternative designs evidence (the third *Morton-Norwich* factor) after the *TrafFix* decision. According to the Federal Circuit, alternative designs evidence was still probative to determine whether a design was essential to the use or purpose of the product. That is, the *TrafFix* opinion had not ruled out the use of alternative designs evidence, but had merely noted that once a product design had been found to be functional (e.g., under the "affects the cost or quality" part of the standard), that finding could not be overcome simply based on a showing that alternative designs were available.

The Federal Circuit employed the *Morton-Norwich* factors in light of *TrafFix* in *In re Becton, Dickinson & Co.*, 675 F.3d 1368 (Fed. Cir. 2012). Regarding the alternative designs factor, the panel majority reasoned that because it had already found factors (1) and (2) of the *Morton-Norwich* test to point towards functionality, there was "no need" to consider alternative designs evidence. Judge Linn, dissenting, chastised the majority for ignoring that evidence.

The Ninth Circuit has likewise ruled that a factors test of the *Morton-Norwich* variety remains viable after the *TrafFix* decision. *Millennium Laboratories, Inc. v. Ameritox, Ltd.*, 817 F.3d 1123 (9th Cir. 2016) (asserting that the Court in *TrafFix* "did not discredit" the factor test for functionality). The trade dress consisted of graphical elements of certain medical reports. Applying the factors test, the court concluded that triable issues of fact remained on the functionality issue. A "key point," according to the court, was the evidence showing alternative graphical arrangements for presenting the information contained in the report. In *Apple Inc. v. Samsung Elecs. Co., Ltd.*, 786 F.3d 983 (Fed. Cir. 2015), the Federal Circuit, applying Ninth Circuit law, invoked the factors test to assess Apple's claims of (1) unregistered trade dress in the overall shapes of its devices at issue (and the arrangement of icons on the devices' displays); and (2) registered trade dress relating to design details of sixteen icons appearing on the home screens of the devices. As to the unregistered trade dress, the court concluded that there was inadequate evidence to support a jury verdict of non-functionality under any of the factors.

Regarding the alternative designs factor specifically, the court acknowledged that Apple had presented evidence of the existence of alternative designs, but concluded that Apple had not shown that the alternatives "offered exactly the same features" as the asserted unregistered trade dress. Regarding the registered trade dress, the court reached the same conclusion on similar reasoning. According to the court, there was no dispute that the appearances of the individual icons should be deemed functional, and Apple had not adequately shown that the appearance of the combination of icons should be viewed any more favorably. *See also McAirlaids, Inc. v. Kimberly-Clark Corp.*, 756 F.3d 307 (4th Cir. 2014) (relying on alternative designs evidence and asserting that that the *TrafFix* holding on alternative designs did not apply "because the facts of this case differ from those presented to the Supreme Court in *TrafFix*.")

In contrast to the preceding cases, in *Eppendorf-Netheler-Hinz GmbH v. Ritter GmbH*, 289 F.3d 351 (5th Cir. 2002), the Fifth Circuit concluded that evidence of alternative designs was "not germane" to the test for mechanical functionality. Eppendorf had asserted trade dress protection in the design of plastic fins on its disposable pipette tips and dispenser syringes. The court found that the trade dress was functional under the "essential to the use or purpose" standard because Eppendorf had failed to prove that the fins were merely arbitrary flourishes serving no purpose. As previously noted, practically all trade dress claims could be thrown out on functionality grounds if courts chose to endorse this approach.

In *Specialized Seating, Inc. v. Greenwich Industries, L.P.*, 616 F.3d 722 (7th Cir. 2010), Judge Easterbrook commented on alternative designs evidence in upholding a ruling that a firm's registration for an X-frame chair design was invalid for functionality. The record included evidence of numerous chair designs. According to Judge Easterbrook, all of the chair designs, including the design at issue, represented compromises along a number of mechanical design parameters (weight, strength, kind of material, ease of setup, ability to connect the chairs, and other parameters). To Judge Easterbrook, this established that *all* of the alternative designs, along with the design at issue, were functional. That is, under this approach, the evidence of alternative designs seemed to establish functionality rather than cutting against it. The X-frame chair at issue was functional "not because it is the only way to do things, but because it represents one of many solutions to a problem." This is an unusual use of alternative designs evidence in the functionality analysis.

In *Arlington Specialties, Inc. v. Urban Aid, Inc.*, 847 F.3d 415 (7th Cir. 2017), the court upheld a grant of summary judgment of functionality. Arlington claimed trade dress in the shape and design of small personal care bags ("Dopp Kits," as they were known in the World War II era). Plaintiff identifies five elements in its claimed trade dress: (1) the bag's cuboidal shape; (2) the bag's softness; (3) the zipper's location on the bag; (4) the "folded and tucked" corners; and (5) the seam halfway up the bag's sides. The court reasoned that the undisputed evidence showed that the five recited elements "determine the bag's shape, its degree of rigidity, and how hard or easy it is to access its contents"—which were "functional aspects" of the product. The fact that Arlington chose the bag's features for their aesthetic appeal, and the fact that some of those features may have had less utility than other options, were not sufficient to raise a triable issue of fact. According to the court, "the right question is whether the design feature affects product quality or cost or is "merely ornamental." Because the undisputed evidence showed that the design features affected product quality, the court did not need to consider the availability of alternative designs. The court also noted that functionality is a question of fact, but stated that "the bar for functionality is so low that it can often be decided as a matter of law, as in this case."

The Sixth Circuit ruled that invoking alternative designs evidence was error in *Groeneveld Transport Efficiency, Inc. v. Lubcore Int'l, Inc.,* 730 F.3d 494 (6th Cir. 2013) (over a dissent).

3. EXAMPLES: APPLYING THE UTILITARIAN FUNCTIONALITY TEST

In a number of cases involving the utilitarian functionality test of *TrafFix* ("essential to the use or purpose" or "affects the cost or quality"), courts have applied the test vigorously to invalidate trade dress on functionality grounds. In *Eco Mfg. LLC v. Honeywell Int'l Inc.*, 357 F.3d 649 (7th Cir. 2003), involving claims to trade dress in the round shape of a thermostat, Judge Easterbrook imagined three ways in which the round shape might be "useful": rectangular products might clash with other decorative choices, or might be less safe (because of their sharp corners), or might be more difficult to use by people with arthritis or other disabilities. Although the court admitted that "[t]he record does not contain much along any of these lines," the court was still persuaded that its observations showed that the round design affected the cost or quality of the product and thus supported a finding of functionality.

In *Dippin' Dots, Inc. v. Frosty Bites Distrib.*, 369 F.3d 1197 (11th Cir. 2004), the court ruled that the appearance of flash-frozen ice cream beads ("dippin' dots") could not be protected as trade dress due to functionality. Applying the mechanical functionality analysis, the court examined the color, size, and shape of the beads, finding that (1) each color signified a flavor (e.g., pink signified strawberry), and hence was functional; (2) the size of the bead "contributes" to the product's creamy taste, because a larger bead would contain more ice crystals; accordingly, the bead size was functional; and (3) the bead shape allowed a quick and even freeze, contributing to the product's consistency; hence, it was functional. The court's finding as to color may have been better framed as a finding that the color lacked distinctiveness.

In a few other cases applying *TrafFix* where no utility patent was involved, the courts have not been quite so quick to accept functionality arguments. For example, in *General Motors Corp. v. Lanard Toys, Inc.*, 468 F.3d 405 (6th Cir. 2006), GM claimed trade dress protection in the exterior appearance of its HUMVEE vehicle. The evidence showed that the military had functional considerations in mind when it formulated the performance specifications for the HUMVEE vehicle, but this alone did not make GM's design choices as to the appearance of the vehicle "essential" to its use or purpose.

4. EXAMPLES: APPLYING THE AESTHETIC FUNCTIONALITY TEST

In *Abercrombie & Fitch Stores, Inc. v. American Eagle Outfitters*, 280 F.3d 619 (6th Cir. 2002), Abercrombie & Fitch alleged that American Eagle had copied various elements of Abercrombie's clothing, its store setup, and its catalog. The court determined that the clothing designs and store setup were aesthetically functional, whereas the overall appearance of the catalog survived an aesthetic functionality challenge. As to the clothing designs, Abercrombie asserted trade dress in the combination of several elements, such as certain words (e.g., "authentic"), various design elements (e.g., lacrosse sticks), combinations of primary colors, and so on. All of these elements in combination conveyed a sense of ruggedness and athleticism, and there was a lack of comparably pleasing alternative designs that would convey that same message for use on casual clothing marketed to young people, according to the court.

Likewise, protecting Abercrombie's store setup would have left rivals without effective alternatives. Abercrombie appeared to be claiming that the use of attractive college students as sales associates comprised an important part of its claimed store setup, and the court was unwilling to relegate competitors to hiring, say, unattractive middle-aged law professors to attempt to sell fashionable clothes to young people.

On the other hand, as to the catalogues, the court decided that the record presented at least a genuine issue of material fact as to aesthetic functionality. Abercrombie's catalogues used "grainy images of exceptionally fit and attractive young people in outdoor (often collegiate) settings," in a way that seemingly attempted to create a "sexual mystique" about the wearer. The court asserted that Abercrombie's rivals could compete effectively while avoiding grainy imagery of "scantily clad college students." Notably, the court proceeded to find that American Eagle's catalogue was not confusingly similar to Abercrombie's catalogue in any event.

As with the clothing designs in *Abercrombie*, a claim to trade dress rights in a round towel failed because the shape was rudimentary and general, according to the court in *Jay Franco & Sons v. Franek*, 615 F.3d 855 (7th Cir. 2010) (discussed above). That fact, coupled with evidence that the trade dress claimant's advertisements had promoted the round shape of the Franek towel as a fashion statement, showed that competitors would be put at a significant non-reputation-related disadvantage and therefore established that the registration at issue was invalid on the ground of aesthetic functionality. The court had also found functionality based on the mechanical functionality test, as discussed above.

In *ERBE Elektromedizin Gmbh v. Canady Technology LLC*, 629 F.3d 1278 (Fed. Cir. 2010), the Federal Circuit (applying Third Circuit law) found that the color blue for flexible endoscopic probes was functional. The evidence showed that the color blue was "prevalent in the medical field," the color made the tip more visible through an endoscopic camera, and "several companies use blue endoscopic probes." The evidence of prevalence and third party usages would seem to be more pertinent to distinctiveness than to functionality. The court recited both the mechanical and aesthetic functionality tests from *TrafFix*, and did not clearly indicate which type of functionality was implicated.

In *Christian Louboutin S.A. v. Yves Saint Laurent America Holding, Inc.*, 696 F.3d 206 (2d Cir. 2012), Louboutin had sought a preliminary injunction to enforce his registered "red sole" trademark. The mark consisted of a lacquered red sole on footwear. The registration included a diagram showing a red sole on a high-heeled shoe, where all aspects of the shoe (except the sole) were depicted in broken lines. Broken lines are ordinarily used to indicate that the registrant considers the features in question to be representative, but not limiting—in other words, that Louboutin here considered the mark to consist of the red sole on any shoe.

Yves Saint Laurent (YSL) sought to market a shoe featuring the same color on the entire shoe. One such shoe was a monochrome red shoe—colored red on the sole and all other features. Louboutin asserted its registered mark against YSL; YSL countered, among other things, that Louboutin's registration should be cancelled because the registered mark was aesthetically functional. YSL succeeded at the District Court, and Louboutin appealed.

The Second Circuit largely disagreed with the District Court's analysis, but it nevertheless upheld the denial of injunctive relief. The Second Circuit's opinion reviewed the evolution of the aesthetic functionality doctrine at some length, concluding that the Supreme Court's decisions in *Qualitex* and *TrafFix* had validated the approach to aesthetic functionality that had been expressed in some prior cases, such as *Wallace Silversmiths* (*see* Section B of this chapter). That is, a mark would be deemed aesthetically functional if protection of the mark would significantly undermine the ability of a competitor to compete in the market, a highly fact-specific inquiry that required the court to balance the mark owner's right to enjoy the benefits of its efforts to distinguish its product against the public's interest in a competitive market. Such a balancing inquiry does not lend itself to the development of per se rules, and, accordingly, the Second Circuit rejected the District Court's conclusion that there should be a per se rule of functionality for color marks in the fashion industry. However, the Second Circuit nonetheless concluded that Louboutin had not been entitled to an injunction. According to the Second Circuit,

Louboutin had established secondary meaning only in the use of a red sole that contrasts in color with the adjoining portion of the shoe. It instructed the Patent and Trademark Office to modify Louboutin's registration to reflect this limitation, citing Lanham Act Section 37, which permits a court in an action involving a registered mark to order the cancellation of a registration "in whole or part." The Second Circuit then concluded that in view of the registration as modified, Louboutin was not likely to succeed in showing that YSL's monochrome shoe infringed, such that it had been proper to deny injunctive relief.

Aesthetic functionality arguments have been asserted, albeit without success, in cases involving trademark merchandising. In *Au-Tomotive Gold, Inc. v. Volkswagen of America, Inc.*, 457 F.3d 1062 (9th Cir. 2006), Au-Tomotive Gold (Auto Gold) sold license plate frames, key chains, and other automobile accessories. Auto Gold's products included the word marks and logos of various car manufacturers, including, for example, the "VW" logo owned by Volkswagen. Auto Gold argued that it should be entitled to use the logos because the logos should be deemed aesthetically functional, at least in the context of Auto Gold's use of them. The argument was one that can be made in most contexts of trademark merchandising: the logo or mark itself is "the actual benefit that the consumer wishes to purchase." The argument can also be framed as an aesthetic compatibility argument: consumers want accessories with the manufacturer's logo because those accessories will then better match the automobile.

This aesthetic functionality argument failed in *Au-Tomotive Gold*. The court recognized that, under *TrafFix*, the relevant question was whether protection of the marks would put competitors at a non-reputation-related disadvantage. A mere argument that the mark was the basis for consumer demand could not suffice to establish aesthetic functionality—this would "eviscerate the very competitive policies that functionality seeks to protect," according to the court. One might also observe that the standard asserted by Auto Gold is much like the discredited *Pagliero* standard, which would have permitted an aesthetic functionality finding whenever a design was an "essential selling feature" of a product.

CHAPTER 4
USE

The concept of "use" plays numerous roles in U.S. trademark law. This chapter focuses on two. First, we briefly consider the link between the concept of use "in commerce" and the exercise of federal jurisdiction over trademark matters (Section A). Second, we consider the role of adoption and use in establishing trademark rights (Section B) and maintaining trademark rights (Section C). The concepts of use that we cover in this chapter are uses undertaken by, or with the permission of, the party claiming trademark rights. Questions may also arise about whether activities undertaken without the trademark owner's consent constitute unauthorized "use," or "use" that should be shielded as permissible. We cover those aspects of use in Chapters 7 and 9, respectively.

A. USE AS A JURISDICTIONAL PREREQUISITE

As we discussed in Chapter 1, the Supreme Court held in *The Trade-Mark Cases*, 100 U.S. 82 (1879) that Congress' authority to establish a federal trademark system springs from the Commerce Clause. Accordingly, the Lanham Act extends only to marks used "in commerce." For example, registration is available only to marks that are used "in commerce" or that the applicant intends to use "in commerce" under the terms of Lanham Act §§ 1(a)(1) and (b)(1), respectively. An action for infringement of registered trademark rights under Lanham Act § 32(1)(A) can only be brought against an alleged infringer who is engaging in an unauthorized use "in commerce," and the "in commerce" limitation also applies to a corresponding action based on unregistered rights under Lanham Act § 43(a)(1)(A).

Despite its constitutional significance, in practice, the "in commerce" limitation is of relatively little practical significance because of its immense breadth. The Lanham Act defines "in commerce" as being coterminous with the reach of the Commerce Clause. *See* Lanham Act § 45 ("in commerce" encompasses "all commerce which may lawfully be regulated by Congress"). Current Supreme Court Commerce Clause jurisprudence extends Congress' Commerce Clause powers to activities that impact interstate commerce, even if no physical goods cross state lines. Accordingly, even marks used by local businesses in small towns might well be engaged in use in commerce for Lanham Act purposes. For example, a barbecue restaurant called BOZO'S in Mason, Tennessee, was deemed to be using the BOZO'S mark in commerce for Lanham Act purposes based on evidence that a modest amount (15%) of the restaurant's patrons were from other states and that BOZO'S had been mentioned in a few publications distributed across state lines. It was not necessary to show that the restaurant was located on an interstate highway or that the majority of its business involved out-of-state travelers. *Larry Harmon Pictures Corp. v. Williams Restaurant Corp.*, 929 F.2d 662 (Fed. Cir. 1991). Similarly, an Illinois church's sale of two ADD A ZERO-marked hats to a

Wisconsin parishioner a part of a fundraising campaign satisfied the "in commerce" requirement. *Christian Faith Fellowship Church v. adidas AG*, 841 F.3d 986 (Fed. Cir. 2016).

As the foregoing discussion indicates, "in commerce" as used in the Lanham Act is not a synonym for "commercial." The phrase "use in commerce," which we examine closely in the next section of this chapter, should not be equated with "commercial use," and should not be understood to impart a requirement of commerciality.

B. USE AS A PREREQUISITE FOR ESTABLISHING RIGHTS

The U.S. trademark system may be considered a "first-to-use" system. In principle, this means that the first to adopt and use a distinctive and non-functional mark in connection with goods or services has the superior claim to rights in the mark. Courts sometimes speak of this principle in terms of "priority": the first user enjoys priority over others who seek to claim rights in the same or a similar mark. Most other major trademark systems in the world are first-to-register systems. These systems operate on the principle that the first to file an application for registration earns priority.

Although the first-to-use principle is straightforward, its implementation in U.S. law has been complicated. The complexity stems primarily from the fact that U.S. law recognizes both registered and unregistered (common law) trademark rights. (*See* Chapter 1). For several decades, it was not clear whether the same rules for determining sufficiency of use should apply both to claims of registered and unregistered rights. Effective 1989, after protracted debate, Congress amended the Lanham Act to change the rules for use in the context of claims to registered rights. Under the amendments, a claim to registered rights can be based either on *actual* use (supported by evidence of the use that has been undertaken) or on *constructive* use (supported by a claim of a bona fide "intent to use," followed eventually by evidence of actual use). A claim to unregistered rights must be supported by evidence of actual use. The following subsections explore these rules in some detail.

1. ACTUAL USE

Claims to registered rights. The owner of a mark that is "used in commerce" is entitled to apply to register its mark on the principal register. Lanham Act § 1(a)(1). The application must verify that the mark is in use in commerce, Lanham Act § 1(a)(3)(C), and must state the date of first use, among other things. Lanham Act § 1(a)(2). The Lanham Act defines "use in commerce" for the purpose of claims to registered rights as follows:

> "Use in commerce" means the bona fide use of a mark in the ordinary course of trade, and not made merely to reserve a right in a mark. For purposes of this chapter, a mark shall be deemed to be in use in commerce—

(1) on goods when—

(A) placed in any manner on the goods or their containers or the displays associated therewith or on the tags or labels affixed thereto, or if the nature of the goods makes such placement impracticable, then on documents associated with the goods or their sale, and

(B) the goods are sold or transported in commerce, and

(2) on services when it is used or displayed in the sale or advertising of services and the services are rendered in commerce, or the services are rendered in more than one State or in the United States and a foreign country and person rendering services is engaged in commerce in connection with the services.

Lanham Act § 45.

The definition requires "bona fide" use, and further specifies that such use must be undertaken "in the ordinary course of trade, and not made merely to reserve a right in a mark." This language responds to (and rejects) the "token use" doctrine, a judicial practice which had developed prior to the 1988 statutory revisions. Under the token use doctrine, courts had permitted mere symbolic uses (such as shipments of small quantities of marked goods within the mark owner's own distribution chain) to serve as evidence of use sufficient to support an application for registration, even though such uses clearly would not have qualified as actual uses for purposes of establishing unregistered rights under the standards prevailing at the time. Accordingly, decisions rendered prior to 1988 on actual use in the context of registered rights should be viewed with some caution, as those decisions may have been relying on the now-discarded notion of token use. *See, e.g., Custom Vehicles, Inc. v. Forest River, Inc.*, 476 F.3d 481 (7th Cir. 2007).

The requirement that use be bona fide and not merely to reserve rights in a mark also responds to fears about trademark warehousing. It is argued that in the absence of a use requirement, firms might amass large portfolios of trademark rights purely for the purpose of asserting them against subsequent market entrants in order to extract license fees. *Central Mfg., Inc. v. Brett*, 492 F.3d 876 (7th Cir. 2007). Trademark warehousing is thought to be undesirable because it does not align with the goal of rewarding producers who invest in developing consistent product quality.

The Lanham Act Section 45 definition of "use in commerce" also specifies what is meant by the use in commerce of a mark on goods and on services, respectively. As for goods, the definition states that if (a) the mark is physically associated with the goods, and (b) those goods are "sold or transported in commerce," then the mark will be "deemed" to be in use on the goods. Regarding provision (a), some older decisions seemed to insist on direct physical affixation of the mark to the goods. Cases such as *In re Marriott Corp.*, 173 U.S.P.Q. 799 (CCPA 1972) adopted a softer rule. There, the applicant had sought to register TEEN TWIST for sandwiches, and the PTO had refused registration on the ground that the applicant had merely used the mark on menus depicting the sandwiches. The CCPA reversed, finding this evidence sufficient to demonstrate affixation. Use of the mark in a catalogue portraying the goods may also suffice.

Regarding provision (b), calling for the goods to be "sold or transported in commerce," no general approach has emerged. Some courts have relied on language from *New England Duplicating Co. v. Mendes*, 190 F.2d 415 (1st Cir. 1951), where the court called for use "in a way sufficiently public to identify or distinguish the marked goods in an appropriate segment of the public mind as those of the adopter of the mark . . . ." Courts have tended to say that the determination of sufficient publicity is to be based on the facts of each case, *New West Corp. v. NYM Co. of Cal., Inc.*, 595 F.2d 1194 (9th Cir. 1979), sometimes explicitly adopting a "totality of circumstances" approach.

Some caution is warranted when invoking the totality of circumstances test in connection with claims to registered rights. If a firm aggressively publicizes its mark through advertising the mark in connection with the firm's goods, some might argue that the advertising alone should establish actual use, and, indeed, some courts seem to have accepted this proposition in the context of claims to unregistered rights (as we discuss below). An objection is that the Lanham Act definition arguably calls for a showing of at least one instance of selling or transporting the marked goods in commerce. A court could address this statutory construction dilemma by concluding that the term "deemed" in the statutory definition merely establishes one set of conditions under which use is to be found, rather than establishing a minimum threshold requirement.

In some cases, the analysis of the "sold or transported" language seems to rest primarily on the quantity of goods sold or transported, rather than on a more open-ended totality of the circumstances approach. *See, e.g., Paramount Pictures Corp. v. White*, 31 U.S.P.Q.2d 1768 (TTAB 1994) (distribution of game in connection with promoting musical group was *de minimis* and insufficient to establish actual use). *But see Custom Vehicles, Inc. v. Forest River, Inc.*, 476 F.3d 481 (7th Cir. 2007) (suggesting in dicta that "one sale of a $150 million airplane" might be sufficient, but concluding that one sale of a van did not suffice in the circumstances of the case).

The foregoing discussion relates to use in connection with goods. The Lanham Act Section 45 definition of use in commerce separately specifies the acts that are deemed to be use in connection with services. The provision sets out two elements, calling for the mark to be "used or displayed in the sale or advertising" of services, and for the services to be rendered in commerce. To analyze the first element, the PTO has developed a "direct association" test: there must be "a direct association between the mark and the services," meaning that the mark is used "in such a manner that it would readily be perceived as identifying the source of the services." *In re Adair*, 45 U.S.P.Q.2d 1211 (TTAB 1997). The direct association test may be viewed as a surrogate for the "affixation" concept that is invoked to test whether a mark is sufficiently associated with goods.

As to the second element—the requirement that services be rendered in commerce—the TTAB has held that there must be at least "an open and notorious public offering of the services to those for whom the services are intended." *Intermed Commc'ns, Inc. v. Chaney*, 197 U.S.P.Q. 501 (TTAB 1977). The TTAB applied this standard with some exuberance in *In re Cedar Point, Inc.*, 220 U.S.P.Q. 533 (TTAB 1983). Cedar Point, a long-established amusement park, was adding a water park that it planned to call OCEANA. Before the water park's grand opening, Cedar Point distributed some 700,000 advertising brochures including the OCEANA mark. One month before the grand opening, Cedar Point applied for a service mark registration for OCEANA. The TTAB upheld a finding that no services had been rendered in commerce as of the time of the application, notwithstanding the extensive distribution of brochures and the fact that construction of the park was at an advanced stage.

The Federal Circuit invoked *Cedar Point* to invalidate a service mark registration in *Aycock Engineering, Inc. v. Airflite, Inc.*, 560 F.3d 1350 (Fed. Cir. 2009). Aycock, the mark owner, had registered AIRFLITE for flight chartering services, defined in the registration as services in the form of "arranging for individual reservations for flights on airplanes."

Aycock formed a company, obtained two toll-free numbers to be used by customers to make flight reservations, and developed a network of air taxi operators who contracted with him to be available to provide flights to customers. However, as of the time the application was filed, Aycock never had actually arranged a flight for a customer, had never (apparently) advertised the availability of the toll-free numbers, and had never had more than twelve air taxi operators in his network (whereas he testified that he needed at least 300 in order to make his business operational). The Federal Circuit held that Aycock's application was void *ab initio* for failure to establish actual use when the application had been filed in 1970. The fact that the registration had existed for some thirty years prior to the ruling did not immunize the registration from invalidity.

In *Couture v. Playdom, Inc.*, 778 F.3d 1379 (Fed. Cir. 2015), the Federal Circuit clarified its language from *Aycock*. The court ruled that an "open and notorious" offering of services to intended customers, without more, is insufficient to satisfy the Lanham Act standard for showing a use in commerce.

Claims to unregistered rights. Some courts have held that the elements of actual use as set forth in the current Lanham Act definition for registered rights also apply to the assessment of actual use in the context of unregistered rights. *Planetary Motion, Inc. v. Techsplosion, Inc.*, 261 F.3d 1188 (11th Cir. 2001); *Allard Enters., Inc. v. Advanced Programming Res., Inc.*, 146 F.3d 350 (6th Cir. 1998). This suggests that a firm asserting unregistered rights ideally should be prepared to show (1) affixation or other association of the mark with the goods or services; and (2) sale or transport of the goods, or rendering of the services, in commerce.

Courts applying this approach in the context of unregistered rights frequently invoke the Lanham Act definition, but still rely on the *Mendes* test (discussed in Section B.1) to show the second element of actual use. Recall that the *Mendes* test asks whether the alleged use was sufficiently public to distinguish the marked goods among relevant consumers, in view of the totality of the circumstances. *See Johnny Blastoff, Inc. v. L.A. Rams Football Co.*, 188 F.3d 427 (7th Cir. 1999) (invoking the totality of circumstances test); *West Florida Seafood, Inc. v. Jet Restaurants, Inc.*, 31 F.3d 1122 (Fed. Cir. 1994) (considering "the evidence as a whole"). For example, *Planetary Motion* involved a dispute about whether the plaintiff had engaged in actual use of the unregistered mark COOLMAIL for software related to e-mail systems. The court found actual use. The plaintiff had posted the software on a UNIX user site online for free download under a standard open-source license agreement (the GNU General Public License), along with manuals and other announcements referencing the software (and the mark), and the software had been incorporated into several versions of a product that had been sold worldwide by a German company. This was all in keeping with the ordinary practice of software distribution under open-source arrangements, and the court asserted that use should be assessed by reference to customary practices in the particular industry.

The sheer quantity of use may be important. In *Zazu Designs v. L'Oreal, S.A.*, 979 F.2d 499 (7th Cir. 1992), a few sales over the counter and by mail of bottles of shampoo bearing the mark did not suffice to establish actual use. On the other hand, a mark owner's sales of over $11 million in SCAR brand rifles over a three-year period sufficed to establish actual use, even though the sales were exclusively to the military. *FN Herstal SA v. Clyde Armory Inc.*, 838 F.3d 1071 (11th Cir. 2016). The fact that the military sales had received extensive media coverage assisted in establishing that the sales were sufficiently public.

A continuing question in such cases is whether evidence falling short of actual sales of the marked goods could support a finding of actual use under the totality of the circumstances. In some older cases, including *Mendes* itself, courts seemed to take the position that advertising activities alone did not suffice, but advertising coupled with other activities might suffice even in the absence of evidence of sales. *See also New West Corp. v. NYM Co. of Cal., Inc.*, 595 F.2d 1194 (9th Cir. 1979).

The Ninth Circuit applied the totality of the circumstances test to service marks in *Chance v. Pac-Tel Teletrac, Inc.*, 242 F.3d 1151 (9th Cir. 2001). The Ninth Circuit affirmed a grant of summary judgment in favor of Pac-Tel, ruling that its use of TELECTRAC for services relating to the radio tracking of fleet vehicles predated Chance's use of TELETRAK for a lost-and-found service. The court discussed the sorts of circumstances that might be considered when deciding whether a service was rendered in commerce, including "the genuineness and commercial character of the non-sales activity," "the scope of the non-sales activity relative to what would be a commercially reasonable attempt to market the service," "the degree of ongoing activity of the holder to conduct the business using the mark," and other factors. Similarly, in *Rearden LLC v. Rearden Commerce, Inc.*, 683 F.3d 1190 (9th Cir. 2012), the Ninth Circuit, applying the totality of the circumstances approach from *Chance*, concluded that "even if a party completes the initial sale of its services only after its opponent has done so, that party still could establish prior use of the contested mark based on its prior non-sales activities." In light of this approach, it was improper to grant summary judgment on the "use" question, the Ninth Circuit determined.

2. CONSTRUCTIVE USE

After a legislative debate that stretched across many decades, the U.S. introduced a statutory concept of constructive use in the 1988 Trademark Law Revision Act. Under the intent-to-use ("ITU") provisions, a firm's bona fide intention to use a mark in commerce can serve as the basis for an application to register the mark, subject to certain conditions discussed below. A firm's bona fide intention to use a mark cannot serve as the basis for establishing unregistered rights.

Lanham Act Section 1(b) provides that a person can apply to register a mark by asserting a bona fide intention to use the mark in commerce, under circumstances showing the person's good faith. The statute does not define the concepts of "bona fide intention" or "good faith" in this context. However, courts are likely to require more than mere assertions of subjective belief. In *M.Z. Berger & Co., Inc. v. Swatch AG*, 787 F.3d 1368, 1376 (Fed. Cir. 2015), the court demanded "objective evidence of intent," although it noted that "the evidentiary bar is not high" and that determinations would be made "on a case-by-case basis considering the totality of the circumstances." *Id*. The court rejected the argument that its standard essentially required evidence that the applicant had actually "promoted, developed, and marketed" the mark in connection with the goods at the time of the application. *Id*. Indeed, in *Berger*, there was no satisfactory documentary evidence to corroborate the alleged intent to use, and there was ample testimony suggesting the lack of any such intent.

Where it is established that a registrant had a bona fide intent to use the mark in connection with some, but not all, of the goods or services specified in the application, it has been held that the application should not be invalidated in its entirety absent fraud. *Kelly Services, Inc. v. Creative Harbor, LLC*, 846 F.3d 857, 875 (6th Cir. 2017). Instead, according to the court in *Kelly Services*, the USPTO should be ordered to cancel the registration in part, to "excise" the goods or services not supported by the requisite intent to use. *Id*. The court acknowledged that its approach might encourage applicants to file "overbroad" ITU applications, but concluded that invalidating the registration in its entirety was too severe a penalty.

In order to perfect the application, the applicant must provide evidence within a prescribed time period that the mark has been put into actual use. Lanham Act § 1(d) (specifying a time period of six months from the notice of allowance of the application, extendable to 24 months). An applicant cannot assign rights in an intent-to-use application prior to filing the Section 1(d) verified statement of actual use. Lanham Act § 10(a)(1). The requirement to show actual use, and the limitation on assignments, both operate to diminish the opportunities for a trademark registration entrepreneur to develop a market in intent-to-use applications.

Lanham Act Section 7(c) specifies that the filing of an application establishes a right of priority in the mark for the goods or services specified in the registration, even if the registration is filed under the intent-to-use provisions. The following example illustrates the importance of Section 7(c). Suppose that a party *A* files an ITU application in January 2010, eventually receives a notice of allowance, and timely files a verified statement of actual use in April 2012. An unrelated party *Z* engages in actual use of the same mark in connection with the same goods in January 2011. Does *A* enjoy Section 7(c) constructive use priority as against *Z*? Yes; this is a permissible defensive use of priority. If *Z* were to oppose the registration of *A*'s mark based on *Z*'s January 2011 use, *A* could defend against the opposition by asserting constructive use priority to January 2010. *Zirco Corp. v. American Tel. & Tel. Co.*, 21 U.S.P.Q.2d 1542 (TTAB 1991). Constructive use priority can also be used offensively. That is, if *A* files an ITU application in January 2010, and *Z* files an ITU application in January 2011, *A* could successfully oppose *Z*'s application based on *A*'s January 2010 date of constructive use priority. *Larami Corp. v. Talk to Me Programs, Inc.*, 36 U.S.P.Q.2d 1840 (TTAB 1995) (noting that a judgment in favor of *A* in such an opposition proceeding would be contingent upon *A* ultimately receiving a registration on its ITU application).

Section 7(c) also plays an important role in priority disputes that arise in connection with trademark litigation. Suppose that *A* files an ITU application in January 2010, and *Z* engages in actual use starting in January 2011. In 2012, *A*'s application matures into a registration, and *A* sues *Z* in federal district court for trademark infringement. *A* is entitled to rely on the January 2010 filing to establish constructive use priority over *Z*. Therefore, assuming that *A* can establish other applicable elements of liability, *A* may succeed in enjoining *Z*'s use of the mark. *But cf. Talk to Me Products, Inc. v. Larami Corp.*, 804 F. Supp. 555 (S.D.N.Y. 1992), *aff'd* 992 F.2d 469 (2d Cir. 1993) (refusing to permit mark owner to claim Section 7(c) priority where mark owner's ITU application had not yet matured into a registration as of the time of the lawsuit).

The Second Circuit applied Section 7(c) in an important case, *WarnerVision Entertainment Inc. v. Empire of Carolina, Inc.*, 101 F.3d 259 (2d Cir. 1996). There, *A* (Empire, through its predecessors) had filed an ITU application in September 1994 (for REAL WHEELS used for model vehicles). *Z* (WarnerVision) filed a use-based application (for REAL WHEELS used for videos featuring autos), claiming its filing date, January 3, 1995, as the date of first use. In November, 1995, before *Z*'s registration issued, *Z* filed a lawsuit to enjoin *A* from engaging in use of the mark, asserting unregistered rights under Lanham Act § 43(a). At the time, *A*'s ITU application was still pending, and *A* had not yet filed its statement of use. Accordingly, if the court had enjoined *A*, *A* would have lost the opportunity to complete the ITU process. Such a ruling also might have encouraged opportunists to monitor the PTO for published ITU applications, choose applications to target, engage in minimal use of the subject marks, and then threaten the ITU application holder with suit, hoping to secure a generous settlement from the ITU holder. Recognizing these prospective problems, the Second Circuit wisely upheld the district court's denial of the preliminary injunction motion.

3. SPECIALIZED DOCTRINES FOR ASSESSING PRIORITY OF USE

Issues of adoption and actual use frequently arise when two or more parties who claim the same (or similar) trademark rights both claim to be the first to adopt and use a mark. They also may arise when an applicant applies to register a mark and the examiner rejects the application on the ground that the mark sought to be registered is confusingly similar to "a mark or trade name previously used in the United States . . . " Lanham Act § 2(d).

The courts and the PTO have developed the following doctrines to deal with particular fact patterns that periodically arise in such disputes. These doctrines operate to liberalize the notion of actual use, essentially injecting some limited constructive use concepts into the actual use analysis. Presumably, the doctrines are based on an impulse to inject considerations of fairness and flexibility into an actual use inquiry that otherwise might become hypertechnical.

Tacking. The doctrine of tacking is designed for cases in which a firm uses similar, but technically distinct, marks over time. Suppose, for example, that a firm adopts and uses an old-fashioned depiction of a pine tree as a logo for camping gear in year 1, then, in year 10, shifts to a simplified, more modern pine tree logo. Should the modern pine tree logo be treated as if it came into actual use in year 1 or year 10? That is, for purposes of establishing a date of first use, should the firm be able to "tack" its use of the old-fashioned logo onto its use of the modern logo? If not, then a mark owner would risk losing its priority of use whenever it sought to alter the mark to respond to new marketing styles.

Courts have held that such tacking is permitted, but only in the "exceptionally narrow instance" where the tacked and tacking marks are "so similar that consumers generally would regard them as essentially the same." *Brookfield Communications, Inc. v. West Coast Ent. Corp.*, 174 F.3d 1036 (9th Cir. 1999). "The marks must create the same, continuing commercial impression, and the later mark should not materially differ from or alter the character of the mark attempted to be tacked." *Van Dyne-Crotty, Inc. v. Wear-Guard Corp.*, 926 F.2d 1156 (Fed. Cir. 1991). In one case, the TTAB concluded that this standard was satisfied when a department store owner sought to tack its first use date of HESS BROTHERS and HESS onto its new mark HESS'S. Consumers had begun referring to the store as HESS'S rather than HESS BROTHERS or HESS; that, indeed, was the reason the store had sought to establish rights in HESS'S. By contrast, THE MOVIE BUFF'S MOVIE STORE for a video store could not be tacked onto MOVIEBUFF.COM. *Brookfield Communications, Inc. v. West Coast Ent. Corp.*, 174 F.3d 1036 (9th Cir. 1999). *See also One Indus., LLC v. Jim O'Neal Dist., Inc.*, 578 F.3d 1154 (9th Cir. 2009) (a firm's prior use of an "O' " logo could not be tacked to the firm's subsequent use of a redesigned "O' " logo).

A similar type of question arises when a firm uses a mark in connection with a first product (say, MOVIEBUFF for software) for a time, and then shifts to using the same mark in connection with a second product (say, MOVIEBUFF for an online database). Should the mark MOVIEBUFF for an online database be treated as if it had first been used when the firm commenced use of the mark MOVIEBUFF for software? This may be understood as another form of a "tacking" argument. It has been argued that tacking should be permitted in this class of cases if it can be shown that the second product is within the scope of the firm's natural zone of product expansion. *Brookfield Communications, Inc. v. West Coast Ent. Corp.*, 174 F.3d 1036 (9th Cir. 1999). The concept of a "natural zone of expansion" more typically refers to a firm's natural *geographic* zone of expansion, a topic discussed in Chapter 6.

The "same, continuing commercial impression" inquiry is a question for the jury. *Hana Financial, Inc. v. Hana Bank*, 135 S.Ct. 907 (2015). The Court reasoned that while the inquiry might be characterized as a mixed question of law and fact, the fact that the inquiry relied on the ordinary consumer's understanding of the "impression" of a mark suggested that the question should be reserved for the jury.

Analogous use. We noted above that in the registration context, a priority of use issue may arise under Lanham Act § 2(d), which bars registration if there exists a confusingly similar mark or trade name previously used in the United States. In determining whether such a mark or trade name is previously used for purposes of Section 2(d), the TTAB has recognized a doctrine of "analogous use." That is, evidence that firm *A* used a term in a manner that is at least analogous to a mark will suffice to preclude another firm *B* from subsequently registering the term as a mark, even though *A*'s use would not qualify under the rules for actual use. For a use to be analogous to a trademark use, the use must be (1) an open and notorious public use; (2) directed to the segment of the purchasing public for whom the product or services are intended; and (3) carried out in a manner sufficient to inform or apprise prospective purchasers of the present or future availability of the adopter's product or service. *Computer Food Stores, Inc. v. Corner Store Franchises, Inc.*, 176 U.S.P.Q. 535 (TTAB 1973). For example, use of a mark in advertisements prior to the actual sale or transport of any marked goods might qualify as an analogous use under the *Computer Food Stores* test. However, even where an alleged analogous use satisfies this test, the cases have imposed an additional requirement: the analogous use must be followed eventually by an actual use. *American Express Co. v. Goetz*, 515 F.3d 156 (2d Cir. 2008); *T.A.B. Sys. v. Pactel Teletrac*, 77 F.3d 1372 (Fed. Cir. 1996) (explaining that the analogous use can be tacked onto the actual use when the actual use follows within a commercially reasonable period of time). The TTAB has cautioned against confusing this concept of "analogous use" with the now-discarded notion of token use. *Shalom Children's Wear Inc. v. In-Wear A/S*, 26 U.S.P.Q.2d 1516 (TTAB 1993). Token use referred to an actual trademark use carried out at a de minimis level and not in the ordinary course of trade, as we described above in Section B.1.

Unlawful uses. Suppose that a mark claimant attempts to rely on instances of actual use that were illegal when undertaken. Should those instances of actual use provide the basis for a claim of registered or unregistered rights? In a case involving registered rights, a Ninth Circuit panel held that a mark owner could not rely on uses of the mark OLIVENOL for a dietary supplement where the evidence showed that the mark owner's label's violated certain labelling restrictions. *CreAgri, Inc. v. USANA Health Sciences, Inc.*, 474 F.3d 626 (9th Cir. 2007). The Trademark Trial and Appeal Board has invoked the doctrine of unlawful use in cases involving efforts to register marks used in connection with marijuana sales, noting that the sales are unlawful under federal law even though they may be legal under various state laws. *In re Morgan Brown*, 119 U.S.P.Q.2d (BNA) 1350 (TTAB 2016).

Foreign use; claims to foreign priority (Lanham Act § 44). Lanham Act Section 44 implements the *telle quelle* obligation of Paris Convention Article 6 *quinquies*. In essence, the *telle quelle* obligation is that a trademark originating from a Convention country must be accepted for filing and protected "as is" in any other Convention country if the trademark is duly registered in the mark owner's country of origin. Lanham Act Section 44(e) provides that a mark duly registered in the country of origin of the foreign applicant may be registered in the U.S. on the principal register if the applicant timely submits a certification or certified copy of the registration in the country of origin, and if the application states "the applicant's bona fide intention to use the mark in commerce, but use in commerce shall not be required prior to the registration." In *Crocker Nat'l Bank v. Canadian Imperial Bank of Commerce*, 223 U.S.P.Q. 909 (TTAB 1984), the TTAB held that foreign nationals who filed U.S. applications based on Lanham Act § 44(e) were under no obligation to show use anywhere in the world. Under prior PTO practice, the PTO had relieved such applicants of any requirement to show use in commerce in the U.S., but had required them to show use at least somewhere in the world. On the other hand, the Federal Circuit has held that a foreign national who files based on Section 44(e) is still subject to other validity conditions of U.S. law, such as distinctiveness. *In re Rath*, 402 F.3d 1207 (Fed. Cir. 2005). The case concerned the U.S. rule that a mark that is "primarily merely a surname" lacks distinctiveness and cannot be registered absent a showing of secondary meaning. Lanham Act § 2(e)(4). The court held that this rule applied equally to foreign nationals filing on the basis of Section 44(e).

Whereas Section 44(e) deals with the effect in the U.S. of foreign *registrations*, Section 44(d) concerns a related issue: priority based on the filing of a foreign *application* for registration. It provides that if a qualifying foreign national applies for registration in an eligible country (such as a Paris Convention country, or other eligible country as specified in Section 44(b)), and then later files an application to register in the U.S., the U.S. application will be treated as having been filed on the filing date of the foreign application if other requirements in Section 44(d) are met. The primary requirements are (1) that the U.S. application be filed within six months of the foreign application filing date (Section 44(d)(1)); and (2) that the applicant file a statement of bona fide intent to use the mark in commerce. (Section 44(d)(2)). Importantly, there is no requirement that the applicant follow up with an eventual statement of actual use, even though applications filed under the Section 1(b) ITU provision are subject to such a requirement.

The rules of constructive use priority embodied in Section 7(c) take into account claims of foreign priority made pursuant to Section 44(d). If a party *A* files an application in Canada in January 2012 and files an application in the U.S. in May 2012, properly claiming priority to the Canadian application under Section 44(d), *A* will receive a date of constructive use priority of January 2012. Accordingly, if a party *Z* files a U.S. application in February 2012, *Z*'s claim of constructive use priority is subject to *A*'s superior claim of priority based on the Canadian application. Lanham Act § 7(c)(3).

4. IDENTIFYING THE USER; USE FOR THE BENEFIT OF ANOTHER

In the usual case, there is little need to question whether the person undertaking the use of a mark is doing so on behalf of the trademark claimant. If Ford employees manufacture a Ford nameplate and affix it to the chassis of a Ford automobile, the trademark law takes the position that Ford is using the mark, recognizing that the employment relationship between Ford and its employees removes any doubt that the employees are acting on behalf of Ford.

In less typical cases, the relationship between the entity actually carrying out the use and the entity claiming ownership of the mark may be less clear. Some rules of trademark law have developed to govern the analysis in such cases.

One such rule is the "related companies" doctrine, codified in Lanham Act § 5. Under that provision, use of a mark by an entity *U* inures to the benefit of another entity *O* if *U* is a "related company" with *O*, a concept that is defined in Section 45 as "any person whose use of a mark is controlled by the owner of the mark with respect to the nature and quality of the goods or services on or in connection with which the mark is used." Where *U* and *O* are in a formal subsidiary/parent relationship, the related company test is satisfied. *May Dept. Stores Co. v. Prince*, 200 U.S.P.Q. 803 (TTAB 1978). Likewise, the test is satisfied where *U* is *O*'s licensee, as long as the license provides for adequate control over the quality of the goods or services that the licensee provides under the mark. *United States Jaycees v. Philadelphia Jaycees*, 639 F.2d 134 (3d Cir. 1981). This is particularly important for franchising relationships, which will ordinarily involve a trademark license between the mark owner/franchisor and the mark user/franchisee. *Dawn Donut Co., Inc. v. Hart's Food Stores, Inc.*, 267 F.2d 358 (2d Cir. 1959) (applying the related companies doctrine to franchising, and discussing the proviso that the franchisee control the quality of the goods).

Consider another scenario in which *O* is a manufacturer of trademarked goods and *U* is its exclusive distributor. In the absence of any express contract, courts are likely to presume that manufacturer *O* is the trademark owner, allowing the distributor *U* to attempt to rebut the presumption. *Covertech Fabricating, Inc. v. TVM*

Building Prods., Inc., 855 F.3d 163 (3d Cir. 2017). Borrowing from McCarthy's treatise, the *Covertech* court adopted a multi-factor balancing test to determine whether the distributor had rebutted the presumption. *Id.* at 171 (specifying that the factors to be considered are: (1) "[w]hich party invented or created the mark"; (2) "[w]hich party first affixed the mark to goods sold"; (3) "[w]hich party's name appeared on packaging and promotional materials in conjunction with the mark"; (4) "[w]hich party exercised control over the nature and quality of goods on which the mark appeared"; (5) "[t]o which party did customers look as standing behind the goods, *e.g.*, which party received complaints for defects and made appropriate replacement or refund"; and (6) "[w]hich party paid for advertising and promotion of the trademarked product."), *quoting* 2 MCCARTHY ON TRADEMARKS § 16:48.

Where the relationship between *U* and *O* is more ambiguous, courts may consider whether there is at least a "substantial relationship" between the two in order to decide whether uses by *U* should inure to the benefit of *O* in accord with the related companies doctrine. *Secular Organizations for Sobriety, Inc. v. Ullrich*, 213 F.3d 1125 (9th Cir. 2000) (no "substantial relationship" established where organizers of national non-profit entity encouraged autonomy among local affiliates). These principles have been especially difficult to apply to informal organizations such as musical groups. Some courts have held that where individual musicians perform together under the name of a group, the individuals do not each establish individual trademark claims to the group name. Rather, the use of the group name by the individual members ordinarily inures to the benefit of some controlling entity—perhaps the manager of the group, for example. Accordingly, musicians who depart the group do not have trademark rights in the group name to carry with them, and this may affect the departing musician's ability to continue to perform under the group name, or to exclude others from doing so. *Robi v. Reed*, 173 F.3d 736 (9th Cir. 1999). In contrast, other courts have suggested that the "norm in the music industry is that an artist or group generally owns its own name." *Bell v. Streetwise Records, Ltd.*, 640 F. Supp. 575 (D. Mass. 1986) (concluding that the performers in the pop group NEW EDITION owned trademark rights in the name superior to any claim of rights made by the group's management). The *Bell* court suggested that courts first identify the "quality or characteristic for which the group is known by the public," and then determine who controls that quality or characteristic. In *Bell*, the public associated the group primarily with the characteristics of the individual performers, helping to persuade the court that the performers should be deemed the initial users (and hence owners) of rights in the mark.

In another series of cases, a problem analogous to the related companies problem arises. Here, the issue is whether the use of a mark by the public could inure to the benefit of a trademark owner. A classic example involves the mark COKE for soft drinks produced by Coca-Cola. Coca-Cola introduced its soft drink under the name COCA-COLA, but, in time, consumers began referring to the drink as COKE.

Eventually, Coca-Cola sought to assert trademark rights in COKE, and succeeded. *Coca-Cola, Co. v. Busch*, 44 F. Supp. 405 (E.D. Pa. 1942). To arrive at this result, the court effectively was treating the public as Coca-Cola, Inc.'s surrogate, permitting the public's adoption and use of the shortened name COKE to inure to Coca-Cola, Inc.'s benefit. It may be convenient to refer to such uses as "surrogate" uses.

On a related point, where the Illinois High School Athletic Association (IHSA) had used the term MARCH MADNESS in reference to the Illinois state high school basketball tournament, but the general public across the United States had subsequently come to use the term to refer to the National Collegiate Athletic Association (NCAA) basketball tournament, the IHSA could not claim exclusive rights in the term sufficient to block the NCAA (or its licensees) from using the mark. *See Illinois High School Ass'n v. GTE Vantage Inc.*, 99 F.3d 244 (7th Cir. 1996). The court referred to the MARCH MADNESS mark as a "dual-use" term and ruled that it should be treated as if it had become generic, but the court did not specify whether that meant that the NCAA had no claim of trademark rights. The court might have said (but did not) that the public's use of MARCH MADNESS in reference to the NCAA basketball tournament constituted a use effective to establish trademark rights.

C. NON-USE AND THE FAILURE TO CONTROL USES

Because trademark rights arise from adoption and use (or their legal equivalents), it follows that trademark rights may be lost if the mark owner discontinues use or fails to control it. The Lanham Act incorporates these principles, defining two forms of trademark abandonment:

A mark shall be deemed to be "abandoned" if either of the following occurs:

(1) When its use has been discontinued with intent not to resume such use. Intent not to resume may be inferred from circumstances. Nonuse for 3 consecutive years shall be prima facie evidence of abandonment. "Use" of a mark means the bona fide use of such mark made in the ordinary course of trade, and not made merely to reserve a right in a mark.

(2) When any course of conduct of the owner, including acts of omission as well as commission, causes the mark to become the generic name for the goods or services on or in connection with which it is used or otherwise to lose its significance as a mark. Purchaser motivation shall not be a test for determining abandonment under this paragraph.

Lanham Act § 45. In this Section, we discuss abandonment through non-use (C.1) and abandonment through failure to control use (C.2).

1. NON-USE

When a mark owner discontinues use of the mark "with intent not to resume such use," the mark is deemed abandoned. Lanham Act § 45. Nonuse for three consecutive years constitutes prima facie evidence of abandonment—effectively creating a "mandatory inference of intent not to resume use." *Emergency One v. American FireEagle*, 228 F.3d 531 (4th Cir. 2000). According to the express language of the statute, intent not to resume use may also be inferred from the circumstances. Lanham Act § 45. In *Emergency One*, the mark challenger made out a *prima facie* case by showing that the mark owner had ceased production of fire trucks bearing the mark at issue, and, during a three-and-a-half year period, had not applied the mark to new fire trucks, although the mark owner had used the mark on some promotional merchandise. *But cf. Community of Christ Copyright Corp. v. Devon Park Restoration Branch of Jesus Christ's Church*, 634 F.3d 1005 (8th Cir. 2011) (record showed that mark owner intended to move away from use of mark, but there was no inference of non-use given that mark's use continued on church's buildings, podiums, and more; mark's use was reduced, but not discontinued).

If a *prima facie* case of abandonment for non-use is made out, the burden of production shifts to the mark owner to provide evidence of intent to resume use, although the ultimate burden of showing abandonment remains with the mark challenger. *Emergency One v. American FireEagle*, 228 F.3d 531 (4th Cir. 2000). To overcome the prima facie case, the mark owner must show something beyond a mere subjective intent to resume use. *Natural Answers Inc. v. SmithKline Beecham Corp.*, 529 F.3d 1325 (11th Cir. 2008). Likewise, evidence of mere "intent not to abandon" is insufficient. *Exxon Corp. v. Humble Exploration Co., Inc.*, 695 F.2d 96 (5th Cir. 1983) ("There is a difference between intent not to abandon or relinquish and intent to resume use in that an owner may not wish to abandon its mark but may have no intent to resume its use.")

Moreover, intent to resume use at some unspecified future date will not be accepted. Courts have held that evidence of intent to resume use "in the reasonably foreseeable future" is needed. *Emergency One v. American FireEagle*, 228 F.3d 531 (4th Cir. 2000). In *Emergency One*, the court commented that a case-by-case analysis was required in order to determine whether the "reasonably foreseeable future" criterion was satisfied. The *Emergency One* case involved the mark AMERICAN EAGLE used on fire trucks, and the court suggested that five to six years might be reasonable for fire trucks given their long lives, whereas the same time period might be unreasonable for a product having a much shorter useful life, such as potato chips. In *Silverman v. CBS Inc.*, 870 F.2d 40 (2d Cir. 1989), CBS had used "Amos 'n Andy" in connection with radio and (later) television broadcasts from the 1920s until 1966, when it ceased the use in response to complaints from civil rights organizations. When it asserted rights in the mark in the late 1980s against Silverman, CBS claimed that it had always intended to resume use of the mark at some unspecified time. This showing was insufficient, according to the court.

Some courts have held that the requisite intent to resume use must be formulated within the three years of nonuse. *Specht v. Google Inc.*, 747 F.3d 929 (7th Cir. 2014); *ITC Ltd. v. Punchgini, Inc.*, 482 F.3d 135, 149 n. 9 (2d Cir. 2007). In *Specht*, the Android Data Company (formed by Specht) had used ANDROID DATA for various software and web-based services starting in 1998, but by 2002, it evidently was no longer providing services in connection with the mark. It maintained a website (androiddata.com) until 2005, but did not sell any services through the site. In 2007, Specht had attempted to license his software, and had delivered a mass mailing to potential customers in 2007, generating no sales. The court ruled that Specht had failed to establish an intent to resume use. The mere maintenance of the website alone was inadequate under the circumstances, and the 2007 activities were mere isolated activities, and in any event occurred more than three years after the discontinuance of use. Hence, those activities could not provide the basis for a determination of intent to resume use.

A few courts have discussed whether a mark owner should be able to present evidence of "residual goodwill" to overcome an inference of non-use. In *Ferrari S.p.A. Esercizio Fabbriche Automobili E Corse v. McBurnie*, 11 U.S.P.Q.2d 1843 (S.D. Cal. 1989), Ferrari asserted trade dress rights in the appearance of its 365 GTB/4 Daytona Spyder, which it had not produced for some fifteen years. The court pointed out that Ferrari had continued to service Daytona Spyder vehicles and supply parts for them. In addition, the court decided that even independent of Ferrari's activities, there remained a "residual goodwill" in the appearance of the Daytona Spyder— that is, consumers still strongly associated the design with Ferrari, perhaps aided by the fact that the vehicles were still driven extensively even though Ferrari was no longer making them, and by the fact that Ferrari continued to make other similar vehicles. The Second Circuit relied on these facts to distinguish *Ferrari* in *L & J.G. Stickley, Inc. v. Canal Dover Furniture Co., Inc.*, 79 F.3d 258 (2d Cir. 1996), a case involving the famed furniture designs of Gustav Stickley. The designs were discontinued in the 1920s and only reintroduced in 1989. The court refused to give Stickley the benefit of residual goodwill even though it seemed probable that some consumers continued to associate Stickley with the designs.

2. FAILURE TO CONTROL USES

As we have noted, the Section 45 definition of abandonment specifies that a mark can be abandoned as a result of a mark owner's conduct:

A mark shall be deemed to be "abandoned" when either of the following occurs . . .

(2) When any course of conduct of owner, including acts of omission as well as commission, cause mark to become generic name for goods or services in connection with which it is used or otherwise to lose its significance as a mark . . .

Lanham Act § 45. There are two primary courses of conduct that are most likely to give rise to a claim of abandonment under prong (2) of the definition. First, when a mark owner simply fails to police uses by unrelated third parties, or attempts to police them but fails, the mark may become generic. This is a reiteration of the genericness doctrine discussed in Chapter 2.

Second, a trademark owner's "naked" licensing of a mark could give rise to abandonment. A naked trademark license is one that does not provide for the licensor to exercise control over the quality of the goods or services that the licensee provides under the mark. *Eva's Bridal Ltd. v. Halanick Enterprises, Inc.*, 639 F.3d 788 (7th Cir. 2011). Without such control, the mark may cease to provide a guarantee of consistent quality, and consumers who rely on the mark may be misled. *Dawn Donut Co., Inc. v. Hart's Food Stores, Inc.*, 267 F.2d 358 (2d Cir. 1959).

There are three ways in which a trademark licensor may demonstrate adequate quality control: (1) by pointing to express quality control provisions in the license agreement; (2) by demonstrating that the licensor in fact exercised control over quality even in the absence of express provisions in the license; or (3) that the licensor reasonably relied upon the licensee to maintain quality control in view of some special relationship among the licensing parties, such as a long-term business relationship. *Stanfield v. Osborne Indus., Inc.*, 52 F.3d 867 (10th Cir. 1995).

In *FreecycleSunnyvale v. Freecycle Network*, 626 F.3d 509 (9th Cir. 2010), the court discussed naked licensing arising out of the use of the marks FREECYCLE and THE FREECYCLE NETWORK by a member group (FreecycleSunnyvale) of a non-profit umbrella organization (Freecycle Network). An e-mail from the umbrella group to the member warning against use of the marks "for commercial purposes" did not amount to an express or implied quality control provision. Moreover, various admonitions and policies such as "Keep it Free, Legal, and Appropriate for all Ages" did not demonstrate that the umbrella group in fact exercised adequate control, because these policies did not necessarily relate to the quality of the member groups' services and there was no adequate evidence that the policies were enforced in any event. Nor was the court persuaded that the quality control requirement should be liberalized in the context of loosely-organized, not-for-profit groups.

In *Eva's Bridal Ltd. v. Halanick Enterprises, Inc.*, 639 F.3d 788 (7th Cir. 2011), Judge Easterbrook determined that the licensing arrangement at issue constituted "the paradigm of a naked license" because the licensor "had, and exercised, *no* authority over the appearance and operations of [the licensee's] business, or even over what inventory to carry or avoid." Although the licensor and licensee were relatives and there had been a longstanding family practice of opening new bridal shops and sharing the EVA'S BRIDAL name among family members, Judge Easterbrook apparently did not see this as sufficient to justify reasonable reliance by the licensor on the licensee's quality control. Likewise, in *Stanfield*, the prior working relationship between the parties was deemed insufficient to justify reasonable reliance. In *Barcamerica Int'l USA Trust v. Tyfield Importers Inc.*, 289 F.3d 589 (9th Cir. 2002), the Ninth Circuit offered four examples of close working relationships that would justify a licensor's reliance on the licensee's quality control efforts:

> (1) a close working relationship for eight years; (2) a licensor who manufactured ninety percent of the components sold by a licensee and with whom it had a ten year association and knew of the licensee's expertise; (3) siblings who were former business partners and enjoyed a seventeen-year business relationship; and (4) a licensor with a close working relationship with the licensee's employees, and the pertinent agreement provided that the license would terminate if certain employees ceased to be affiliated with the licensee.

The court decided that the mark owner in *Barcamerica* had failed to show reasonable reliance on the licensee's efforts, resulting in the abandonment of the mark LEONARDO DA VINCI for wine. The fact that the licensee's wine made under the DA VINCI label was allegedly of high quality did not matter; the question was whether the mark owner undertook efforts to ensure that the product quality remained consistent.

Notwithstanding the helpful guidance from cases like these, it remains difficult to predict how judges will resolve issues of abandonment via alleged uncontrolled licensing. Judges have split over the standard of evidence for a showing of abandonment through naked licensing, sometimes in the same case. *Grocery Outlet Inc. v. Albertson's Inc.*, 497 F.3d 949 (9th Cir. 2007) (debating the use of the "clear and convincing" standard—advocated by one judge—and the "preponderance" standard—advocated by another). In some cases involving formal franchise arrangements, judges have seemed to place a particularly heavy burden on terminated franchisees seeking to establish that their own failure to control quality resulted in abandonment of the franchisor's marks. *Kentucky Fried Chicken Corp. v. Diversified Packaging Corp.*, 549 F.2d 368 (5th Cir. 1977).

In some other cases, especially those outside the franchising context, courts have seemed to apply more relaxed standards, although each case must be taken on its facts. In *Tumblebus Inc. v. Cranmer*, 399 F.3d 754 (6th Cir. 2005), the court decided that a Louisville, Kentucky small business owner's acquiescence in the use of her mark by others in various parts of the country was not a license at all, and hence there had been no need for the business owner to police quality in order to preserve rights in her mark. Because the other users were geographically remote, their uses would not have given rise to consumer deception and would have required no license from the mark owner. The consumer protection rationale for imposing a quality control requirement would not be applicable under such circumstances.

Similarly, in *University Book Store v. University of Wisconsin Board of Regents*, 33 U.S.P.Q.2d 1385 (TTAB 1994), the TTAB rejected abandonment arguments in an opposition proceeding, in which a number of retailers opposed the University of Wisconsin's application to register WISCONSIN BADGERS and other marks for various products and services. There was evidence that the University had permitted scores of third-party uses over a long period of time, but the TTAB concluded that these uses should be treated as having been carried out under an implied license from the university. Satisfactory quality control under this implied license arrangement in fact had been maintained, according to the TTAB, even though it was difficult to point to affirmative steps undertaken by the University to effectuate that goal. The precedential value of this ruling outside the collegiate marks context is unclear. The TTAB's approach may be viewed more as a pragmatic response to universities' attempts to secure trademark rights than as a general pronouncement on the law of abandonment through uncontrolled licensing. Moreover, the TTAB's approach did not set the stage for trademark liability for businesses that had used the marks at issue for many years. Those businesses could invoke the equitable doctrine of laches against the university in any future trademark infringement litigation. See Chapter 12 for a discussion of the laches doctrine.

Another trademark law concept warrants mention here because it is reminiscent of the naked licensing cases, although it does not necessarily result in abandonment. United States trademark law permits trademark rights to be assigned, but only along with "the goodwill of the business in which the mark is used, or with that part of the goodwill of the business connected with the use of and symbolized by the mark." Lanham Act § 10(a)(1). This rule reflects the traditional conception of trademark rights as limited property rights in marks—limited in the sense that the rights only exist to the extent that the marks symbolize the owner's goodwill when used in connection with particular goods and services. An assignment unaccompanied by the goodwill that the mark represents is characterized as an "in gross" assignment and is deemed invalid. *See, e.g., Sugar Busters v. Brennan*, 177 F.3d 258 (5th Cir. 1999). The most direct consequence of invalidating an assignment is that the transfer of rights that the assignment purports to effectuate is deemed not to have occurred. While an invalidated assignment could conceivably result in abandonment, more typically the would-be assignee takes up use of the mark, and the chief question is whether the assignee can claim the benefit of the assignor's prior use.

For example, in *Clark & Freeman Corp. v. Heartland Co. Ltd.*, 811 F. Supp. 137 (S.D.N.Y. 1993), an assignment from Sears Roebuck (which had been selling HEARTLAND women's boots) to Clark (which began selling HEARTLAND men's shoes and boots) made in the context of the settlement of opposition proceedings was deemed an invalid assignment in gross. After the purported assignment, Sears discontinued use of the mark, but the would-be assignee Clark began using it on its products. In subsequent litigation, Clark sought to claim entitlement to the benefit of Sears' prior use for establishing a date of first use. Clark argued that because Sears had immediately discontinued use after the purported assignment, the assignment should be deemed to have transferred goodwill ipso facto. Alternatively, Clark argued that because it had started using the mark on "substantially similar goods" after the purported assignment, the assignment should be treated as a transfer of both the mark and the requisite goodwill. The court rejected the first argument as too "mechanistic," pointing out that the goal of protecting consumers from deception would not be achieved if assignments could be validated merely because the assignor discontinued use. As to the alternative argument, the court acknowledged that goodwill might be deemed to have transferred if the assignee's goods are in fact "substantially similar," presumably allowing the assignee to claim the benefit of the assignor's date of first use. However, the court decided that the respective products at issue were not substantially similar: the women's "pixie" boots that Sears had made and the Clark men's shoes and hiking boots were directed to "substantially distinct" markets. Similarly, in *PepsiCo, Inc. v. Grapette Co.*, 416 F.2d 285 (8th Cir. 1969), the court invalidated the assignment of the mark PEPPY from a failing small soft drink manufacturer to Grapette, which sought to use the mark on a pepper-flavored drink. The products were not substantially similar, and allowing such transfers to proceed would present too great a risk that assignees would attempt to deceive the public.

CHAPTER 5
REGISTRATION

In the U.S., an applicant may register a mark under either the Principal or the Supplemental Register. Designations are registrable on the Principal Register if they function as trademarks or service marks in accordance with the relevant definitions in Lanham Act § 45; and if the mark owner complies with the relevant application procedures (described in this Chapter, Section A); and if the designations are not barred from protection under Lanham Act § 2 (described in this Chapter, Section B). Registration on the Principal Register confers three significant benefits. First, Principal Register registrations constitute *prima facie* evidence of (1) the validity of the registered mark and the validity of the registration; (2) the registrant's ownership of the mark; and (3) the registrant's exclusive right to use the registered mark in commerce on or in connection with the goods or services specified in the registration. Lanham Act §§ 7(b), 33(a). Second, the filing of such an application for registration confers on the applicant a nationwide right of priority as of the application filing date, subject to the exceptions specified in Lanham Act § 7(c) (discussed in Chapters 4 and 6). Third, Principal Register registrations may become incontestable as specified in Lanham Act §§ 14–15. We discuss incontestability below in Section A.4.

Designations that do not yet function as trademarks or service marks, but are *capable* of distinguishing the applicant's goods and services, may be registrable on the Supplemental Register. *See* Lanham Act §§ 23–28. The Supplemental Register was established to enable U.S. applicants to satisfy the home registration prerequisite for obtaining protection in some foreign trademark systems, but it is sometimes used as an interim form of registration (for marks that may eventually develop secondary meaning) or even as a second-best form of registration for marks that may never satisfy the requirements for Principal Register registration. Registrations on the Supplemental Register are not accorded the registration benefits discussed in the preceding paragraph.

A. PROCEDURAL ASPECTS OF REGISTRATION

The Principal Register registration process may be divided into four parts: initial application; examination; publication and opposition; and post-registration process. The Lanham Act specifies some of the procedural rules, while many others reside in the PTO's trademark regulations, found in 37 C.F.R. Part 2.

1. APPLICATION: BASES FOR REGISTRATION

To obtain a U.S. trademark registration, a mark owner must file an application for registration. There are five alternative bases for filing an application for registration. 37 C.F.R. § 2.34.

Use in commerce: section 1(a) application. An applicant may file a registration based on actual use of the mark in connection with goods or services. Such an application must include (or be amended to include) a verified statement that the mark is in use in commerce on or in connection with the goods and services designated in the application, an indication of the date of first use, and a specimen showing how the applicant actually uses the mark in commerce. *See* Chapter 4 for a discussion of the concept of use.

Intent-to-use: section 1(b) application. Alternatively, an applicant may file a registration based on constructive use. A Section 1(b) "intent to use" (ITU) application must include (or be amended to include) a verified statement that the applicant had a bona fide intention to use the mark in commerce on or in connection with the goods or services listed in the application as of the application filing date. As discussed in Chapter 4, an ITU applicant must ultimately show actual use in commerce in accordance with Section 1(d) in order to receive a registration.

Foreign registration: section 44(e) application. Section 44(e) provides an independent basis for registration. Section 44 implements the so-called *telle quelle* obligation found in Art. 6 *quinquies* of the Paris Convention. That is, Section 44(e) provides that a foreign national of a Paris Convention country can acquire a U.S. registration based strictly on a foreign filed registration, assuming that the mark is otherwise eligible for registration under U.S. standards. An application based on Section 44(e) must include a copy of the applicant's foreign registration and must include (or be amended to include) a verified statement the applicant had a bona fide intention to use the mark in commerce on or in connection with the goods or services listed in the application as of the application filing date. Applicants invoking Section 44(e) are not required to assert actual use; Section 44(e) expressly provides that "use in commerce shall not be required prior to registration." *See also Crocker Nat'l Bank v. Canadian Imperial Bank of Commerce*, 228 U.S.P.Q. 689 (TTAB 1986) (breaking with prior practice to hold that Section 44 provides foreign nationals with an independent basis of registration, such that foreign nationals were under no obligation to prove use in Section 44 applications). Section 44 does not have the effect of eliminating other substantive requirements for registration, however—in particular, the other section 2 bars (discussed in Part B of this chapter). For example, the Federal Circuit has held that an applicant who files an application based on a foreign registration under Section 44(e) is not excused from the rule requiring a showing of secondary meaning for a mark that is merely a surname. *In re Rath*, 402 F.3d 1207 (Fed. Cir. 2005).

Foreign application: section 44(d) claim to priority. Section 44(d) provides another filing basis, but one that must be coupled with one of the other filing bases discussed above. Section 44(d) is a typical "foreign priority" provision. It provides that if a qualifying national (one who meets the requirements of Section 44(b)) first files an application for registration of a mark in an eligible country and later files an application for U.S. registration, the U.S. application will be treated as having been filed on the filing date of the foreign application, if the other requirements of Section 44(d) are satisfied. Among these other requirements, Section 44(d)(1) imposes a time limitation: the U.S. application must be filed within six months of the foreign application filing date. An application invoking Section 44(d) must include a claim of priority (and must provide identifying information about the foreign application to which priority is claimed), and must also include (or be amended to include) a verified statement the applicant had a bona fide intention to use the mark in commerce on or in connection with the goods or services listed in the application as of the application filing date. Before the application can be approved for publication, the applicant must establish a basis under section 1(a), section 1(b) or section 44(e) of the Act. Section 44(d) does not require that the statement of bona fide intention to use be followed by any evidence of actual use, and if the applicant chooses to establish a basis under Section 44(e), no evidence of use would be required prior to registration, as noted above.

International registration: section 66(a) extension of protection under the Madrid Protocol. The Madrid Protocol (the "Protocol Relating to the Madrid Agreement Concerning the International Registration of Marks") establishes a system under which trademark owners in member countries may secure trademark rights in other member countries by a single filing with their home country's trademark office. The United States joined the Madrid Protocol system in late 2003 and added implementing provisions to the Lanham Act at

§§ 60–74. Under those provisions, qualifying trademark applicants can file an international application with their home trademark office and then use that international application as a basis for a U.S. application by requesting "an extension of protection" of their international registration to the United States. The request for extension of protection is then forwarded via the International Bureau of WIPO (the World International Property Organization) to the PTO, and the PTO examines the request as it would any domestic application. The international application (or the request for extension) must contain a declaration stating that the applicant has a bona fide intent to use the mark in commerce, and making other representations as detailed in the PTO's regulations. 37 C.F.R. § 2.33. A registration based on a Section 66(a) request for extension of protection may be issued without proof of use in the United States.

2. EXAMINATION; FRAUDULENT PROCUREMENT

In its initial stages, trademark registration is an *ex parte* process in which an applicant negotiates with an examiner, but no formal adversary to the applicant is present. It has long been understood that *ex parte* processes present opportunities for abuse by those applicants who are inclined to misrepresent or omit relevant facts in order to procure trademark registrations. Accordingly, the trademark laws include rules designed to deter fraudulent procurement. If a registration was procured fraudulently, the registration will be cancelled, and

Lanham Act § 14(3) provides that a petition for cancellation based on fraudulent procurement may be filed at any time. In addition, even after a registration becomes incontestable (through the process discussed below in A.4), the registration is subject to challenge on the ground that the registration (or the incontestable right to use the mark) was obtained fraudulently. Lanham Act § 33(b)(1).

Fraudulent procurement under the Lanham Act is said to occur when (1) the applicant makes a false statement to the USPTO; (2) the false statement is material to the registrability of a mark; (3) the applicant had knowledge of the falsity of the statement; and (4) the applicant made the statement with intent to deceive the USPTO. *ShutEmDown Sports, Inc. v. Lacy*, 102 U.S.P.Q.2d 1036 (TTAB 2012); *see also L.D. Kichler Co. v. Davoil, Inc.*, 192 F.3d 1349 (Fed. Cir. 1999); *Metro Traffic Control, Inc. v. Shadow Network, Inc.*, 104 F.3d 336 (Fed. Cir.1997). Between 2003 and 2009, the TTAB had adopted a rule that misrepresentations that the applicant "knows or should know to be false or misleading" were sufficient for a showing of fraudulent procurement. *Medinol Ltd. v. Neuro Vasx, Inc.*, 67 U.S.P.Q.2d 1205 (TTAB 2003). However, in 2009 the Federal Circuit put an end to the TTAB's practice, holding that fraudulent procurement can only be shown "if the applicant or registrant knowingly ma[de] a false material representation to deceive the PTO," *In re Bose Corp.*, 580 F.3d 1240 (Fed. Cir. 2009), a standard that is summarized in the "intent to deceive" requirement (element (4) above). The trend in other circuits is to follow the *Bose* requirement for a showing of intent to deceive. *See, e.g., MPC Franchise, LLC v. Tarntino*, 826 F.3d 653 (2d Cir. 2016); *Sovereign Military Hospitaller Order of Saint John of Jerusalem of Rhodes & of Malta v. Fla. Priory of the Knights Hospitallers of the Sovereign Order of Saint John of Jerusalem, Knights of Malta, the Ecumenical Order*, 702 F.3d 1279 (11th Cir. 2012).

The *Bose* court also pointed out that a party seeking to cancel a registration on the basis of fraudulent procurement bears a "heavy burden of proof." Fraudulent procurement must be "proven to the hilt" with evidence satisfying the clear-and-convincing evidence standard.

In *Bose*, the Federal Circuit did not specify the standard for assessing whether the misrepresentation was material (element (2) above). However, the court seemed to analogize the doctrine of fraudulent procurement in trademark practice to the doctrine of inequitable conduct in patent practice, and inequitable conduct requires a showing of "but-for" materiality in most cases according to *Therasense v. Becton Dickinson & Co.*, 649 F.3d 1276 (Fed. Cir. 2011) (*en banc*). "But-for" materiality means that there is a causal connection between the misrepresentation and the issuance of the registration; but for the misrepresentation, the registration would not have issued. The court in *Therasense* rejected less rigorous standards for materiality, including the "important to a reasonable examiner" standard. Nonetheless, one court upheld a finding of fraudulent trademark procurement on the basis of a showing that the misrepresentation at issue would have been important to a reasonable examiner. *Fair Isaac Corp. v. Experian Information Solutions, Inc.*, 650 F.3d 1139 (8th Cir. 2011). One might expect other circuits to reject this approach in favor of but-for materiality.

Acts of fraudulent procurement not only demolish the involved registration, but also may expose the applicant to a civil action for damages according to Lanham Act Section 38. *See East Iowa Plastics, Inc. v. PI, Inc.*, 832 F.3d 899 (8th Cir. 2016) (discussing the issue of standing to pursue a Section 38 action).

3. APPEAL

Individual trademark examiners have responsibility for the initial determination of registrability. Applicants who are dissatisfied with the examiner's decision can appeal to an administrative tribunal, the Trademark Trial and Appeal Board (TTAB). Lanham Act § 20. Applicants who receive an adverse decision from the TTAB can appeal to court via either an appeal to the Court of Appeals for the Federal Circuit (Lanham Act § 21(a)) or by a civil action against the PTO on de novo record in federal district court (Lanham Act § 21(b)). In an action under Section 21(b), the district court acts as the finder of fact. While the district court, in its discretion, may consider the record of the proceedings before the PTO, the court owes the PTO's factual findings no deference, because the PTO would not have been able to consider any new evidence that the parties have added to the record in court. *Swatch AG v. Beehive Wholesale*, LLC, 739 F.3d 150 (4th Cir. 2014).

4. PUBLICATION; OPPOSITION

If the PTO determines that the mark is entitled to registration, it publishes the mark in the Official Gazette of the United States Patent and Trademark Office. Lanham Act § 12. Within thirty days of the publication date (extendable up to a total of 180 days under 37 C.F.R. § 2.102(c) (2003)), interested members of the public may file a petition opposing the PTO's decision to register a mark. Lanham Act § 13. A trademark opposition is an inter partes administrative proceeding which exists to "remedy oversight or error" that may have occurred in ex parte examination, *In re Shell Oil Co.*, 992 F.2d 1204 (Fed. Cir. 1993). It is conducted before the TTAB. Although the Lanham Act does not specify the types of errors that may be corrected by way of an opposition, the general practice is to allow the opposer to raise any legal defect in the registration. Frequently, the opposer alleges that the registration should have been barred under one or more of the Section 2 bars.

Lanham Act Section 13 states that "[a]ny person who believes that he would be damaged by the registration of a mark upon the principal register" has standing to initiate an opposition proceeding. The Federal Circuit has interpreted Section 13 to confer standing where the opposer has (1) a "real interest" in the outcome of the proceedings and (2) an objective basis for believing that damages will accrue (the "reasonable belief" prong). *See Ritchie v. Simpson*, 170 F.3d 1092 (Fed. Cir. 1999). A "real interest" means a "direct and personal stake in the outcome," but it need *not* include a showing of some specific commercial interest not shared by the general public. A "reasonable belief" entails a showing that the opposer possesses an inherent characteristic implicated by the mark, or that others share the belief in harm as demonstrated by survey evidence or the like. In *Ritchie*, opposer had standing to challenge the registration of O.J. SIMPSON and related marks for a variety of goods on grounds of disparagement under Section 2(a); opposer had a "real interest" because he was a "family man" whose values were disparaged by the mark, and he had a "reasonable belief" because he had collected affidavits from others who shared his views. By contrast, a male individual lacked standing to oppose the registration of DYKES ON BIKES for a women's motorcycle group because even if the opposer had alleged a "real interest," he possessed neither an inherent trait implicated by the mark nor any evidence that others shared his views that the mark disparaged the male gender. *McDermott v. San Francisco Women's Motorcycle Contingent*, 81 U.S.P.Q.2d 1212 (TTAB 2006).

5. POST-REGISTRATION PROCESS: RENEWAL; CANCELLATION; INCONTESTABILITY

When a registrant succeeds in receiving a Principal Register registration, the registrant may use the familiar ® ("R-in-circle") trademark notice in connection with the registered mark. While the Lanham Act does not mandate use of the notice, registrants who fail to use the notice cannot collect profits or damages for infringement unless the infringement defendant had actual notice of the registration, Lanham Act § 22, or unless the mark owner prevails on a parallel claim for damages under Lanham Act § 43(a).

Trademark registrations on the Principal Register have no definite expiration date. However, the registrant must take certain steps to maintain the registration in force, as summarized below.

Renewal. A Principal Register registration remains in force for ten years, renewable indefinitely, if the registrant satisfies two basic conditions. First, starting five years after registration, the registrant has a one-year period (plus a six-month grace period after expiration of the one-year period) within which to file an affidavit attesting to the continued use of the mark in connection with the goods and services recited in the registration, or provide an excuse for nonuse. Lanham Act § 8(a) and (b). Second, within one year before the registration expires (plus a six-month grace period after expiration), the registrant must file a renewal application complying with the requirements of Lanham Act Section 9(a); *see also* 37 C.F.R. § 2.182. Subsequently, the registrant may renew the registration for successive ten-year periods without limitation if the registrant timely files a renewal application, along with a Section 8 affidavit of continued use. Lanham Act § 8(a)(3).

Cancellation. All registrations are subject to the possibility of cancellation under various circumstances. Under Lanham Act Section 37, a court properly vested with jurisdiction "in any action involving a registered trademark" is authorized to direct the PTO to cancel a registration in whole or in part. Section 37 may be asserted as a defense in a trademark infringement action; it does not create an independent basis for federal court jurisdiction. *Airs Aromatics, LLS v. Opinion Victoria's Secret Stores Brand Mgmt., Inc.*, 744 F.3d 595 (9th Cir. 2014).

In addition, Lanham Act §§ 14–15 authorize third parties to initiate administrative "cancellation" proceedings at the PTO. Lanham Act Section 14 provides that any person who believes he is or will be damaged by a registration may petition to cancel a registration. According to Section 14(3), a cancellation petition may be filed at any time after registration if the cancellation is based on one or more of the following grounds: (1) genericness; (2) functionality; (3) abandonment; (4) fraud in obtaining the registration; (5) violation of Section 4 (relating to collective marks and certification marks); or (6) violation of Section 2(a), (b), or (c). A petition for cancellation based on any other grounds must be filed within five years from the date of registration. Lanham Act § 14(1). After the five-year period expires, a party cannot initiate a cancellation proceeding based on common objections such as the prior use of a confusingly similar mark (Section 2(d)) or descriptiveness (Section 2(e)).

Like oppositions, cancellations are heard before the TTAB, and are subject to judicial review in the same manner as other TTAB judgments.

Incontestability and the time limit on cancellations. The Lanham Act contains two related sets of provisions that serve to quiet title to Principal Register registrations. In Lanham Act Section 14, Congress provided a five-year time limit for initiating cancellation proceedings, subject to exceptions specified in Lanham Act Section 14(3)–(5). This provision applies to all Principal Register registrations, regardless of whether the registrant has followed the procedures for achieving incontestable status. In addition, the Lanham Act provides a limited concept of incontestability via Sections 15 and 33(b). Lanham Act Section 15 lists four prerequisites for obtaining incontestability status for a Principal Register registration: (1) there has been no final decision adverse to registrability or the registrant's claim of ownership; (2) there is no proceeding involving the registered rights that is pending in either the PTO or the courts; (3) an affidavit is timely filed stating that the mark has been in continuous use for five years in connection with the goods (and stating other matters as specified in Section 15(3)); and (4) the mark is not generic. The preamble of Section 15 also carves out a number of exceptions (including the Section 14(3) and (5) exceptions). If the registrant satisfies the requirements of Section 15, and no exception applies, the registrant's *right to use* the registered mark in connection with those goods and services for which five years' use has been demonstrated becomes incontestable. Section 33(b), in turn, specifies that the registration presumption (established separately in Section 33(a)) is "conclusive" for incontestable registrations, but only to the extent that the right to use properly became incontestable under Section 15. Thus, for example, a mark that is the subject of an incontestable registration can be challenged for genericness on the grounds that the registration never satisfied Section 15(4) and thus never properly became incontestable to begin with. In addition, Section 33(b) proceeds to narrow the scope of incontestability even further by setting forth nine defenses that can be raised even as to incontestable registrations. For example, an incontestable registration can be challenged for functionality pursuant to Section 33(b)(8). However, incontestable status does cut off challenges based on the mark's alleged mere descriptiveness. In *Park 'n Fly, Inc. v. Dollar Park and Fly, Inc.*, 469 U.S. 189 (1985), the Court confirmed that the defense of mere descriptiveness was not a preserved defense to an incontestable registration under Section 33(b). The mark owner held a registration for PARK 'N FLY in connection with long-term parking lots near airports, and the registration had achieved incontestable status. The defendant argued that notwithstanding incontestability, the registration should be subject to challenge on grounds of mere descriptiveness—at least in the context of trademark infringement litigation, even if not in the context of a cancellation proceeding. The Court rejected this distinction: both Section 15 and Section 33(b) expressly provided that incontestable registrations could only be challenged on specified grounds, and descriptiveness was not among them. The Court's decision had good footing in the legislative history—it appeared that Congress had considered and rejected the idea of listing descriptiveness among the preserved defenses. However, it remains uncertain whether the rule from *Park 'N Fly* also applies to many other "extra-textual" defenses—i.e., other defenses that were not preserved under Section 33(b), perhaps for the reason that Congress simply did not consider them. Questions about whether functionality was a preserved defense prompted Congress to amend Section 33(b) to list it explicitly. For example, it has been held that incontestable status does not foreclose a challenge to the validity of an assignment agreement. *Federal Treasury Enterprise Sojuzplodoimport v. Spirits Int'l N.V.*, 623 F.3d 61 (2d Cir. 2010).

According to *Park 'n Fly*, the effect of establishing one of the preserved defenses is merely to alter the registration presumption—instead of a "conclusive" presumption as to the registrant's right to use the mark, the registration serves only as *prima facie* evidence of the right to use. However, once a litigant has established a Section 33(b) defense, a number of courts simply treat the Section 33(b) defense as a defense on the merits, and conclude that the registrant's claim for liability cannot stand.

B. SUBSTANTIVE ASPECTS OF REGISTRATION: SECTION 2 BARS

Lanham Act Section 2 provides that no trademark (or, specifically, no trademark "by which the goods of the applicant may be distinguished from the goods of others") may be refused registration on the Principal Register unless the PTO (in ex parte examination) or the mark challenger (in oppositions, cancellations, or litigation) demonstrates that a substantive bar to registration applies. Sections 2(a)–(f) spell out those substantive bars. Some of the Section 2 bars incorporate common law concepts of distinctiveness, functionality, and priority of use, topics that we discussed in Chapters 2–4, respectively. Other Section 2 bars augment the common law.

There are three basic questions to be answered with respect to each Section 2 bar. First, do any procedural rules prevent the invocation of the bar? Second, what is barred? Third, is the bar absolute, or may it be overcome by evidence of secondary meaning? The first question is relatively straightforward to answer. All of the Section 2 bars, except for the Section 2(f) dilution bar, apply in all procedural contexts—*ex parte* examination, *inter partes* administrative proceedings (oppositions and cancellations), and litigation. Section 2(f) is not a ground of objection in *ex parte* examination, but is available in *inter partes* proceedings. In addition, all Section 2 grounds may be invoked for five years after the registration, but thereafter the grounds are limited as a consequence of the restrictions in

Lanham Act Sections 14–15 (discussed in the preceding section).

In the remainder of this Chapter, we discuss several of the Section 2 bars, focusing on the "second" and "third" questions—what is barred, and whether the bar is absolute. Although we discuss most of the Section 2 bars, the reader should be aware that a small subset of the bars tends to be invoked most frequently. The Section 2(d) bar (confusingly similar prior mark or trade name) and the Section 2(e)(1) bar (merely descriptive mark) are perhaps the most frequently encountered of all of the Section 2 bars.

1. SECTION 2(a) SCANDALOUS/ DISPARAGING MARKS

Section 2(a) bars from registration any mark which "[c]onsists of or comprises immoral, deceptive, or scandalous matter; or matter which may disparage or falsely suggest a connection with persons, living or dead, institutions, beliefs, or national symbols, or bring them into contempt, or disrepute . . . ." The TTAB construed Section 2(a) as imposing separate bars for "scandalous matter," "matter which may disparage," deceptive matter, and "matter which may falsely suggest a connection." (The TTAB treated matter which may bring persons "into contempt or disrepute" as equivalent to disparaging matter.) The following is a discussion of the scandalousness and disparagement bars. Other Section 2(a) bars are discussed elsewhere. In particular, *see infra* Section 2 of this chapter for a discussion of the deceptiveness bar, and *see* Section B.4 of this chapter for a discussion of the false connection bar.

The Supreme Court struck down the Section 2(a) disparagement bar as facially unconstitutional in *Matal v. Tam*, 137 S.Ct. 1744 (2017). An applicant, the lead singer of an Asian-American rock group called THE SLANTS, was barred from registering the band's name on the ground that the mark disparaged Asian Americans. The Federal Circuit had overturned the rejection on First Amendment grounds, and the Supreme Court granted certiorari. The Court unanimously ruled that Section 2(a)'s disparagement prohibition violated the First Amendment's free speech clause on its face. But the Court split over the reasons for this conclusion. Justice Alito's opinion was joined (in part) by Chief Justice Roberts and Justices Thomas and Breyer. Alito's opinion considered and dismissed three arguments in support of the constitutionality of the disparagement provision: (1) the act of registering a trademark was not a form of government speech, because trademarks have not traditionally been used to convey government messages and trademarks are not ordinarily identified in the public mind with the government; (2) while the government can decline to subsidize activities it does not wish to promote, trademark registration is not akin to a government subsidy (so refusing registration is not akin to declining to subsidize); and, (3) trademark registration could not be characterized as a type of government program under which some speech restrictions would be constitutionally permissible. The opinion sidestepped the question of whether a trademark is commercial or noncommercial speech, and accordingly whether a bar to registration would be subject to relaxed or strict scrutiny. According to Justice Alito's opinion, the disparagement bar would not pass even relaxed scrutiny (which requires that the restriction be "narrowly drawn" to serve a "substantial interest"). The disparagement bar was not narrowly drawn to suppress invidious discrimination, Justice Alito concluded, but instead was a "happy talk" clause that purported to bar registration of marks that disparaged *any* person, group, or institution. Justices Kennedy, Ginsburg, Sotomayor, and Kagan concurred in part. They viewed the disparagement provision as a straightforward example of viewpoint discrimination, triggering strict scrutiny, irrespective of the commercial/noncommercial distinction.

Only the disparagement language of Section 2(a) was before the Court, and, accordingly, the Court did not speak explicitly to the constitutionality of the Section 2(a) bar to "scandalous" marks, although it surely must be understood as casting the viability of that bar into doubt. Nor did the Court comment on how its decision might affect other potentially speech-restrictive aspects of trademark law, such as the prohibition on dilution by tarnishment (discussed in Chapter 8). Additionally, the Court did not clarify whether its analysis also applied to efforts to bar the enforcement of unregistered rights under Section 43(a).

2. SECTION 2(a) DECEPTIVENESS

In addition to the prohibition against scandalous and disparaging marks, Section 2(a) of the Lanham Act also bars registration of any mark which "consists of or comprises ... deceptive ... matter ...." The Federal Circuit has adopted a three-part test for analyzing claims of Section 2(a) deceptiveness: (1) Is the term misdescriptive of the character, quality, function, composition or use of the goods? (2) If so, are prospective purchasers likely to believe that the misdescription actually describes the goods? (3) If so, is the misdescription likely to affect the decision to purchase? *In re Budge Mfg. Co., Inc.*, 857 F.2d 773 (Fed. Cir. 1988). Applying its test, the court affirmed the rejection of an application to register LOVEE LAMB for automotive seat covers that were made from synthetic fibers, not natural lambskin.

Section 2 also contains another bar that is similar to the deceptiveness bar—namely, the Section 2(e)(1) bar for marks that are "deceptively misdescriptive." It is critical to distinguish between Section 2(a) deceptiveness and Section 2(e)(1) deceptive misdescriptiveness. A Section 2(a) deceptiveness bar, like the other Section 2(a) bars, is absolute—it cannot be overcome by a showing of secondary meaning. However, the Section 2(e)(1) deceptive misdescriptiveness bar can be overcome if secondary meaning can be shown. The PTO has suggested that a term that satisfies the first two prongs of the *Budge* test will be deemed deceptively misdescriptive under section 2(e)(1). That is, if (1) a mark is misdescriptive of the goods/services, and (2) prospective purchasers are likely to believe the misdescription, the mark is Section 2(e)(1) deceptively misdescriptive. TMEP § 1203.02(a); *In re Shniberg*, 79 U.S.P.Q.2d 1309 (TTAB 2006). In *Shniberg*, the TTAB concluded that the mark SEPTEMBER 11, 2001 for books and entertainment services *not* dealing with the September 11 terrorist attacks was deceptively misdescriptive. In that case, the TTAB suggested that where the misdescription is merely a *relevant factor* in the consumer's purchase decision, the mark may be deceptively misdescriptive under the test articulated above, whereas if the misdescription is *material* to the consumer's purchase decision, the mark might fall under the *Budge* test for Section 2(a) deceptiveness.

3. SECTIONS 2(a) AND 2(e): GEOGRAPHIC INDICATIONS AND GEOGRAPHIC MARKS

Section 2 contains a number of provisions that relate to marks containing geographic terms. Two major provisions are found in Section 2(e). Section 2(e)(2) bars registrations for any geographically descriptive mark (any mark which "when used on or in connection with the goods of the applicant is primarily geographically descriptive of them, except as indications of regional origin may be registrable under [Lanham Act] section 4 . . . "). Section 2(e)(3) bars registrations for any mark that contains what may be described informally as misleading geographic terms (any mark which "when used on or in connection with the goods of the applicant is primarily geographically deceptively misdescriptive of them").

The following discussion explains the Section 2(e)(2) and (3) case law.

Section 2(e)(2) geographically descriptive marks. The test for a *prima facie* case under Section 2(e)(2) is composed of three elements: (1) the primary significance of the mark is geographic to the relevant public (i.e., the mark is the name of a place known generally to the public); (2) purchasers would be likely to make a goods/place or services/place association, i.e., to think that the goods or services originate in the geographic place identified in the mark; and (3) the mark identifies the geographic origin of the goods or services. *In re the Newbridge Cutlery Co.*, 776 F.3d 854 (Fed. Cir. 2015); Trademark Manual of Examining Procedure § 1210.01(a) (rev. April 2005) (internal citations omitted).

In applying the first element, it is important to remember that the mere inclusion of an arguably geographic term in a mark will not necessarily require a conclusion that the primary significance of the mark is geographic. For example, even though the term American is often used in its geographic sense, it does not follow inevitably that the mark THE AMERICAN GIRL is of primarily geographic significance. *Hamilton-Brown Shoe Co. v. Wolf Bros. & Co.*, 240 U.S. 251 (1916) (noting that "American" as used here did not signify the origin of manufacture or likely place of sale or use; AMERICAN SHOES would present a different case). The mark must be considered as a whole, and this is particularly important if the mark is a composite mark including geographic and non-geographic elements. For example, the mark SWISS ARMY KNIFE for a multi-function knife is not likely to be perceived as primarily of geographic significance despite the inclusion of the geographic term "Swiss." *See Forschner Group v. Arrow Trading Co.*, 30 F.3d 348 (2d Cir. 1994). On the other hand, in *Burke-Parsons-Bowlby Corp. v. Appalachian Log Homes, Inc.*, 871 F.2d 590 (6th Cir. 1989), the court agreed that the mark APPALACHIAN LOG STRUCTURES for log homes sold in Tennessee and Florida was primarily geographically descriptive, even though the geographic term "Appalachian" was coupled with other terms that might have indicated a style of construction rather than geographic origin.

It is also important to consider the group constituting the "relevant public" in any given case. For example, in *In re Joint-Stock Co. "Baik"*, 80 U.S.P.Q.2d 1305 (TTAB 2006), the mark at issue was BAIKALSKAYA for vodka made near Lake Baikal in Russia. The applicant argued that it was unlikely that average Americans would have any knowledge of Lake Baikal. The Board dismissed this argument; the relevant public for purposes of the inquiry was the subset of Americans who purchase vodka, including Russian vodka. In any event, the "relevant public" for purposes of the analysis is the purchasing public in the United States only. *Newbridge*, 776 F.3d at 861.

The second element, the requirement for showing a goods/place association, is an important one. The Court of Customs and Patent Appeals in *In re Nantucket, Inc.*, 677 F.2d 95 (CCPA 1982), is generally credited with adopting the goods/place association requirement—insisting, that is, upon more than merely a showing that a term had a geographic connotation. Subsequently, the Federal Circuit stated that it was not necessary to show that a place was famous or "noted" for the goods in order to establish a goods/place association; rather, there merely need be a "reasonable predicate" for the conclusion that "the public would be likely to make the particular goods/place association" that is alleged. *In re Loew's Theatres, Inc.*, 769 F.2d 764 (Fed. Cir. 1985).

The TTAB has adopted a limited presumption as to the goods/place association. Where elements (1) and (3) of the Section 2(e)(2) test are met, and the geographic place referred to in a primarily geographic mark is "neither obscure nor remote," the presumption of a goods/place association is triggered. *In re Trans Continental Records, Inc.*, 62 U.S.P.Q.2d 1541 (TTAB 2002). In the context of *ex parte* examination, where the examiner has established a goods/place association, the applicant may rebut this showing with additional evidence establishing that the public would not actually believe the goods derive from the geographic location identified by the mark. *In re Save Venice New York, Inc.*, 259 F.3d 1346 (Fed. Cir. 2001).

Where the geographic mark at issue is a service mark, the second element of the Section 2(e)(2) test would require a showing of a services/place association. The Federal Circuit discussed the requirements for showing a services/place association in *In re Les Halles de Paris, J.V.*, 334 F.3d 1371 (Fed. Cir. 2003), in which applicant sought to register LE MARAIS for restaurant services for a restaurant located in New York serving French kosher cuisine. (The Jewish quarter of Paris is known as Le Marais.) The court took the view that a showing of a services/place association required some additional showing beyond mere evidence that the consumer identified the place as a known source of the services. For example, concerning the restaurant services at issue, the court stated that "the PTO might find a services/place association if the record shows that patrons, though sitting in New York, would believe the food served by the restaurant was imported from Paris, or that the chefs in New York received specialized training in the region in Paris, or that the New York menu is identical to a known Parisian menu, or some other heightened association between the services and the relevant place." Evidence showing merely that LE MARAIS "conjures up memories or images of the Le Marais area of Paris" was insufficient to establish the sort of additional showing that the court required.

A Section 2(e)(2) bar is not absolute—it can be overcome by a showing of secondary meaning. Moreover, the Section 2(e)(2) bar does not reach "indications of regional origin" that "may be registrable" under Lanham Act § 4, the certification mark provision. For example, suppose that the state of Indiana seeks to register the mark INDIANA MELONS as a certification mark for cantaloupes certified as Indiana-grown by an Indiana state agency. Under Section 4, the mark could receive protection as a geographical certification mark if the certifier exercises control over the designation and limits it to those products meeting the certifier's standards of regional origin. If those conditions were met for INDIANA MELONS, then the geographical certification mark would be exempt from the requirement to show secondary meaning even if it were otherwise deemed to be geographically descriptive.

Section 2(e)(3) primarily geographically deceptively misdescriptive marks. As noted, Section 2(e)(3) bars registrations for any mark which "when used on or in connection with the goods of the applicant is primarily geographically deceptively misdescriptive of them." In *In re California Innovations, Inc.*, 329 F.3d 1334 (Fed. Cir. 2003), the court held that in order to establish a Section 2(e)(3) bar, the PTO must show that "(1) the primary significance of the mark is a generally known geographic location, (2) the consuming public is likely to believe the place identified by the mark indicates the origin of the goods bearing the mark, when in fact the goods do not come from that place, and (3) the misrepresentation was a material factor in the consumer's decision." The third element—materiality—derives from the law of Section 2(a) deceptiveness. The court reasoned that including a materiality element in the requirements for a Section 2(e)(3) bar was sensible because the Section 2(e)(3) bar (like the Section 2(a) deceptiveness bar) was absolute. The court explained that the backdrop for its decision was the statutory revision brought about by the U.S. implementation of the NAFTA agreement. Before NAFTA, marks that were deceptively misdescriptive and marks that were primarily geographically descriptive were treated alike: both were barred under then-existing Section 2(e)(2), and as to both, the bar could be overcome by a showing of secondary meaning. As a result of NAFTA, Congress revised Sections 2(e) and (f) to bring them into their current form, leaving geographically descriptive marks in Section 2(e)(2), moving geographically deceptively misdescriptive marks to Section 2(e)(3), and revising Section 2(f) to state that a Section 2(e)(2) bar for geographic descriptiveness could still be overcome with a showing of secondary meaning, but a Section 2(e)(3) bar for geographic deceptive misdescriptiveness could not be overcome by a showing of secondary meaning.

The Federal Circuit has ruled that to prove materiality under the California Innovations formulation, one must prove that a substantial portion of relevant consumers are likely to be deceived, the relevant consumer group being "the entire U.S. population interested in purchasing the product or service." *In re Spirits Int'l N.V.*, 563 F.3d 1347 (Fed. Cir. 2009) (vacating and remanding rejection on the ground that the TTAB had incorrectly analyzed materiality). The case involved the mark MOSKOVSKAYA for vodka that did not originate in Moscow. "Moskovskaya" is a Russian term that translates to "of or from Moscow."

In *In re Les Halles de Paris, J.V.*, 334 F.3d 1371 (Fed. Cir. 2003), involving a service mark as noted above, the court concluded that evidence of a very strong services/place association (under the second prong of the § 2(e)(3) test) could give rise to an inference of materiality (the third prong of the test).

Geographic indications. A geographic indication is not quite like a trademark. Whereas a trademark identifies goods as originating from a particular producer, a geographic indication indicates that the goods originate from any of a variety of producers located in a particular geographic region—such as "Georgia" for peaches or "Idaho" for potatoes. The TRIPS agreement defines geographical indications as "indications which identify a good as originating in the territory of a Member, or a region or locality in that territory, where a given quality, reputation or other characteristic of the good is essentially attributable to its geographic origin." TRIPS Art. 22(1). The TRIPS agreement does not require member states to provide for the registration of geographical indications. The U.S. trademark system does not provide a registry for geographical indications, although the EU does. The TRIPS agreement does require member states to offer protection against designations that mislead the public as to the geographic origin of goods. The bars to registering certain geographic marks in Lanham Act Section 2(e), and the prohibitions against trademark infringement and false designation of origin in Lanham Act Sections 32 and 43(a), respectively, may support a conclusion that the U.S. complies with this TRIPS obligation.

As noted above in connection with the discussion of Section 2(e)(2), a geographic term that is used as a certification mark may be registered without evidence of secondary meaning, so long as the requirements of Lanham Act Section 4 are met. Thus, for example, the Idaho Potato Commission owns various certification marks for potatoes grown in Idaho.

Section 2(a) also contains language pertaining to geographic indications used in connection with wine and spirits. Specifically, a Section 2(a) bar is appropriate for an application to register "a geographical indication which, when used on or in connection with wines or spirits, identifies a place other than the origin of the goods and is first used on or in connection with wines or spirits by the applicant on or after [January 1, 1996]." The provision is intended to bring the U.S. into compliance with TRIPS Art. 23.

4. SECTIONS 2(c); 2(a); 2(e)(4): NAME MARKS

Marks that consist of personal names may raise a number of Section 2 issues. Section 2(c) prohibits one person from registering another person's name as a mark without the other person's consent. In particular, registration is barred for any mark which "[c]onsists of or comprises a name, portrait, or signature identifying a particular living individual except by his written consent, or the name, signature, or portrait of a deceased President of the United States during the life of his widow, if any, except by the written consent of the widow." For example, Section 2(c) barred an applicant from registering OBAMA PAJAMAS for sleepwear, where President Barack Obama had not given consent. *In re Hoefflin*, 97 U.S.P.Q.2d 1174 (TTAB 2010). In some cases, questions arise about whether the mark at issue identifies a particular living individual. For example, while it is clear that Section 2(c) would bar Professor Janis from registering GRAEME DINWOODIE for expensive silk neckties (in the absence of Graeme Dinwoodie's consent), it is less clear whether Section 2(c) would similarly bar Professor Janis from registering DINWOODIE, or Professor Dinwoodie's various nicknames (G-DIN, G-MAN, WOODIE), or other variations like GRAEME D., for the same goods, because there may be an issue about whether the nicknames or partial names identify Professor Dinwoodie. The TTAB has held that a name, nickname or the like will be deemed to "identify" a particular living individual for purposes of Section 2(c), only if the "individual bearing the name in question will be associated with the mark as used on the goods, either because that person is so well known that the public would reasonably assume the connection, or because the individual is publicly connected with the business in which the mark is used." *Martin v. Carter Hawley Hale Stores, Inc.*, 206 U.S.P.Q. 931 (TTAB 1979). A Section 2(c) bar cannot be overcome by a showing of secondary meaning.

In addition to possible Section 2(c) objections, one who attempts to register another's name as a mark (even with consent) may face a bar under section 2(a). We have already considered Section 2(a)'s scandalousness/disparagement bars (in B.1. above) and its deceptiveness bar (in B.2. above), but Section 2(a) also bars a mark that "[c]onsists of or comprises ... matter ... which may ... falsely suggest a connection with persons, living or dead." The TTAB has applied a four-part test to determine whether a name mark falsely suggests a connection under § 2(a): (1) the mark must be the same as or a close approximation of the person's previously used name or identity; (2) there must be evidence that the mark (or part of it) would be recognized as such; (3) there must be a showing that the person in question is not connected with the goods or services of the applicant; and (4) "the person's name or identity must be of sufficient fame that when it is used as part or all of the mark on applicant's goods, a connection with that person is likely to be made by someone considering purchasing the goods." *In re Sauer*, 27 U.S.P.Q.2d 1073 (TTAB 1993), *aff'd* 26 F.3d 140 (Fed. Cir. 1994), *citing Buffett v. Chi-Chi's, Inc.*, 226 U.S.P.Q. 428 (TTAB 1985). As with other Section 2(a) bars, the Section 2(a) "false connection" bar is absolute; it cannot be overcome by a showing of secondary meaning.

The TTAB applied the four-part test to bar registration under Section 2(a) of MOHAWK for cigarettes. *In re White*, 80 U.S.P.Q.2d 1654 (TTAB 2006). The applicant was a member of the Mohawk tribe, and the applicant's licensee held contractual rights to sell cigarettes (of any brand) on the Mohawk reservation. The applicant argued that these connections sufficed to show that there was a connection between the mark and the applicant's goods, such that element (3) of the test was not satisfied. Nonetheless, the TTAB upheld the rejection. Evidence showing a mere "general commercial connection" between the applicant and the named institution was not enough. Instead, the commercial connection had to relate to the applicant's goods or services. That is, there needed to be evidence of "a specific endorsement, sponsorship or the like of the particular goods and services, whether written or implied." *Id.*

Where an applicant seeks to register a mark that would be perceived as "primarily merely a surname," Section 2(e)(4) is implicated. As the foregoing discussion demonstrates, if the surname identifies some other living individual, Section 2(c) would also be implicated, and if the surname falsely suggests a connection with a living or dead individual, Section 2(a) would be implicated. Thus, Section 2(e)(4) is primarily important when an individual seeks to register a mark that is his or her own surname.

In some cases, it will not be clear whether a mark will in fact be perceived as primarily merely a surname by the relevant public. The TTAB uses a multi-factor analysis to make the determination, considering factors that include "(i) whether the surname is rare; (ii) whether anyone connected with applicant has the involved term as a surname; (iii) whether the term has any other recognized meaning; and (iv) whether the term has the 'look and feel' of a surname." *In re United Distillers, PLC,* 56

U.S.P.Q.2d 1220 (TTAB 2000) (reversing a rejection of HACKLER for alcoholic beverages).

A Section 2(e)(4) surname bar is not absolute—it can be overcome if the applicant establishes secondary meaning. That is, a mark that is primarily merely a surname is treated analogously to a descriptive mark. As with descriptive terms, there is an impulse to keep surnames free for use absent a showing that the mark owner has built up market recognition in the surname as a designation for particular goods or services. The PTO may hesitate to award trademark rights in surnames on the grounds that it might limit third parties who have the same surname from going into business under their names. However, the courts may be able to alleviate this concern by recognizing a broad fair use defense if the surname mark is asserted in litigation. We discuss the fair use defense in Chapter 9. Another concern is that some surnames may be so common that consumers will not be likely to rely on them as source indicators. For example, it seems quite likely that a consumer encountering SMITH'S CAR SALES in Indianapolis, Indiana, will not immediately assume that SMITH'S CAR SALES in Louisville, Kentucky is affiliated with the Indianapolis SMITH'S. *See Peaceable Planet, Inc. v. Ty, Inc.*, 362 F.3d 986 (7th Cir. 2004) (laying out these rationales for requiring secondary meaning for trademark protection of surnames).

The Lanham Act rules pertaining to name marks can be particularly difficult to apply when an applicant seeks to register an historic name or surname. For example, where an applicant sought to register SOUSA for fireworks, the examiner rejected the application on the ground that SOUSA would be perceived as merely a surname, and hence would be barred prima facie under Section 2(e)(4). In response, the applicant successfully argued that SOUSA would be perceived as a reference to the historic figure (John Philip Sousa, composer of patriotic music), especially in view of the connection between the composer's music and the products at issue—fireworks. *In re Pyro-Spectaculars Inc.*, 63 U.S.P.Q.2d 2022 (TTAB 2002). But it may seem that the applicant's own argument might give rise to a further concern that the mark falsely suggests a connection with an individual, and hence should be barred under Section 2(a). In an earlier case, a court recognized trademark rights in WYATT EARP in connection with a television series where the television program had "battered [the name Wyatt Earp] into the public consciousness . . . to an extent far beyond any fame or notoriety ever previously attached to the [person's] name." *Wyatt Earp Enters., Inc. v. Sackman, Inc.*, 157 F. Supp. 621 (S.D.N.Y. 1958). Courts have not adequately explored the interaction between Sections 2(e)(4), 2(a), 2(c) pertaining to name marks.

5. SECTION 2(d) CONFUSION BAR

Section 2(d) is perhaps the most commonly invoked of the Section 2 bars. Under Section 2(d), a mark is barred from registration if it is confusingly similar to previously used or registered marks, or previously used trade names. Specifically, a Section 2(d) bar arises for any mark which "[c]onsists of or comprises a mark which so resembles a mark registered in the Patent and Trademark Office, or a mark or trade name previously used in the United States by another and not abandoned, as to be likely, when used on or in connection with the goods of the applicant, to cause confusion, or to cause mistake, or to deceive."

Section 2(d) presents two broad issues. First, there may be a question about whether the prior mark or trade name was in fact "previously used or registered" and not abandoned. The rules relevant to answering this question are discussed in Chapter 4. Second, there may be a question about whether the prior mark or trade name in fact presents a likelihood of confusion. Likelihood of confusion under Section 2(d) is analyzed by way of a multi-factor test. Courts use variations of the multi-factor test for determining likelihood of confusion in trademark infringement cases. We discuss the multi-factor tests in Chapter 7.

Section 2(d) also refers to the possibility that more than one registrant will hold rights to use a mark concurrently (typically in separate geographic territories). We discuss geographic limitations on the scope of trademark rights in more detail in Chapter 6.

A Section 2(d) confusion bar cannot be overcome by a showing of secondary meaning, as specified in Section 2(f).

6. SECTION 2(e) DESCRIPTIVENESS BAR

Section 2(e)(1) incorporates the common law rule that marks that are merely descriptive of the goods or services with which they are used are *prima facie* not protectable. Under the common law distinctiveness rules, marks that are deemed merely descriptive may nonetheless be protectable if the mark owner can establish secondary meaning. Section 2(e)(1) is understood as incorporating the common law rules for distinguishing between inherently distinctive marks and merely descriptive marks. Likewise, under Section 2(f), a Section 2(e)(1) descriptiveness bar can be overcome by a showing of secondary meaning. Section 2(f) also provides the mark owner with a presumption of secondary meaning where the mark owner proves that he or she engaged in substantially exclusive and continuous use of the mark in commerce for the five years before the date on which secondary meaning is claimed.

7. OTHER SECTION 2 BARS

Section 2(b) government insignia. Section 2(b) bars applicants from registering government insignia—i.e., any mark which "[c]onsists of or comprises the flag or coat of arms or other insignia of the United States, or of any State or municipality, or of any foreign nation, or any simulation thereof." A Section 2(b) bar cannot be overcome by a showing of secondary meaning, as specified in Section 2(f).

Section 2(e)(5) functionality. Under Section 2(e)(5), a mark is barred from registration if it "comprises any matter that, as a whole, is functional." The provision offers no definition of functionality, leaving the PTO and the courts to incorporate common law concepts of functionality discussed in Chapter 3. A Section 2(e)(5) functionality bar cannot be overcome by a showing of secondary meaning, as specified in Section 2(f).

Section 2(f) dilution. According to Section 2(f), dilution is a ground for barring registration, but only in the context of opposition or cancellation proceedings, not in the context of *ex parte* examination. Specifically, a person who can satisfy the requirements for standing may petition to oppose the registration of a mark, or to cancel a registered mark, if the mark would be likely to cause dilution by blurring or dilution by tarnishment. The Lanham Act defines those concepts of dilution in Section 43(c), as we discuss in Chapter 8.

CHAPTER 6
GEOGRAPHIC LIMITS ON TRADEMARK RIGHTS

As we saw in Chapter 4, to establish entitlement to United States federal trademark rights, a party must establish use in commerce, either by showing actual use or, where permitted, by relying on constructive use. The use in commerce requirement also presents a number of issues having to do with the *scope* of trademark rights—in particular, the geographic scope of those rights. In Sections A and B, we discuss the rules that dictate whether one party's use of a mark in commerce in one geographic region of the United States is sufficient to establish trademark rights that are superior to the rights of someone who has long been using the same or a similar mark in another geographic region of the United States. The rules differ depending upon whether the marks at issue are asserted at common law (*see* Section A) or under a federal registration (*see* Section B).

In Sections C and D, we discuss the U.S. trademark rules that govern the extent to which trademark rights can extend across national boundaries. Section C covers scenarios in which a party who has used a mark outside the U.S. seeks to prevent another party from using the mark within the United States. Finally, Section D analyzes whether it is possible for a U.S. trademark holder to restrain conduct occurring abroad on the basis of his or her U.S. trademark rights.

A. GEOGRAPHIC LIMITS ON COMMON LAW RIGHTS: *TEA ROSE* DOCTRINE

In a pair of decisions, *United Drug Co. v. Theodore Rectanus Co.*, 248 U.S. 90 (1918) and *Hanover Star Milling Co. v. Metcalf*, 240 U.S. 403 (1916), the Supreme Court established the governing rule for the geographic scope of common law trademark rights. The rule is frequently referred to as the "Tea Rose" doctrine in reference to the mark that was at issue in the *Hanover Star Milling* case. Under the *Tea Rose* doctrine, a senior user of a mark who has established common law rights in that mark in a given geographical area cannot enjoin a good faith junior user of the mark who is operating in a geographically remote area. In this context, the "senior" user is the party that first used the mark *somewhere* in the United States, even if that use was not in the geographical area in dispute.

In *Hanover Star Milling*, the senior user had adopted the mark TEA ROSE for flour in about 1872, and had used the mark in various northern states (Ohio, Pennsylvania, and Massachusetts) by 1912. The junior user had begun using TEA ROSE for flour in the south in 1904, and by 1912, was using the mark in Mississippi, Alabama, Georgia, and Florida. In 1912, the senior user sued, claiming that its status as the senior user entitled it to exclusive use throughout the United States. The Court acknowledged that if two parties were using the same mark in the same geographic market, priority of appropriation would resolve the issue: the senior user would prevail. However, where two parties "independently" were using the same mark "in separate markets wholly remote" from one another, the Court declared that priority of appropriation was "legally insignificant, unless at least it appears that the second adopter has selected the mark with some design inimical to the interests of the first user." *Id.* As applied here, the senior user could not enjoin the junior user in the southern states.

The Court revisited and restated the rule in *United Drug*. In *United Drug*, the senior user (United Drug and its predecessors) had adopted and used the mark REX in connection with a medicine in Massachusetts, beginning as early as about 1877. Theodore Rectanus, the junior user, began using the mark REX for a medicine in Louisville, Kentucky in 1883. There was no evidence that Rectanus was aware of United Drug's prior Massachusetts use as of that time. In 1912, United Drug sought to use the mark in Louisville; Theodore Rectanus was still using the mark there. In the subsequent lawsuit between United Drug and Rectanus, the District Court held that United Drug was entitled to injunctive relief; the Court of Appeals reversed, holding that United Drug was not entitled to enjoin Rectanus' use in Louisville. At the Supreme Court, the main question was whether the Court should adopt a strict rule of priority in time with no geographic limitations (in which case United Drug would prevail as the senior user) or whether the Court should adopt a more flexible approach under which geographic considerations, coupled with other equitable considerations, could trump priority in time (in which case Theodore Rectanus might prevail). The Court chose the latter approach. Although Rectanus was the junior user, Rectanus was the first to use the mark in Louisville. Rectanus had presumably invested in building up goodwill in Louisville, and consumers in Louisville would have identified the mark with Rectanus, especially because Louisville was geographically remote from Massachusetts. Moreover, Rectanus appeared to have adopted the mark in good faith, without knowledge of United Drug's Massachusetts use. Under those circumstances, the Court concluded, United Drug should not be entitled to enjoin Theodore Rectanus' use of the mark in the disputed territory—Louisville. The Court did not invalidate United Drug's rights, nor, strictly speaking, did the Court deny United Drug's status as the senior user. Thus, the case is best understood as one about limiting the scope of United Drug's rights, coincident with the geographic scope of United Drug's established use.

Courts applying the *Tea Rose* doctrine have encountered a number of issues, discussed briefly below.

Injunction against senior user. One concern is the precise nature of the remedy that results from applying the *Tea Rose* doctrine. The Court in *United Drug* refused to allow the senior user United Drug to enjoin the junior user Rectanus in Louisville, but the Court did not rule on whether Rectanus could have enjoined United Drug in Louisville. Apparently, Rectanus had made no such claim for relief, so the Court refrained from commenting on the issue. Subsequent courts have had to confront the issue, and they have held that a good faith junior user can enjoin the senior user in the disputed geographic area. *See National Ass'n for Healthcare Comm'n's, Inc. v. Central Arkansas Area Agency on Aging, Inc.*, 257 F.3d 732 (8th Cir. 2001).

Good faith. Another issue concerns the assessment of the junior user's good faith. The junior user's mere awareness of the senior user's use of the mark may be relied upon as a factor cutting against good faith, but is not alone sufficient to demolish a good faith claim. *See C.P. Interests, Inc. v. California Pools, Inc.*, 238 F.3d 690 (5th Cir. 2001). This is likely to be important in the modern cases. With the rise of online commerce and the ease with which online searches can be conducted, many would-be junior users have the tools to become aware of uses by senior users. If awareness at this level destroyed any argument of good faith, the *Tea Rose* doctrine would become virtually a dead letter. Thus, it is sensible to have a rule that requires a showing of more than mere awareness to undermine a claim of good faith.

On the other hand, it has been said that if the junior user undertakes the use expecting to trigger a likelihood of confusion with the goods or services of the senior user, the junior user cannot be deemed to be acting in good faith. RESTATEMENT (THIRD) OF UNFAIR COMPETITION § 19, cmt. (d) (1995). This likewise strikes us as a sensible rule, except that it may be tricky to administer. It is not likely that direct evidence of the junior user's subjective expectations will be available, suggesting that proof will usually be by way of inference from circumstantial evidence.

That inference should not be triggered merely by the junior user's awareness of the senior user's use.

Geographic remoteness. There is no simple rule of geographic distance for determining whether competing users are geographically remote from one another for purposes of the *Tea Rose* doctrine. The question at issue in a determination of geographic remoteness is not one of mere distance, but rather one of the extent of consumer recognition. The extent of consumer recognition derives from a combination of many factors, certainly including the nature of the underlying goods or services and the nature and extent of the parties' advertising efforts. The geographic location of a party's use is a rough proxy for the geographic extent of consumer recognition. The date for assessing geographic remoteness is the date when the junior user adopts and begins use of the mark at issue. *Bright Beginnings v. Care Comm.*, 30 U.S.P.Q.2d 1712 (C.D. Cal. 1994).

Some courts determine the geographic location of a party's use by analyzing market penetration—that is, by asking whether the party's use has penetrated a particular geographic region in question. The Eighth Circuit has developed a multi-factor test for market penetration, under which the court is to weigh "all the factors including plaintiff's dollar value of sales at the time defendants entered the market, number of customers compared to the population of the state, relative and potential growth of sales, and length of time since significant sales." *Sweetarts v. Sunline, Inc.*, 380 F.2d 923 (8th Cir. 1967). Courts should approach this test with caution, keeping in mind that it is only a rough measure of the scope of consumer recognition. A mark owner's reputation might extend beyond the geographic market that the mark owner has actually penetrated as measured by the *Sweetarts* test, and, if that is the case, the court should not treat the *Sweetarts* test as dispositive.

The court applied the *Sweetarts* market penetration test in *National Ass'n for Healthcare Communications, Inc. v. Central Arkansas Area Agency on Aging, Inc.*, 257 F.3d 732 (8th Cir. 2001). The National Association for Healthcare Communications ("Healthcare"), the senior user, had adopted and used CARELINK for emergency response services starting in 1991 (apparently outside Arkansas). Starting in 1992, Healthcare attempted to market its services in Arkansas, but made only one sale between 1992 and April 1994, and no sales between April 1994 and September 1995. At that time, Healthcare began contracting with several customers in northwest Arkansas and built up its business there. A competitor, Central Arkansas, adopted and used the mark in a six-county region in central Arkansas in 1995. When Healthcare sought to enjoin Central Arkansas' use of the mark in the six-county region, the court applied the market penetration test to determine whether Central Arkansas' use (a good faith, junior use) was geographically remote. The court determined that it was; Healthcare had never made a sale in the six-county region, and it did not appear that Central Arkansas was likely at the time to expand beyond the six-county region, so there was no reason to expect that consumers would be likely to be confused. The court ruled that Healthcare could not enjoin Central Arkansas' operation in the six-county region.

Even if the senior user has not shown actual market penetration or existing reputation in the geographic area at issue, the senior user may still claim that the area is within the senior user's "zone of natural expansion." The idea is that a senior user who is engaged in a business that is not inherently local (e.g., the manufacture of automobile parts) should be given breathing space to secure exclusive rights beyond the strict confines of the geographic area where the senior user has already established actual market penetration or goodwill. In *Tally-Ho, Inc. v. Coast Community College Dist.*, 889 F.2d 1018 (11th Cir. 1989), the court adopted Professor McCarthy's four criteria for defining the zone of natural expansion: (1) How great is the geographical distance from the senior user's actual location to a point on the perimeter of the zone of expansion? (2) What is the nature of the business? Does it already have a large or small zone of actual market penetration or reputation? (3) What is the history of the senior user's past expansion? Has it remained static for years, or has it continually expanded into new territories? Extrapolating prior expansion, how long would it take the senior user to reach the periphery of the expansion zone he claims? (4) Would it require an unusual "great leap forward" for the senior user to enter the zone, or is the zone so close to existing locations that expansion would be (or is) a logical, gradual, step of the same length as those previously made?

The natural expansion doctrine is looked upon with disfavor by a number of authorities. *See, e.g.,* RESTATEMENT (THIRD) OF UNFAIR COMPETITION § 19, cmt. (c) (1995). One court rejected the doctrine altogether. *Raxton Corp. v. Anania Assocs.*, 668 F.2d 622 (1st Cir. 1982). In *Raxton*, the court argued that it would be "unworkable" and "unfair" to penalize a good faith junior user of a mark just because the junior user "occupied what for them would be a largely undiscoverable path of some remote prior user's expansion."

Partial geographic abandonment. The *Tea Rose* doctrine defines the geographic limits of a party's common law trademark rights. Analogously, some courts accept the proposition that there can be a geographic dimension to a party's abandonment of its common law trademark rights. For example, in *Tumblebus Inc. v. Cranmer*, 399 F.3d 754 (6th Cir. 2005), the plaintiff used the TUMBLEBUS mark itself in Louisville, Kentucky, and arguably engaged in naked licensing in various other parts of the United States. The question was whether the naked licensing should result in *nationwide* loss of the plaintiff's common law rights, or only a loss of rights in those areas where the naked licensing occurred. The court chose the latter, recognizing that common law rights in a mark could be lost in certain geographic areas but retained in others. The court in *Tumblebus* tied this notion of "partial geographic abandonment" to the Lanham Act Section 45 definition of abandonment. That definition specifies that abandonment occurs when a term "lose[s] its significance as a mark." In *Tumblebus*, the plaintiff's

TUMBLEBUS mark had retained its significance in the greater Louisville area, even if it may have lost its source-indicating significance in the areas where naked licensing occurred. Accordingly, the plaintiff retained common law rights in Louisville even if the plaintiff would be deemed to have abandoned them elsewhere. For another example in applying this principle to registered rights, *see Patsy's Italian Restaurant, Inc. v. Banas*, 658 F.3d 254 (2d Cir. 2011) ("[I]f a restaurant operates in both New York and California, but engages in naked licensing only in California, the restaurant's registered mark may lose its significance in California while retaining its significance in New York.")

B. GEOGRAPHIC LIMITS AND REGISTERED RIGHTS

1. THE *DAWN DONUT* RULE

Whereas the *Tea Rose* doctrine governs the determination of the geographic scope of unregistered rights, the rule from *Dawn Donut Co., Inc. v. Hart's Food Stores, Inc.*, 267 F.2d 358 (2d Cir. 1959) governs the analogous determination for registered rights. In *Dawn Donut*, the plaintiff, Dawn Donut, began using the mark DAWN on large bags of donut mix made at its plant in Jackson, Michigan in 1922. Dawn Donut sold the mixes to bakers in various states, including New York, shipping the mix either directly from its Michigan plant or from its warehouses. One such warehouse had been located in Jamestown, New York, but subsequently had shut down. Dawn Donut also apparently had licensed various bakers to sell donuts at retail under the DAWN DONUT mark. Some of these retail licensees were in New York, but none were in the Rochester, New York area. Defendant, Hart, operated a grocery store chain in the Rochester area and sold donuts through its bakeries associated with those stores. It started using the mark DAWN on its donuts in 1951. There was no evidence that Hart had knowledge of Dawn Donut's prior use of the mark when Hart adopted it in Rochester.

If Dawn Donut had been asserting rights at common law, the *Tea Rose* doctrine would have dictated the outcome. However, Dawn Donut had obtained a federal registration for the mark in 1927, and had renewed the registration in 1947, after the passage of the Lanham Act. Under the provisions then in force (in Lanham Act Section 22), the registration had the effect of providing constructive notice as of July 5, 1947, the effective date of the Lanham Act. The court in *Dawn Donut* concluded that this constructive notice should extend nationwide, regardless of the locations of the registrant's actual uses of the mark. Accordingly, Hart could not claim good faith adoption without knowledge after July 5, 1947, because Hart was constructively on notice as to Dawn Donut's rights even though Dawn Donut had not actually used or licensed the mark in the Rochester area. Put another way, Dawn Donut's failure to use or license the mark in the Rochester area could not, as a matter of law, give rise to a partial geographic abandonment under Lanham Act Section 45; the fact that Dawn Donut had obtained federally registered rights precluded any such claim of partial abandonment.

Note that under the current Lanham Act provisions, a registration confers nationwide priority as of the application *filing* date. This is the concept of constructive use priority, codified in Lanham Act Section 7(c), which became effective in 1989. We discussed this concept in Chapter 4.

However, while Dawn Donut had thereby prevailed in establishing superior rights, it did not follow that Dawn Donut should be entitled to enjoin Hart from operating in the Rochester area. If there was no evidence of any likelihood that Dawn Donut would expand into the Rochester area, then it was unlikely that Hart's operations in that area would give rise to a likelihood of consumer confusion. If Dawn Donut and Hart merely continued to operate in their separate respective geographic areas, then there was no consumer interest at stake that would trigger the need for an injunction.

The facts of *Dawn Donut* are especially important in understanding this second part of the *Dawn Donut* rule. In many instances, it may seem that the senior registrant (here Dawn Donut) could easily prove a likelihood of expanding into the disputed area—after all, the senior registrant went to the trouble of suing to enforce rights in the disputed area. In *Dawn Donut*, however, there was strong evidence that Dawn Donut's business was in decline. The number of Dawn Donut's licensees had dropped from nearly 80 during the 1920s to only 16 as of the time of trial. During the 1920s, 11 of the licensees were in New

York; as of the time of trial, none were. Dawn Donut had not shown a likelihood of expanding into the disputed area, and was not entitled to an injunction, although the court noted that "the plaintiff may later, upon a proper showing of an intent to use the mark at the retail level in defendant's market area, be entitled to enjoin defendant's use of the mark." *Id.*

Indeed, to resolve disputes of the sort discussed in this chapter, courts frequently will need to answer close questions about the proper geographical scope of any injunctive relief, and those answers are likely to be tightly bound to the facts of the case and the associated equities. For example, in *Guthrie Healthcare System v. Contextmedia, Inc.*, 826 F.3d 27 (2d Cir. 2016), the senior registrant (Guthrie) was a relatively large healthcare system, but it operated in a rather confined geographic area (the "Twin Tiers" area of New York and Pennsylvania, referred to in the case as the "Guthrie Service Area"). The junior registrant (Contextmedia) was a smaller company, but it had a nationwide customer base for its network that provided digital content to healthcare facilities. After a bench trial on infringement, the district court enjoined Contextmedia from providing services under the disputed mark in the Guthrie Service Area, but declined to extend the injunction further, and expressly authorized Contextmedia to continue using its marks online. On appeal, the Second Circuit vacated and remanded to the extent that the injunction order left Contextmedia free to use its marks outside the Guthrie Service Area and online. The district court should have tailored the scope of the injunction more carefully to give "due weight" to

Guthrie's interest in forestalling confusion, balanced against other case-specific equitable factors, the appellate court concluded. In general, the court considered both the balance of harms to the parties and the impact on the public interest. Specifically, as to the harm to the mark owner, if Guthrie could show plausibly foreseeable harm to its reputation arising from Contextmedia's use of the marks outside the Guthrie Service Area, or if Guthrie could show that those uses impaired Guthrie's prospects for growth beyond the Area, the lower court would be justified in extending the geographic reach of the injunction. Likewise, the lower court would be justified in extending the injunction to bar Contextmedia's online usages, although the Second Circuit emphasized that "innumerable variable factors" controlled this determination, and those factors might vary from case to case.

In summary, the rule from *Dawn Donut* has two equally important components, which may be stated together as follows: (1) a senior registrant does have the right to enjoin a junior user even where the junior user adopted the mark in good faith in a geographically remote disputed area, (2) but only where the senior registrant shows a likelihood of expanding into the disputed area.

2. JUNIOR REGISTRANT VS. SENIOR USER

Lanham Act Section 7(c), covering constructive use priority, provides that a registrant does *not* enjoy nationwide priority as against another person who used the mark prior to the registrant's filing date (and who has not abandoned the mark). *See* Chapter 4. Lanham Act Section 15 specifies that a registrant's right to use the registered mark cannot become incontestable to the extent to which that use "infringes a valid right acquired under the law of any State or Territory" as a result of actual use prior to the registrant's constructive use date. As a consequence of these provisions, cases may arise in which courts must mark out the respective geographic areas in which the junior registrant and the senior user may operate. For example, in *Dorpan S.L. v. Hotel Melia, Inc.*, 728 F.3d 55 (1st Cir. 2013), Dorpan had registered marks including the term MELIA for hotel services in the late 1990s. In 2007, Dorpan opened a hotel in Coco Beach, Puerto Rico, under the name GRAN MELIA. However, for many decades beforehand, dating back to the 1890s, Hotel Melia, Inc. ("HMI") had operated a hotel under the name HOTEL MELIA in Ponce, Puerto Rico. The court reasoned that in order to determine the geographic scope of HMI's pre-existing unregistered trademark rights arising under Puerto Rican law, it needed to apply a likelihood-of-confusion factors analysis, asking whether Dorpan's use of the mark in Coco Beach would give rise to a likelihood of confusion in light of HMI's senior use in Ponce. Only after doing so would the court be able to decide the geographic boundaries of HMI's and Dorpan's respective rights under Lanham Act Section 15, the court concluded.

3. SENIOR REGISTRANT VS. "INTERMEDIATE" JUNIOR USER: LANHAM ACT SECTION 33(b)(5)

The *Dawn Donut* rule applies to a dispute between a senior registrant and a junior user, where a "junior" user is one who adopts and begins use of a mark after the senior registrant's date of nationwide priority. As we have noted, under Lanham Act Section 7(c), a registrant's date of nationwide priority is the *application filing date*, assuming that the application eventually issues as a registration. (We discussed constructive use priority in Chapter 4.)

A slightly different rule applies to a dispute between a senior registrant and an "intermediate" junior user. The following example explains the concept of the intermediate junior user and illustrates the applicable rule. Suppose that a registrant **SR** begins using a mark in northwestern Iowa in 1992, and files an application for federal registration in 1999. Under Section 7(c), **SR**'s date of *nationwide* priority is the application filing date, in 1999. Suppose that another party, **JR**, adopts and uses the mark in central Indiana in 1995. **JR**'s use is after **SR**'s 1992 use, but before **SR**'s 1999 date of nationwide priority. It may be useful to call **JR** an *intermediate* junior user to signify that **JR** adopted and first used the mark in the interim time period between **SR**'s first use and **SR**'s nationwide priority date. The Lanham Act sets forth a rule for resolving disputes between a senior registrant and an intermediate junior user. Lanham Act Section 33(b)(5) grants the intermediate junior user a "limited area" defense to infringement. Specifically, if the intermediate junior user adopted the mark without knowledge of the senior registrant's prior use, and if the intermediate junior user has used the mark continuously starting before the senior registrant's nationwide priority date, then the intermediate junior user may continue to use the mark in the limited geographic area in which the continuous use has been proven. This defense is preserved even as against incontestable registrations.

Arguably, the Section 33(b)(5) limited area defense for intermediate junior users is a codification of the *Tea Rose* doctrine. Courts have split on this question. A Ninth Circuit decision concludes that Section 33(b)(5) includes no element of geographic remoteness, and thus differs from the *Tea Rose* doctrine. *Quiksilver, Inc. v. Kymsta Corp.*, 466 F.3d 749 (9th Cir. 2006). A Sixth Circuit decision, by contrast, reads a geographic remoteness element into Section 33(b)(5). *Champions Golf Club, Inc. v. The Champions Golf Club, Inc.*, 78 F.3d 1111 (6th Cir. 1996).

4. REGISTRANT VS. REGISTRANT: CONCURRENT USE REGISTRATIONS; LIMITED AREA DEFENSE

When a good faith junior user prevails under the *Tea Rose* doctrine, the probable result is that both the senior user and the junior user will continue their respective uses of the mark concurrently, albeit in their separate geographic regions. Similarly, the

Dawn Donut rule may result in the senior registrant and the junior user continuing their uses of the mark concurrently, in a case where the senior registrant cannot prove a likelihood of expanding into the junior user's territory. There is one additional permutation to consider: the prospect that two holders of federal registrations would operate concurrently.

Under Section 2(d), the PTO is empowered to grant "concurrent registrations" if a court has finally determined that more than one person is entitled to use the same or similar marks in commerce. The PTO is required to "prescribe conditions and limitations as to the mode or place of use" of the concurrently registered mark or underlying goods. Concurrent registrations may also issue from an inter partes administrative proceeding at the PTO called a "concurrent use proceeding." *See* Lanham Act §§ 17–18. For an example, see *Weiner King, Inc. v. The Wiener King Corp.*, 201 U.S.P.Q. 894 (TTAB 1979) (granting applications for concurrent use registrations).

A related rule is codified in Section 33(b)(6). It provides that if a registrant sues a competitor for infringement, and it turns out that the competitor had registered and used the mark prior to the registrant's registration (or publication of the registrant's application) and had not abandoned it, then the competitor has a defense to infringement even if the registrant's registration is incontestable. However, the defense only applies for the geographic area in which the competitor used the mark prior to the registrant's registration. This is sometimes referred to as the "limited area" defense.

C. THE TERRITORIAL NATURE OF U.S. TRADEMARK RIGHTS

Trademark rights are said to be territorial, but modern commercial activities are rarely confined within national boundaries. In the cases discussed below, a mark owner has adopted and used a mark overseas, and then subsequently has sought to enjoin a competitor who is using the mark in the United States. Disputes such as these challenge traditional notions of the territoriality of the trademark right.

1. TERRITORIALITY AND THE RULE FROM *PERSON'S*

Some cases have taken the view that territorial limits are basic to the concept of U.S. trademark rights. *Person's Co. Ltd. v. Christman*, 900 F.2d 1565 (Fed. Cir. 1990) is an important case on point. The relevant facts are summarized on the accompanying timeline (*see* figure on page 186). A Japanese company, Person's Co., had adopted and used the mark PERSON'S for clothing in Japan starting as early as 1977. Larry Christman, a U.S. citizen, purchased some PERSON'S clothing on a trip to Japan. Returning to the U.S., he developed a line of clothing bearing the PERSON'S mark and began selling it in the northwestern U.S. in April 1982. In April 1983, Christman filed an application to register the mark for clothing in the United States, which duly issued in 1984. The evidence indicated that

Christman had consulted with counsel prior to adopting the mark and had received a clearance opinion, and was unaware of any plans on the part of the Japanese company to begin selling in the United States.

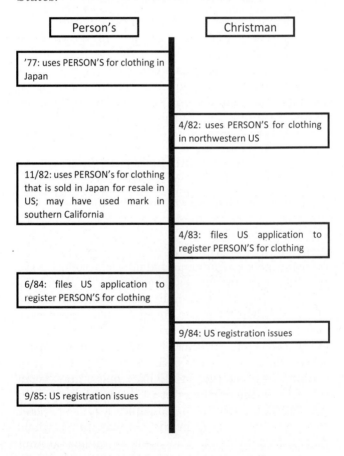

Around November 1982, Person's Co. began sales to buyers for resale in the United States. About a year later, Person's filed an application to register PERSON'S for clothing and other goods in the U.S., and Person's registration issued in August 1985. (Person's did not claim the benefit of any Japanese registration under Lanham Act Section 44.) Not surprisingly, as Person's expanded its sales activity in the U.S., Person's and Christman came into conflict. Person's petitioned to cancel Christman's registration, Christman counterclaimed to cancel Person's registration. Christman prevailed at the TTAB, and Person's appealed.

Person's first argued that it was the senior user based on its use in Japan. The Federal Circuit held that Person's could not rely on overseas use to establish priority in the United States. The court took the view that "[t]he concept of territoriality is basic to trademark law; trademark rights exist in each country solely according to that country's statutory scheme." Accordingly, Christman was the senior user for purposes of U.S. rights, because Christman was the first to adopt and use the mark "in U.S. commerce."

Person's offered an alternative argument: that Christman had proceeded in bad faith. Here, Person's seemed to be invoking a transboundary equivalent to the *Tea Rose* doctrine, arguing that Christman's bad faith disqualified him from being treated as a geographically remote good faith junior user. There were two problems with the argument. First, the record did not support a claim of bad faith on

Christman's part. Christman had procured a clearance opinion from counsel, and Christman's mere awareness of Person's Japanese use did not give rise to an inference of bad faith. Moreover, based on the court's view of the territoriality of trademark rights, there was no international equivalent to the *Tea Rose* doctrine in any event.

The court did acknowledge that there were two circumstances under which an inference of bad faith might be proper: (1) the foreign mark is well-known in the U.S.; or (2) the U.S. party's use "is a nominal one made solely to block the prior foreign user's planned expansion into the United States." However, it is not clear why bad faith would be relevant in any event if no analog to the *Tea Rose* doctrine exists.

Cases such as *Person's* might be easier to resolve if there were a simpler way for an overseas mark owner to establish that overseas activities constituted use in the United States. The Fourth Circuit considered the matter in *International Bancorp LLC v. Societe des Bains de Mer et du Cercle des Etrangers a Monaco*, 329 F.3d 359 (4th Cir. 2003), *cert. denied* 540 U.S. 1106 (2004). Societe Des Bains ("SBM") operated the CASINO DE MONTE CARLO in Monaco. SBM operated a small New York office through which it advertised the casino in the United States, but did not operate a casino in the U.S. or own a relevant U.S. trademark registration.

International Bancorp operated a number of online gambling websites, including websites associated with the name CASINO DE MONTE CARLO (e.g., a website located at casinodemontecarlo.com).

International Bancorp sued for a declaration that it was entitled to the domain names at issue; SBM counterclaimed for various Lanham Act trademark violations. At the trial court, SBM prevailed on one of its counterclaims (trademark infringement). On appeal, the principal issue was whether SBM had established protectable trademark rights in CASINO DE MONTE CARLO for casino services. There were two grounds of challenge to protectability: distinctiveness and use in commerce. As to use in commerce, the question was whether SBM had satisfied the elements of the Section 45 definition of use in commerce for service marks. SBM had certainly used the mark at issue in advertising its services in the U.S., but the Section 45 definition requires an additional element: that services be rendered "in commerce." The Fourth Circuit held over a dissent that evidence that U.S. citizens went to and gambled at the casino sufficed to show that SBM's casino services were rendered in commerce. Commerce encompassed trade between U.S. citizens and the subjects of foreign nations (and SBM was such a subject). The Fourth Circuit distinguished *Person's* on two grounds: (1) that in *Person's*, there had been no evidence that the Japanese company had used or displayed its mark to advertise or sell products to U.S. consumers; and (2) that *Person's* involved marks used on goods, not on services. The first ground may rest on a dubious reading of the *Person's* facts, and the second ground may present a distinction that makes no real difference in this context. In any event, it is not clear that *International Bancorp's* view of foreign use will prevail. *See First Niagara Ins. Brokers Inc. v. First Niagara Financial Group, Inc.*, 77 U.S.P.Q.2d 1334 (TTAB 2005), *rev'd on other grounds* 476 F.3d 867 (Fed. Cir. 2007). The TTAB invoked *Person's* and effectively declined to follow *International Bancorp.* The TTAB reaffirmed that promoting a mark that is used on goods marketed outside the United States does not create priority inside the United States.

2. WELL-KNOWN MARKS

As noted above, the *Person's* court hinted that its analysis of geographic priority in that case might be different if the Japanese company's mark had been well-known in the United States. The following cases deal with the doctrine of well-known marks, showing that the doctrine is not yet well-entrenched in trademark jurisprudence in the United States.

International standards for well-known marks: Paris Convention Art. 6bis. Treaties to which the U.S. formally adheres contain obligations that require the U.S. to provide special protections for well-known marks. Specifically, Paris Convention Article 6*bis*(1) provides that "[t]he Countries of the Union undertake . . . to refuse or to cancel the registration, and to prohibit the use, of a trademark which constitutes a reproduction . . . liable to create confusion, of a mark considered by the competent authority of the country of registration or use to be well known in that country . . . and used for identical or similar goods . . . ." In addition, Article 2(2) of the TRIPS agreement requires WTO members to comply with specified Articles of the Paris Convention, including Article 6*bis*. TRIPS Articles 16(2) and (3) expand upon Paris Art. 6*bis*, extending it to service marks and to uses of marks on goods/services that are unrelated to those of the mark owner, but would still "indicate a connection" with the mark owner. TRIPS Art. 16(2) additionally provides that "[i]n determining whether a trademark is well-known, Members shall take account of the knowledge of the trademark in the relevant sector of the public, including knowledge in the member concerned which has been obtained as a result of the promotion of the trademark."

However, these treaty obligations are not self-executing. Congress must incorporate them explicitly into the Lanham Act, unless the obligations are already embodied implicitly in existing trademark law. Because Congress has not explicitly enacted a well-known marks doctrine, the question under the cases discussed below is whether some other implicit Lanham Act basis for the doctrine exists.

Conflicting U.S. authority on well-known marks. The well-known marks doctrine does not have a solid pedigree in U.S. law. A New York state court appeared to rely on a well-known marks doctrine in *Vaudable v. Montmartre, Inc.*, 123 U.S.P.Q. 357 (Sup. Ct. N.Y. Co. 1959), where the court granted an injunction against a New York restauranteur who had sought to use MAXIM'S for a restaurant in New York, on the ground that a Paris firm had used the mark for several decades for a restaurant in Paris. Although the Paris firm had not used the mark in the U.S., its mark was deemed to be well-known among

New York consumers. The TTAB invoked the well-known marks doctrine in a few cases, relying on *Vaudable* as authority. *See, e.g., Mother's Restaurants, Inc. v. Mother's Other Kitchen, Inc.*, 218 U.S.P.Q. 1046 (TTAB 1983). This was essentially the extent of the case law until the decisions in two major appeals in the federal courts, *Grupo Gigante* and *ITC*.

In *Grupo Gigante v. Dallo & Co., Inc.*, 391 F.3d 1088 (9th Cir. 2004), a Mexican firm, Grupo Gigante, had adopted and used GIGANTE for grocery stores in Mexico starting in 1962. Grupo registered the mark in Mexico in 1963. By 1990s, Grupo had its grocery store operations expanded across Mexico, including in border cities (e.g., Tijuana). In June 1998, Grupo obtained a California state registration for GIGANTE for grocery stores, and in 1999, Grupo opened a GIGANTE store in the Los Angeles area.

Dallo had previously entered the California market. In 1991, Dallo opened a grocery store under the name GIGANTE MARKET in San Diego. Dallo's business had come to Grupo's attention in 1995, but Grupo did not open negotiations with Dallo until June 1998. In July 1998, Dallo obtained a California state registration. *See* the accompanying timeline (*see* figure on page 186) for a summary of the relevant facts.

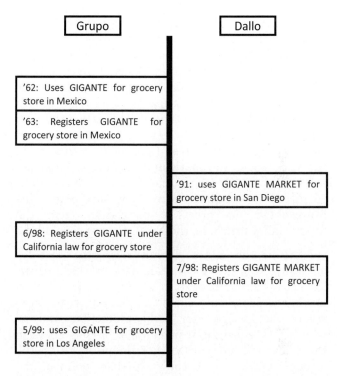

In subsequent trademark litigation between Grupo and Dallo, the trial court granted summary judgment in favor of Grupo. On appeal, the case centered around whether Grupo could rely on the well-known marks doctrine, which the court characterized as an exception from the principle of territoriality. Dallo had conceded that a well-known marks doctrine existed; the controversy concerned whether the GIGANTE mark qualified for well-known status (and what the test should be for making this determination). The trial court had analyzed the question by assessing whether Grupo's GIGANTE mark had attained secondary meaning in the San Diego area. The Ninth Circuit rejected this approach on the ground that it gave too much significance to the foreign activities. That is, the trial court's approach treated U.S. activities under the mark and foreign activities equivalently for purposes of establishing priority, given that a firm operating in the U.S. under the mark and seeking to establish priority over Grupo would likewise have been required to establish secondary meaning. This represented too great a derogation from the territoriality principle, the Ninth Circuit concluded.

Instead, the Ninth Circuit held, the test for assessing whether the well-known marks doctrine applies required the court to consider (1) whether the mark has achieved secondary meaning in the area where the foreign user seeks protection; and (2) whether "a substantial percentage of consumers in the relevant American market is familiar with the foreign mark." The court further defined the "relevant American market" as that geographic area "where the defendant uses the alleged infringing mark." Finally, the court identified two factors that courts should include in analyzing familiarity under the second prong of the test: "the intentional copying of the mark by the defendant, and whether customers of the American firm are likely to think they are patronizing the same firm that uses the mark in another country." These factors, of course, could also be used in a secondary meaning analysis, so it may be more difficult to distinguish between the secondary meaning test and the well-known marks test than the Ninth Circuit anticipates.

The court vacated and remanded to permit the lower court to determine whether Grupo's evidence satisfied the court's two-pronged standard. Judge Graber, concurring, agreed with the majority's articulation of the standard, but would have found that Grupo's evidence was insufficient to satisfy it. Judge Graber took issue with Grupo's survey evidence, which had assumed that Mexican-Americans in the San Diego area comprised the relevant audience. According to Judge Graber, Grupo should not have limited the survey to Mexican-Americans given that the grocery store's services were presumptively directed to the general population. Moreover, Judge Graber found that a 20–22% familiarity rate would have been inadequate; instead, Judge Graber would have required a showing that a *majority* of the relevant customers were familiar with Grupo's mark. This is an exceptionally stringent standard unmatched elsewhere in U.S. trademark law.

The Second Circuit rejected the reasoning of *Grupo Gigante* and took a dramatically different view of the status of the well-known marks doctrine in *ITC Ltd. v. Punchgini, Inc.*, 482 F.3d 135 (2d Cir. 2007). ITC, an Indian corporation, had operated the BUKHARA restaurant in India starting in 1977. In the 1980s, ITC opened BUKHARA restaurants in several cities around the world, including Chicago and New York City. ITC also obtained a federal trademark registration in the U.S. for BUKHARA for restaurant services in 1987. However, ITC closed the New York restaurant in 1991 and the Chicago restaurant in 1997, so at the time of the litigation, it was only operating BUKHARA restaurants in Asia. In 1999, defendant Punchgini opened a restaurant in New York under the name BUKHARA GRILL and sought to emulate elements of the décor of ITC's BUKHARA restaurants. ITC sued in 2003.

This is not the usual fact pattern that gives rise to a dispute over the well-known marks doctrine, because here, the owner of the allegedly well-known mark actually had used it in the U.S., and even had registered it, but thereafter had discontinued use. Accordingly, the well-known marks doctrine was invoked in an unusual context here. The Court of Appeals concluded as a matter of law that ITC had abandoned its U.S. registered rights as of about 2000. (*See* Chapter 4 for a discussion of the rules of abandonment.) ITC sought to rely on the well-known marks doctrine to save its U.S. rights from abandonment. Specifically, ITC claimed that because its mark was well-known before it ever opened its New York City restaurant, and before it ever sought U.S. registration, that its efforts to penetrate the U.S. market should not matter—its efforts outside the U.S. should suffice to establish priority for purposes of an assertion of common law rights within the United States.

The Second Circuit displayed little sympathy for this argument, and its skepticism may have carried over into its refusal to recognize the well-known marks doctrine as a viable doctrine in U.S. law. The

Second Circuit noted that *Vaudable* had relied on New York state common law, not federal law, and that TTAB decisions recognizing a well-known marks doctrine had simply invoked *Vaudable* uncritically, without considering whether federal law provided a basis for the doctrine. According to the court, *Grupo Gigante* had proceeded in much the same way, providing no searching analysis of the doctrine's basis in federal law and apparently recognizing the doctrine purely on the basis of policy.

The Second Circuit thus turned to the Lanham Act, and found no statutory basis for a well-known marks doctrine codified there. ITC had argued that Lanham Act Section 44(b) (which guarantees foreign mark owners the benefits of certain treaty rights, including those of the Paris Convention and TRIPS Agreement) coupled with Section 44(h) (which protects foreign mark owners from unfair competition) effectively created a well-known marks doctrine. The Second Circuit rejected this construction of Section 44, saying that Section 44(b) was cabined by the principle of territoriality and Section 44(h) could afford foreign mark owners protection no greater than that conferred by Section 44(b). The absence of a Lanham Act basis for the well-known marks doctrine was fatal, because the international treaty obligations in the Paris Convention and TRIPS were not self-executing.

Finding no textual basis for the doctrine, the court turned to policy. While the court acknowledged that there might be sound reasons of trademark policy for supporting a well-known marks doctrine, the court declined to recognize the doctrine solely on policy grounds, because doing so would offend notions of judicial restraint.

While the foregoing analysis disposed of the federal law claims, ITC continued to press its New York state law claims. Here, the Second Circuit certified to the New York Court of Appeals (the state's highest court) the question whether New York law should recognize a well-known marks doctrine. That court declined to recognize the doctrine, but did "reaffirm" that a trademark owner's goodwill could cross national boundaries, and this phenomenon could be taken into account in deciding claims of misappropriation under New York common law, as the court had done in *Vaudable*. *ITC Ltd. v. Punchgini*, 9 N.Y.3d 467 (2007). The New York court then specified that the elements of such a claim were (1) "actual goodwill" in New York (i.e., consumer association); and (2) appropriation (i.e., deliberate copying) of that goodwill. Relevant factors for assessing whether such goodwill existed included "evidence that the defendant intentionally associated its goods with those of the foreign plaintiff in the minds of the public, such as public statements or advertising stating or implying a connection with the foreign plaintiff; direct evidence, such as consumer surveys, indicating that consumers of defendant's goods or services believe them to be associated with the plaintiff; and evidence of actual overlap between customers of the New York defendant and the foreign plaintiff." Returning to the federal courts, ITC emphasized the evidence of Punchgini's deliberate copying in an attempt to sustain the claim of misappropriation under New York Law. Again, the Second Circuit was unimpressed, dismissing ITC's claim on summary judgment with the comment that evidence of deliberate copying was not sufficient by itself to show that actual goodwill existed in New York. *ITC, Ltd. v. Punchgini*, 518 F.3d 159 (2d Cir. 2008).

By contrast, the Cuban mark owner in *Empresa Cubana Del Tabaco v. Culbro Corp.*, 587 F. Supp. 2d 622 (S.D.N.Y. 2008) succeeded in showing misappropriation under New York law pursuant to the *ITC* test. Evidence that the Cuban mark (COHIBA for cigars) had "acquired recognition consistent with 'secondary meaning' in the U.S., that is, it was 'uniquely associated' with the Cuban COHIBA, or that this was its 'primary significance'" sufficed to satisfy the "actual goodwill" prong of the *ITC* test.

In *Belmora, LLC v. Bayer Consumer Care AG*, 819 F.3d 697 (4th Cir. 2016), the Fourth Circuit rendered a ruling on standing that has important implications for claims under the well-known mark doctrine. Bayer had sold naproxen sodium pain relievers under the mark FLANAX in Mexico for several decades, but had sold the product under the name ALEVE in the United States. Belmora adopted and registered the mark FLANAX in the U.S. for its naproxen sodium pain relievers and began selling its products in the United States, using packaging that resembled Bayer's FLANAX packaging. Belmora's advertisements, which seemed to be directed to Latinos living in the U.S., arguably claimed that

Belmora's FLANAX product was connected with Bayer's Mexican product.

Bayer sought to have Belmora's U.S. registration for FLANAX cancelled, invoking Lanham Act 14(3), which provides that a registrant's mark can be cancelled if the registrant has used the mark to misrepresent the source of the goods. Bayer also sued Belmora in a separate action, alleging that Belmora's marketing of FLANAX pain relievers in the U.S. gave rise to a claim for unfair competition under Section 43(a)(1)(A) and false advertising under Section 43(a)(1)(B).

In the cancellation proceeding, the TTAB ruled for Bayer, and Belmora sought review by civil action under Lanham Act Section 21(b), and Bayer's Section 43(a) suit was consolidated with this action. In the consolidated matter, the district court ruled for Belmora on both the cancellation and Section 43(a) claims, on the ground that Bayer had lacked standing to pursue those claims. In particular, the district court accepted the argument that because Bayer had never used the FLANAX mark in United States commerce, Bayer lacked statutory standing to bring Lanham Act claims, under the two-part test established in *Lexmark International, Inc. v. Static Control Components, Inc.,* 134 S.Ct. 1377 (2014). (*See* Chapter 10 for additional discussion of the *Lexmark* decision.)

A Fourth Circuit panel vacated and remanded. According to the court, one's use of one's own mark within the U.S. was not a condition precedent for standing to bring either a Section 43(a) claim or a cancellation claim, given that the relevant statutory language extended to "any person" who was likely to have suffered damage. Moreover, Bayer satisfied both prongs of the *Lexmark* test for both the Section 43(a) claims and the cancellation claim. The allegations that Belmora targeted its marketing to Latino residents of the U.S. (and residents of Mexico who live near the U.S. boarder and shop in the U.S.) demonstrated that Bayer's commercial reputation in the U.S. was implicated (relevant to the "zone of interests" prong of the *Lexmark* test). Similarly, these allegations showed that Belmora's marketing practices in the U.S. might proximately cause Bayer to lose sales of FLANAX in Mexico. Therefore, the court reasoned, Bayer had established standing. A contrary ruling presumably would have foreclosed many claims under the well-known marks doctrine in the U.S., because mark owners ordinarily would invoke the doctrine when they have established use outside the United States but have made minimal or no actual uses inside the United States. On the other hand, the court emphasized that it was ruling only on standing, and that Bayer would need to prove deception among U.S. consumers in order to prevail on the merits.

D. THE EXTRATERRITORIAL ENFORCEMENT OF U.S. TRADEMARK RIGHTS

The cases in this section deal with the circumstances under which the owner of U.S. trademark rights can enforce those rights against activities occurring abroad. This is, in a sense, the reverse of the issue discussed in Section C above, where the issue was whether activities carried on outside the U.S. could give rise to trademark rights enforceable within the U.S.

In *Steele v. Bulova Watch Co.*, 344 U.S. 280 (1952), defendant Steele was a U.S. citizen who operated a business in Mexico City selling watches stamped with plaintiff's BULOVA mark, for which Bulova owned a U.S. registration. The district court concluded that it lacked subject matter jurisdiction because the defendant's activities had occurred outside the United States. The Court of Appeals reversed, and the Supreme Court took the case on *certiorari*. The Supreme Court noted that Congress' power to regulate under the Lanham Act was coextensive with its Commerce Clause powers, but the Court did not lay out an explicit test for determining when it would be proper to apply the Lanham Act to commercial activities occurring outside the United States. Instead, the Court appeared to rely on three factors, without placing them into any hierarchy. First, the Court took account of the fact that Steele's activities carried out in Mexico City were likely to have a substantial effect within the United States. For example, the Court noted that Steele had apparently purchased some watch components in the U.S., and that Bulova's Texas sales representative had received complaints from retail jewelers along the Texas/Mexico border about defective watches marked with the BULOVA mark that apparently originated with Steele. Second, the Court's analysis also seemed to rely on Steele's U.S. citizenship, because it made the question before the Court essentially one of domestic law, as the Court saw it. Congress (and the U.S. courts) had authority to regulate unfair trade practices in foreign commerce carried out by U.S. citizens, according to the Court. Third, the Court concluded that because Steele's Mexican registration had been cancelled, the Court did not need to consider whether the exercise of jurisdiction over Steele's activities would conflict with Steele's Mexican trademark rights.

In *Vanity Fair Mills, Inc. v. T. Eaton Co., Ltd.*, 234 F.2d 633 (2d Cir.), *cert. denied* 352 U.S. 871 (1956), the Second Circuit restated the *Bulova* analysis as a three-factor test: "(1) the defendant's conduct had a substantial effect on United States commerce; (2) the defendant was a United States citizen . . . ; and (3) there was no conflict with trade-mark rights established under foreign law. . . ." The court observed that the absence of the second factor was likely to preclude a court from exercising jurisdiction extraterritorially, given that the Court in *Bulova* had relied heavily on Steele's U.S. citizenship to justify jurisdiction. In *Vanity Fair*, the defendant was a Canadian company (thus, factor (2) was not satisfied) that held a Canadian registration on the mark at issue (and so it appeared that factor (3) was also not satisfied). The court declared that the Lanham Act should not be applied extraterritorially "against foreign citizens acting under presumably valid trademarks in a foreign country," apparently even if there was a showing of a substantial effect on U.S. commerce.

In *Sterling Drug, Inc. v. Bayer AG*, 14 F.3d 733 (2d Cir. 1994), the court applied the Lanham Act extraterritorially while still attempting to keep faith with the *Vanity Fair* factors. The defendant was a German company, which counseled against extraterritorial application according to the *Vanity Fair* factors, but the court was impressed by the evidence that suggested that the defendant's activities had a substantial effect on U.S. consumers. It would be problematic to apply the *Vanity Fair* factors "mechanically," the court reasoned, because doing so would imperil the Lanham Act's goal of protecting the interests of U.S. consumers. In any event, the court asserted, *Vanity Fair* was not on all fours, because the plaintiff there had sought a blanket injunction, while the plaintiff in *Sterling Drug* merely sought to limit foreign uses that reached the United States. The "stringent" *Vanity Fair* test was appropriate when the plaintiff sought an absolute bar against the defendant's use, but was "unnecessarily demanding" when plaintiff sought a domestic injunction.

The court in *McBee v. Delica Co.*, 417 F.3d 107 (1st Cir. 2005) definitively moved away from using the *Vanity Fair* factors as the sole test for assessing extraterritorial application of the Lanham Act. According to *McBee*, the *Vanity Fair* factors were appropriate for cases in which the defendant was a U.S. citizen, where the rationale for applying the law extraterritorially was Congress' power to regulate the overseas conduct of its citizens. However, where the defendant was not a U.S. citizen, the rationale shifted: the trademark law could be invoked extraterritorially if doing so fell within Congress' power to regulate foreign commerce. To develop a test for use in these cases, the *McBee* court turned to antitrust law, where the Supreme Court had already held that overseas conduct by foreign defendants could be subject to U.S. antitrust law only if the conduct had a "substantial effect" on U.S. commerce. The "substantial effect" test was one of the *Vanity Fair* factors, but, according to *McBee*, it should be the sole test for determining whether to apply the Lanham Act to the overseas conduct of foreign defendants. To show a substantial effect, the mark owner must show that there are impacts within the United States, and that these impacts are "of a sufficient character and magnitude to give the United States a reasonably strong interest in the litigation." If the substantial effects test is met, only then should the court analyze comity considerations (that is, considerations as to whether the defendant was acting under color of the law of his or her own country) under the *McBee* court's approach. Applying its test, the court found that it would be improper to apply the Lanham Act to defendant's Japan-based website, and to defendant's sales in Japan, because there was no substantial effect on U.S. commerce as to either activity.

Similarly, the Ninth Circuit borrowed antitrust law rules to analyze a question of the extraterritorial application of the Lanham Act in *Trader Joe's Co. v. Hallatt*, 835 F.3d 690 (9th Cir. 2016). Hallatt, a Canadian resident, had opened a store in Canada called "Pirate Joe's." At the store (and through his website), Hallatt sold TRADER JOE'S-branded goods that he had purchased at TRADER JOE'S stores in the U.S. and transported to Canada. Trader Joe's asserted Lanham Act claims against Hallatt in a U.S. federal district court, seeking damages and an injunction that would prevent Hallatt from reselling the goods in Canada or using the Pirate Joe's name for the Canadian store.

To determine whether to apply the Lanham Act to Hallatt's activities in Canada, the court considered a set of factors borrowed from *Timberlane Lumber Co. v. Bank of America National Trust & Savings Ass'n,* 549 F.2d 597 (9th Cir. 1976)—namely, whether (1) the alleged violations created some effect on American foreign commerce; (2) the effect was sufficiently great to present a cognizable injury to the plaintiffs under the Lanham Act; and (3) the interests of and links to American foreign commerce were sufficiently strong in relation to those of other nations to justify an assertion of extraterritorial authority. The court concluded that Trader Joe's had satisfied this test. As to prongs (1) and (2), Trader Joe's could show an adequate effect on commerce without needing to show that foreign-purchased goods trickled back into the United States. Instead, it was sufficient for Trader Joe's to show that Hallatt's activities could affect Trader Joe's reputation and the value of its U.S. marks, primarily through Hallatt's alleged failure to comport with quality control practices that Trader Joe's observes in its U.S. operations. Moreover, some of Hallatt's activities (e.g., his bulk purchases from Trader Joe's stores) occurred within the U.S. in any event. As to the third prong—essentially an analysis of international comity considerations using a seven-factor balancing analysis—the fact that there was no pending Canadian trademark action between the parties, and that the TRADER JOE'S mark was well-known in Canada, counseled in favor of extraterritorial application. In addition, Hallatt had allegedly engaged in his activities with the intent to harm Trader Joe's. Furthermore, Hallatt held legal permanent resident status in the United States and allegedly held assets in the United States, and purchased his goods from U.S. stores, suggesting that an injunction issuing from a U.S. court could realistically be enforced to remedy the alleged harm.

CHAPTER 7
CONFUSION-BASED TRADEMARK LIABILITY THEORIES

Likelihood of confusion is the touchstone for trademark infringement liability (for registered rights) and false designation of origin liability (for unregistered rights). In this Chapter, we detail the elements of those liability theories, with a special focus on the likelihood of confusion element. We first introduce the topic (Section A) and discuss the requirement that the alleged infringer's unauthorized use qualifies as actionable use (Section B). We next take up the likelihood of confusion factors analysis, discussing its general application both in infringement matters and in the registration context (Section C), its use in theories of confusion away from the point of sale (Section D), and in the theory of reverse confusion (Section E). We conclude with a discussion of liability for facilitating another's direct infringement, primarily under the theory of contributory infringement (Section F).

A. INTRODUCTION

A trademark infringement claim under Lanham Act Section 32(1)(a) has three elements: (1) the plaintiff owns a valid, registered mark; (2) the defendant is engaged in unauthorized use of the mark; and (3) that use causes a likelihood of confusion. A claim of unfair competition by false designation of origin under Lanham Act Section 43(a)(1)—which may be conceived of as a claim for infringement of unregistered trademark rights—has three similar elements: (1) the defendant is engaged in unauthorized use of a mark; (2) the plaintiff owns valid rights in the mark; and (3) the defendant's use causes a likelihood of confusion. *See, e.g., Checkpoint Sys., Inc. v. Check Point Software Technologies, Inc.*, 269 F.3d 270 (3d Cir. 2001) (providing a slightly different three-element test). This chapter deals with the unauthorized use element (element (1)) and the likelihood of confusion element (element (3)), with an emphasis on the latter.

Under modern U.S. trademark law, likelihood of confusion is the touchstone for determining liability. This was not always the case. Under the Trademark Act of 1905, it was not clear that liability turned on consumer confusion at all. Section 16 of the 1905 Act, the primary infringement provision, imposed liability on anyone who copied another's trademark without consent and affixed it to merchandise "of substantially the same descriptive properties" as the merchandise set forth in the registration. This language did not preclude the use of a confusion inquiry, but it certainly did not require it, either. Similarly, in cases involving unregistered marks, decided under the rules of common law unfair competition, it was not clear that consumer confusion was the dominant inquiry. The decision in *Borden Ice Cream Co. v. Borden's Condensed Milk Co.*, 201 Fed. 510 (7th Cir. 1912) illustrates the point, although the case was sufficiently extreme that it was probably anomalous even when decided. Borden's Condensed Milk Co. (the "old company") sought to enjoin Borden Ice Cream Co. (the "new company") from marketing ice cream under the BORDEN name. The old company had sold many dairy products under the BORDEN name, but not ice cream. The new company was well aware of the old company and its products, and even had brought in an individual named Charles F. Borden and had given him a share of stock as an apparent pretext for adopting the "Borden" name. The old company sued, asserting unfair competition. The District Court held for the old company, but the Seventh Circuit reversed. According to the appellate court, the fundamental question before it was not whether the public was likely to be deceived as a result of the new company's actions. Rather, the question was whether the new company's actions had actually diverted sales away from the old company. In the absence of evidence of such diversion, whether or not the public had been deceived was "no concern" of the court. This was true even if the new company was shown to have proceeded with fraudulent intent. The court had "no right to interfere" unless the old company had actually lost sales. Nor would the court look ahead to the prospect that the old company might well expand into ice cream sales in the future. The old company's marks only had legal significance insofar as they had actually offered goods for sale under them. This meant, the court observed, that the new company could make anything under the name "Borden" that the old company had not already made and offered to the public. Under this severely restricted view, the old company and the new company were not currently in competition at all, so there could be no remedy for alleged unfair competition.

The views expressed in *Borden's* have been definitively rejected. By the time Congress enacted the Lanham Act in 1946, the fundamental inquiry in trademark infringement and unfair competition claims was whether the alleged infringer had caused a likelihood of confusion. Congress incorporated the phrase "likely to cause confusion" into Lanham Act Section 32. Courts recognized that likely confusion had become the dominant inquiry, and that, unlike the 1905 Act, the Lanham Act "made plain that infringement might be found and prohibited, though the use of the registered mark was upon goods having different descriptive properties than those set forth in the registration, and though in consequence there was no actual competition between the parties." *Fleischmann Distilling Corp. v. Maier Brewing Co.*, 314 F.2d 149 (9th Cir. 1963), *cert. denied* 374 U.S. 830 (1963). In *Fleischmann*, the court found that defendant's adoption and use of BLACK & WHITE for beer infringed plaintiff's registered mark BLACK & WHITE for Scotch whiskey because the defendant's use would have been likely to cause confusion among consumers. The court took into account factors such as defendant's intent to trade off plaintiff's goodwill, the strength of the plaintiff's mark, and the fact that the relevant purchasers were "unskilled" members of the general public who would rely on general impressions in selecting products.

This brings us to the modern analysis for confusion-based liability, which we analyze in the remaining Parts.

B. ACTIONABLE USE

Section 32(1)(a) imposes liability on anyone "who shall, without the consent of the registrant . . . *use in commerce* any reproduction . . . of a registered mark *in connection with the sale, offering for sale, distribution, or advertising of any goods or services* . . . " if "*such use* is likely to cause confusion." Section 43(a) renders liable anyone "who, *on or in connection with any goods or services* . . . *uses in commerce* any word, term, name, symbol, or device, or any combination thereof . . . " if "*such use* is likely to cause confusion." (Emphasis supplied.) The italicized language in Sections 32(1)(a) and 43(a) expresses the requirement of "actionable use." We have adopted this terminology to distinguish actionable use from the use required to establish trademark rights (discussed in Chapter 4). Some courts and commentators use the phrase "trademark use" to refer to both varieties of use—the use that a mark owner undertakes in order to establish rights in a mark, and the unauthorized use that an alleged infringer carries out. This practice risks conflating two concepts that should be distinct, as we discuss in this Section.

Most trademark cases do not involve close questions about actionable use. Suppose that Alpha, Inc. owns the mark HOOSIERS for basketballs. Beta, Inc., then introduces HOOSIER brand basketballs, and sells them in competition with Alpha, without Alpha's authorization. The word HOOSIER is printed in large letters on Beta's basketballs, and also appears on Beta's packaging and advertising materials. Beta has unquestionably engaged in actionable use because Beta is affixing the term HOOSIER to its products and selling those products in commerce. Of course, Beta's activities go even further—they exceed what is required for actionable use, in that Beta is probably using the term HOOSIER as a brand for Beta's own products. That is, Beta is surely engaging in the sort of use that would have qualified Beta to assert trademark rights in HOOSIER for basketballs, had Beta been able to establish that its activities preceded Alpha's.

Actionable use has been an issue in a minority of cases having less traditional fact patterns, although some of the cases have had important commercial implications. In *Holiday Inns, Inc. v. 800 Reservation, Inc.*, 86 F.3d 619 (6th Cir. 1996), *cert. denied* 519 U.S. 1093 (1997), the court concluded that plaintiff Holiday Inns owned unregistered trademark rights in the vanity phone number 1-800-HOLIDAY used in connection with its hotel services, the defendant Call Management's reservation and use of a complementary number (that is, 1-800-405-4329, which is the number corresponding to 1-800-H[zero]LIDAY) for hotel reservation services did not give rise to Section 43(a) liability. Call Management had only used 1-800-405-4329 in promoting its services; it had never expressed the number as 1-800-H[zero]LIDAY. Thus, the question was whether the reservation and use of only the 405 number constituted actionable use. The court concluded that there was no actionable use; Call Management was only taking advantage of existing confusion among the misdialing public, and Holiday Inns should have taken the precaution of reserving complementary numbers. Although the court did not say as much, the court's opinion might be understood to say that there must be some minimum threshold of activity for the actionable use requirement to be satisfied, and that, at least on the facts before it, where the defendant did not associate the plaintiff's mark with the defendant's services, there could be no Lanham Act Section 43(a) liability notwithstanding the commercial advantage that the defendant derived. *See also DaimlerChrysler AG v. Bloom*, 315 F.3d 932 (8th Cir. 2003) (licensing of vanity number 1-800-637-2333 to automobile dealers did not constitute actionable use, even though the number could be translated to 1-800-MERCEDES and might have misled consumers).

Actionable use issues have also arisen in cases involving online advertising practices, especially in cases involving the sale and purchase of keywords that trigger online advertisements. In a relatively early case, defendant WhenU sold software that triggered pop-up advertisements to appear on a computer user's screen in response to search terms entered by the user. The software used an internal directory that correlated users' search terms with product or service categories. Thus, a user who conducted a search to access the website of plaintiff 1-800 Contacts might encounter a pop-up advertisement from any one of a number of competing providers of eye care services. The software code apparently included the URL for plaintiff's website (www.1800contacts.com) and presumably many others. The court found that

WhenU had not engaged in actionable use. The listing of plaintiff's website in defendant's code was not actionable use because it was merely an "internal utilization of a trademark in a way that does not communicate it to the public." In addition, the use of the plaintiff's URL to trigger pop-up advertisements was not actionable use. The pop-up advertisements did not "display" 1-800's mark, and WhenU did not "sell" keywords to its customers or "otherwise manipulate which category-related advertisement will pop up in response to any particular terms on the internal directory."

Although the *1-800 Contacts* case appeared to provide the foundation for a rather strict test for actionable use, the case was largely superseded by *Rescuecom Corp. v. Google Inc.*, 562 F.3d 123 (2d Cir. 2009), which now appears to have emerged as the leading enunciation of the actionable use requirement. *Rescuecom* involved commercial transactions relating to keywords. In particular, Google had operated an "Adwords" program in which particular keywords corresponding to a Google user's search terms triggered the appearance of advertisements on the Google search results page. For example, competitors of Rescuecom could purchase from Google the keyword "Rescuecom" so that competitors' advertisements would appear in the Google search results when a Google user entered "Rescuecom" as a search term. Google had also used a "Keyword Suggestion Tool" which recommended particular keyword purchases to particular advertisers, including recommendations that a given advertiser purchase the keyword corresponding to a particular competitor's trademark. Rescuecom alleged that Google's activities violated the Lanham Act, and the District Court dismissed the complaint on a Rule 12(b)(6) motion, finding, on authority of *1-800 Contacts*, that Google had not engaged in any actionable use.

The Second Circuit vacated and remanded. The panel opinion attempted to distinguish *1-800 Contacts*. The court relied on the dubious distinction between WhenU's use of the 1-800 Contacts URL in the software code and Google's acts of "recommending and selling to advertisers" the keyword corresponding to the actual RESCUECOM mark. The court also concluded that in *1-800 Contacts*, the defendant had never "displayed" the plaintiff's mark, whereas Google "displays, offers, and sells Rescuecom's mark to Google's advertising customers when selling its advertising services." Google's activities could not be characterized as "internal" uses akin to those in *1-800 Contacts*, according to the court.

The *Rescuecom* panel opinion is relatively brief, but the court also issued a lengthy "Appendix" containing a much more extensive analysis of the actionable use issue, undoubtedly a strategy to avoid the need for an en banc rehearing. The Appendix rejects any reading of *1-800 Contacts* that would lead to a strict requirement for actionable use, and, in fact, all but eviscerates the effect of *1-800 Contacts* as precedent, although the Appendix indicates that the judges on the *1-800 Contacts* panel reviewed and agreed with the analysis in the Appendix. The

Appendix declares itself to be dictum, but nonetheless seems to be taken as authoritative.

At its core, the *Rescuecom* Appendix analyzed whether the test for actionable use should conform to the definition of use that determines whether a party can establish trademark rights. As we saw in Chapter 4, Lanham Act Section 45 defines "use in commerce" as follows:

> The term "use in commerce" means the bona fide use of a mark in the ordinary course of trade, and not made merely to reserve a right in a mark ... a mark shall be deemed to be in use in commerce—
>
> **(1)** on goods when—
>
> > **(A)** it is placed in any manner on the goods or their containers or the displays associated therewith or on the tags or labels affixed thereto, or if the nature of the goods makes such placement impracticable, then on documents associated with the goods or their sale, and
> >
> > **(B)** the goods are sold or transported in commerce, and
>
> **(2)** on services when it is used or displayed in the sale or advertising of services and the services are rendered in commerce . . .

The *Rescuecom* Appendix observed that the language "bona fide use of a mark in the ordinary course of trade, and not made merely to reserve a right in a mark" should not apply in the context of the unauthorized use of a mark by an alleged infringer; those concepts would make no sense in that context, and there was a statement in the legislative history that indicated that Congress did not intend to change the rules for infringement when it incorporated the "bona fide" use language into the definition. However, the Appendix reasoned that the remainder of the definition should be applicable in the context of infringement, although the court acknowledged that this divided interpretation of the statutory definition was not altogether satisfactory, and that it might be preferable for Congress to intervene. It appears that courts will follow the *Rescuecom* analysis in holding that the sale of keywords constitutes actionable use, and that they will apply the same analysis to find that the purchase of keywords likewise constitutes actionable use. *Network Automation, Inc. v. Advanced Systems Concepts, Inc.*, 638 F.3d 1137 (9th Cir. 2011) (applying the *Rescuecom* standard in a case involving keyword purchases).

It is important to remember that a finding of actionable use does not equate to a finding of liability. There still must be evidence of likelihood of confusion based on the factors analysis, and its variants, discussed in the following sections.

C. THE FACTORS ANALYSIS

1. OVERVIEW; INTRODUCTION TO THE FACTORS ANALYSIS

Key principles. Students of trademark law should keep three general principles in mind as they approach a likelihood of confusion analysis. First, the analysis is inherently forward-looking. The likelihood standard is necessarily a prediction about the future. This should not be troubling in cases in which the requested relief is injunctive relief, which is likewise inherently forward-looking. In cases in which the requested relief includes actual damages for past infringement, the mark owner must prove actual confusion. The "likelihood" standard is necessarily speculative to a degree, but it cannot be pure guesswork. Evidence of a bare "possibility" of confusion does not suffice. *A & H Sportswear Inc. v. Victoria's Secret Stores Inc.*, 166 F.3d 197 (3d Cir. 1999) (en banc) (rejecting the argument that a relaxed "possibility of confusion" standard should apply in some cases).

Second, the modern likelihood of confusion analysis extends beyond confusion as to source of origin. As enacted in 1946, Lanham Act Section 32 proscribed acts that were "likely to cause confusion or mistake or to deceive purchasers as to the source of origin" of the goods or services at issue. Congress amended the language in 1962, eliminating the phrase "source of origin." This suggests, at least implicitly, that likely confusion as to the alleged infringer's affiliation with the plaintiff, or its sponsorship by the plaintiff, are also cognizable forms of likely confusion, in addition to traditional confusion as to source. This is a critical argument in cases involving trademark "merchandising"—that is, cases in which the owner of a mark (say, a university that owns a logo used in connection with its athletic teams) asserts a claim of infringement against the unauthorized sales of promotional items (say, t-shirts) bearing the mark. Consumers who purchase the t-shirts may have no particular perceptions about the manufacturing origin of the t-shirts, but they may believe that the t-shirt seller is affiliated with the university (as its licensee, for example). The modern Lanham Act Section 32 does not explicitly preclude such a claim of likely confusion, and the deletion of "source of origin" reinforces the argument that Congress intended for the provision to sweep more broadly than merely to source confusion. This principle came into play in *Boston Professional Hockey Association, Inc. v. Dallas Cap & Emblem Mfg., Inc.*, 510 F.2d 1004 (5th Cir. 1975), *cert. denied* 423 U.S. 868 (1975), in which the defendant was found liable for trademark infringement for the sale of cloth emblems bearing logos of National Hockey League teams. According to the Fifth Circuit, the trial court had erred in finding no likelihood of confusion; the trial court had "overlooked the fact that the [Lanham Act] was amended to eliminate the source of origin as being the only focal point of confusion." Here, the confusion requirement was met because the purchasers of defendant's emblems would associate the depicted logos with the hockey teams. It was not necessary to show that purchasers were confused about who manufactured the emblems.

Third, the 1962 amendment also deleted the word "purchasers" from Section 32. One consequence is that claims of likely confusion need not necessarily be limited to acts that occur at the point of purchase. As we discuss in Section D, claims of pre-sale and post-sale likely confusion are at least theoretically viable as a result of the amended language. Relatedly, the deletion of purchasers might suggest that confusion among the general public, even those who are not purchasers and have no prospect of ever becoming purchasers, could be actionable. This proposition is more controversial, perhaps because an impact on a mark owner's customers is the most readily understandable manifestation of reputational harm. Characterizing (and then proving) the general reputational harm that might accrue as a result of an alleged infringer's impact on persons who will never be the mark owner's customers is more challenging.

Introduction to the multi-factor tests. In all federal jurisdictions in the U.S., courts have adopted some variation of a multi-factor test for assessing likelihood of confusion. For example, the Second Circuit's test calls for courts to balance the following factors in order to make a determination as to the likelihood of confusion:

> [Likelihood of confusion] is a function of many variables: the strength of [the] mark, the degree of similarity between the two marks, the proximity of the products, the likelihood that the

prior owner will bridge the gap, actual confusion, and the reciprocal of defendant's good faith in adopting its own mark, the quality of the defendant's product, and the sophistication of the buyers. Even this extensive catalogue does not exhaust the possibilities—the court may have to take still other variables into account.

Polaroid Corp. v. Polarad Electronics Corp., 287 F.2d 492 (2d Cir. 1961). Each Circuit's multi-factor test differs slightly. We have compiled all of the governing tests in Figure 7–1 of GRAEME B. DINWOODIE & MARK D. JANIS, TRADEMARKS AND UNFAIR COMPETITION: LAW AND POLICY (3d ed. 2010). For discussion purposes in the present book, it will be convenient to refer to the following likelihood of confusion test, which calls for the balancing of six factors:

1. Similarity of the marks

2. Strength of plaintiff's mark

3. Relatedness of the products/services (competitive proximity)

4. Defendant's intent

5. Actual Confusion

6. Purchaser Care/Purchaser Sophistication

This particular test does not exactly mimic any of the tests currently used in the Circuits, although it most closely resembles the Eighth Circuit's test from *SquirtCo. v. Seven-Up Co.*, 628 F.2d 1086 (8th Cir. 1980). We have created this test for discussion purposes because it succinctly expresses the characteristic factors found in all of the tests. That is, it includes as factors the alleged infringer's intent (factor 4); actual confusion (factor 5); and a variety of additional factors that might be lumped together as "other market factors" (factors 1, 2, 3, and 6). *See* RESTATEMENT (THIRD) OF UNFAIR COMPETITION §§ 21–23 (1996) (identifying these three categories of factors).

The multi-factor tests for likelihood of confusion probably originate with the Restatement of Torts § 731 (1938). The tests were originally developed for cases in which the alleged infringer's goods were not identical to those of the mark owner—"related goods" cases, as we discuss in more detail below in Section C.2.d of this Chapter. Eventually, multi-factor tests in various forms came to be adopted for all trademark infringement cases.

Many of the cases discussed in this chapter provide illustrations of the application of the modern standard. For one helpful illustration, see *Virgin Enterprises Ltd. v. Nawab*, 335 F.3d 141 (2d Cir. 2003) (finding that defendant's use of VIRGIN WIRELESS for wireless communications was likely to cause confusion in view of plaintiff's use of VIRGIN for electronics stores, recording label, airlines, and many other goods).

Primacy of the factor tests. Courts have cautioned that the factors "operate only as a heuristic device to assist in determining whether confusion exists," *Sullivan v. CBS Corp.*, 385 F.3d 772 (7th Cir. 2004), that the factors are intended as "an adaptable proxy for consumer confusion" and that "the factors are non-exhaustive." *Network Automation, Inc. v. Advanced Systems Concepts, Inc.*, 638 F.3d 1137 (9th Cir. 2011); *Rosetta Stone Ltd. v. Google, Inc.*, 676 F.3d 144 (4th Cir. 2012) (noting that "this judicially created list of factors is not intended to be exhaustive or mandatory"). Notwithstanding these pronouncements, the factors tests have tended to take on talismanic significance. It is relatively rare that courts add factors to the analysis. *But see Tana v. Dan Tanna's*, 611 F.3d 767 (11th Cir. 2010) (discussing the addition of geographic separation between the parties as a confusion factor).

It has also been rare for courts to short-circuit the factors analysis, elevating some subset of factors to dispositive significance. However, arguments for departing from the factors test in this fashion do periodically arise. The most prominent short-cut is that sanctioned by Article 16 of the TRIPS agreement. That Article specifies that when the alleged infringer uses the identical mark on identical goods or services as those of the mark owner, a likelihood of confusion shall be presumed. It is not clear whether U.S. courts actually adhere to the Article 16 presumption, although the decisions in many cases certainly appear to be consistent with the presumption. Some courts have applied, in effect, a reverse presumption, holding that evidence of dissimilarity might alone be enough to justify a finding of no likely confusion. We are skeptical about such an approach, as we discuss below in Section C.2.a. A series of cases in the Ninth Circuit advanced the view that in cases involving online uses of trademarks, a subset of three of the confusion factors—the similarity of the marks, the relatedness of the goods or services, and the "simultaneous use of the Internet as a marketing channel"—should form the basis of the likelihood of confusion analysis. *See, e.g., GoTo.com, Inc. v. Walt Disney Co.*, 202 F.3d 1199 (9th Cir. 2000) (referring to these factors as the "Internet troika"). In time, the Ninth Circuit discarded this approach, recognizing that "it makes no sense to prioritize the same three factors for every type of potential online commercial activity" in light of "the multifaceted nature of the Internet and the ever-expanding ways in which we all use the technology." *Network Automation, Inc. v. Advanced Systems Concepts, Inc.*, 638 F.3d 1137 (9th Cir. 2011).

Procedural contexts—infringement; priority. The likelihood of confusion inquiry and the factors test for assessing that inquiry arise in two distinct procedural contexts. The first, which is the subject of the bulk of this chapter, is in the determination of liability for trademark infringement or false designation of origin in litigation, as governed by Lanham Act Sections 32(1)(a) and 43(a)(1), respectively. The second is the determination of priority of use for the purposes of establishing valid rights, governed by Section 2(d) in the case of registered rights. In the first context, the mark owner may be in the position of calling for a generous and flexible application of the factors analysis in order to achieve a relatively broad scope of protection. In the second context, it is likely to be in the mark owner's interest to call for a more confined application of the factors test in order to avoid a determination that the mark creates a likelihood of confusion with prior marks. In the second context, the factors test of the Court of Appeals for the Federal Circuit is often at issue, since that court takes appellate jurisdiction over appeals from PTO determinations in both *ex parte* registration proceedings and *inter partes* administrative determinations (oppositions and cancellations).

The existence of these two procedural settings for the application of the likelihood of confusion test suggests that there may be the potential for conflicting determinations of confusion regarding the same marks. One potential conflict occurs when an examiner has made a Section 2(d) confusion determination in ex parte examination, and the same parties subsequently seek to litigate the Section 32 confusion issue in an infringement trial. In *Progressive Dist. Services, Inc. v. United Parcel Service, Inc.*, 856 F.3d 416 (6th Cir. 2017), the court addressed the conflict by asking to what extent the district court owed deference to the trademark examiner's decision. The majority approach among circuits that have confronted the issue is to decline any deference where the evidence before the court differs from the evidence that the examiner considers. Where the record before the examiner did not include evidence on the manner in which the mark is actually used in the marketplace, courts have refused to accord the examiner's decision any significant weight, on the ground that evidence of actual marketplace use should be integral to the likelihood of confusion determination in the context of infringement.

A more robust potential conflict arises when the TTAB has made a determination on confusion under Section 2(d) in an opposition or cancellation proceeding, and the same parties subsequently seek to litigate the Section 32 confusion issue in an infringement trial. Here, the question is whether issue preclusion should apply.

In *B&B Hardware, Inc. v. Hargis Indus., Inc.*, 135 S.Ct. 1293 (2015), B&B had successfully opposed Hargis's application to register SEALTITE for fasteners, on the ground that Hargis's mark was confusingly similar under Section 2(d) to B&B's previously-registered mark, SEALTIGHT for fasteners. In B&B's subsequent trademark infringement action against Hargis, the district court refused to give preclusive effect to the TTAB's Section 2(d) determination made in the opposition, and the Eighth Circuit affirmed. The Supreme Court vacated and remanded. The Court held 7–2 (Justices Thomas and Scalia dissenting) that "[s]o long as the other ordinary elements of issue preclusion are met, when the usages [of a mark] adjudicated by the TTAB are materially the same as those before the district court, issue preclusion should apply." But the Court also remarked that "many registrations will not satisfy those ordinary elements," *id.* at 1306, and that therefore "for a great many registration decisions issue preclusion obviously will not apply." *Id.* In particular, the Court stated that if the TTAB was not in a position to consider the parties' actual marketplace usages of their respective marks (which might occur if, for example, the mark owner used its mark in ways that were "materially unlike the usages in its application"), then the TTAB decision should not have preclusive effect. *Id.* at 1308. Nonetheless, on remand in *B&B Hardware*, the Eighth Circuit determined "the usages of the marks adjudicated before the TTAB were materially the same as the usages before the district court," and ruled that the requirements for giving preclusive effect to the TTAB's ruling were met. *B&B Hardware, Inc. v. Hargis Indus., Inc.*, 800 F.3d 427 (8th Cir. 2015).

Another potential conflict might arise when a district court makes a confusion determination and the Trademark Trial and Appeal Board is asked to give that determination preclusive effect in a subsequent opposition or cancellation proceeding involving the same parties. In two decisions rendered prior to *B&B*, the Federal Circuit declined preclusive effect, emphasizing the likelihood that the court proceedings and the TTAB proceedings were likely to be based on different factual records. *Mayer/Berkshire Corp. v. Berkshire Fashions, Inc.*, 424 F.3d 1229 (Fed. Cir. 2005) (jury determination of no likely confusion did not have preclusive effect in a subsequent opposition proceeding); *Jet, Inc. v. Sewage Aeration Systems*, 223 F.3d 1360 (Fed. Cir. 2000) (determination of no likely confusion did not have preclusive effect in a subsequent cancellation proceeding).

Standard of review. Most circuits treat the likelihood of confusion factors analysis as a fact determination to be reviewed under the clearly erroneous standard of review (the First, Third,

Fourth, Fifth, Seventh, Eighth, Ninth, Tenth, and Eleventh circuits). A minority of circuits (the Second, Sixth, and Federal circuits) treat the weighing and balancing of the factors, and the ultimate conclusion as to confusion, as a question of law subject to *de novo* review, although they purport to treat the underlying evaluation of the individual factors as fact questions to which the clearly erroneous standard applies.

2. APPLYING THE FACTORS ANALYSIS: RULES OF THUMB

As we have noted above, it would be a mistake to analyze a complex phenomenon such as likelihood of confusion by engaging in a mere recitation of the confusion factors and tacking on a cursory conclusion about liability. A confusion factors analysis entails more than checking a "yes" or "no" box next to each factor and then totaling up the results. It should be a rigorous analysis that addresses individual factors thoughtfully, recognizing that each factor may provide a slightly different insight into the relevant consumer's encounter with the marks at issue. It is likely to be very fact-specific.

Even so, courts have analyzed the likelihood of confusion factors in so many cases that, by sheer common law accretion, rough general guidelines can be identified for the analysis of each individual factor. A likelihood of confusion analysis that proceeds without an appreciation for these guidelines may appear to be little more than a superficial "gut reaction" to the facts, and is best avoided.

a. Similarity of Marks

All likelihood of confusion factors tests call for an analysis of the similarity of the marks registered and/or used by the mark owner and those used by the alleged infringer. It is important to keep in mind that the objective of this similarity analysis is not to detect the extent of copying, as might be the case in a substantial similarity analysis carried out for purposes of assessing copyright infringement. Rather, the objective is to assess how consumers of the relevant products or services would encounter the marks at issue. Thus, some courts have emphasized that the similarity of marks factor requires a court to assess similarity "in light of the way in which the marks are actually displayed in their purchasing context." *Malletier v. Burlington Coat Factory Warehouse, Corp.*, 426 F.3d 532 (2d Cir. 2005). Accordingly, a mechanistic similarity analysis—a "know it when I see it" rule—is not recommended.

Instead, courts assess mark similarity by considering the full range of characteristics of the marks at issue—the "sight, sound, and meaning" rule. A visual comparison of the marks is usually relevant, especially, of course, in cases in which the protected mark has visual elements. For example, in a case involving Lacoste's "alligator" logo for clothing and Everlast's "flying dragon" logo on judo uniforms, it was appropriate to consider the visual similarities (or, in this case, dissimilarities) between the two. *Lacoste Alligator S.A. v. Everlast World's Boxing Headquarters*, 204 U.S.P.Q. 945 (TTAB 1979). In a case involving SMIRNOFF for vodka, it was appropriate for the court to consider the aural similarity between the mark and defendant's SARNOFF for vodka. *David Sherman Corp. v. Heublein, Inc.*, 340 F.2d 377 (8th Cir. 1965). Where the evidence indicates that consumers tend to order the product by asking for it over the telephone or in person, or when the products are routinely advertised by radio or television, the sound of the marks may well be critical. Additionally, courts should consider the meaning associated with marks, as this is another characteristic that might bear on similarity in any given case. It was sensible for the court to place some weight on similarity of meaning where plaintiff's mark was CYCLONE for wire fencing and defendant's mark was TORNADO for wire fencing. *Hancock v. American Steel & Wire Co.*, 203 F.2d 737 (CCPA 1953).

In carrying out these comparisons, especially comparisons for visual similarity, it should not be assumed that displaying the respective marks side by side is probative. If the products are never sold side by side, then such a display would be nothing more than an artificial construct for litigation purposes rather than an effort to simulate the consumer's actual encounter with the marks. For example, a side-by-side comparison of the trade dress of Louis Vuitton's high-end handbags and the defendant's more modestly-priced handbags was erroneous when the evidence demonstrated that the parties' respective handbags would never have been sold in the same stores. *Louis Vuitton Malletier v. Dooney & Bourke*, 454 F.3d 108 (2d Cir. 2006). *See also Libman Co. v. Vining Indus., Inc.*, 69 F.3d 1360 (7th Cir.

1995) (speculating whether a side-by-side comparison of the stripe trade dress on the parties' respective brooms was probative if the evidence showed that stores typically did not stock more than one brand of broom).

When the similarity analysis involves a registered mark, particularly a registered word mark, there may be a question about how to translate the subject matter of the registration into a real-world mark. In particular, when a mark is registered in standard characters, it would be typical for the registrant to assert that this signifies that the mark might appear in a variety of different fonts, any of which should be considered to fall within the scope of the registration for purposes of conducting a similarity of marks analysis. In a series of decisions, the TTAB had developed the rule that the "reasonable manners" in which a standard character word mark could be depicted would be considered for purposes of a similarity of marks analysis. In *Citigroup*, the Federal Circuit rejected this rule as too restrictive. *Citigroup Inc. v. Capital City Bank Group*, 637 F.3d 1344 (Fed. Cir. 2011). According to the Federal Circuit, the TTAB should carry out the similarity of marks factor by considering "depictions of standard character marks that vary in font, style, size and color" rather than attempting to limit the analysis to that subset of depictions that the TTAB deemed to be "reasonable." The court also directed the TTAB to consider illustrations of the mark as actually used. In a subsequent case, the Federal Circuit extended this approach to a comparison between a standard character mark and a composite mark that included both verbal and design elements, although the court cautioned that "[i]n rejecting the 'reasonable manners' test, we are not suggesting that a standard character mark encompasses all possible design elements of the mark." *In re Viterra Inc.*, 671 F.3d 1358 (Fed. Cir. 2012) (noting that it was leaving for future cases the task of articulating the test for comparing standard character marks with composite marks containing design elements).

Ordinarily, a fair comparison of mark similarity, properly taking the marks in their appropriate commercial context, will include consideration of accompanying labels, disclaimers, or "house marks" (marks that a vendor uses on all of its products—for example, the term CHEVROLET in proximity to CORVETTE for automobiles, where CORVETTE indicates the car model and CHEVROLET may operate as a "house mark" indicating the name of the manufacturer of numerous car models). This guideline is especially prominent in cases involving product design trade dress. For example, in *Nora Beverages v. Perrier Group*, 269 F.3d 114 (2d Cir. 2001), the plaintiff asserted product design trade dress in the ribbed shape of its plastic water bottles, but in conducting a similarity of marks analysis, it was proper for the court to take into account not only the appearance of the parties' respective water bottles, but also the differences in the labels applied to those bottles, on the premise that consumer attention was focused on the appearance and content of the labels.

Some marks are "composite" marks—they include multiple elements, such as a string of words or a combination of verbal and non-verbal aspects. The courts and the TTAB routinely invoke the "anti-dissection" principle when they perceive that an argument as to similarity of the marks improperly focuses on individual elements of a composite mark to the exclusion of other elements. For example, in *Packard Press, Inc. v. Hewlett-Packard Co.*, 227 F.3d 1352 (Fed. Cir. 2000), it was error for the TTAB to conclude that PACKARD TECHNOLOGIES for data processing services was similar to HEWLETT-PACKARD for computer products by focusing on the common element PACKARD. On the other hand, the anti-dissection principle should not be applied when the evidence demonstrates that consumers in fact subdivide the mark into its elements and give some elements more attention than others when actually encountering the marks. For example, it was not error to identify GASPAR as the dominant portion of applicant's mark JOSE GASPAR GOLD for tequila, and to assess similarity between that mark and the prior registered mark GASPAR'S ALE for ale by focusing on the common use of "Gaspar." *In re Chatam Int'l, Inc.*, 380 F.3d 1340 (Fed. Cir. 2004). In addition, where the owner of a registered mark has formally disclaimed protection over some aspect of a mark, the court is to give the disclaimed matter little weight in rendering its similarity of marks determination. *M2 Software Inc. v. M2 Communications Inc.*, 450 F.3d 1378 (Fed. Cir. 2006) (reciting the rule, but asserting that the disclaimed term nonetheless should not be "ignored").

In some cases, a mark owner may be able to demonstrate that it owns a group of marks that include a common element, and that consumers rely on the common element to form perceptions about source. This is commonly referred to as the "family of marks" argument. For example, in various cases, McDonald's has succeeded in proving that it owns a family of marks that uses the "MC" prefix appended to various products—MCMUFFIN, MCNUGGETS, and even, based on our observations, MCLOBSTER. In *J & J Snack Foods Corp. v. McDonald's Corp.*, 932 F.2d 1460 (Fed. Cir. 1991), the court concluded that to prove that a mark family exists, a mark owner must show that "it owns a group of marks having a recognizable common feature, where (1) the group of marks is used and promoted together in such a way that the public associates the common feature with the mark owner; and (2) the common feature is distinctive." The significance of this determination for the similarity of marks factor is that if a mark family exists, it is proper for the court to dissect the mark and focus on the common element. So, in a case in which McDonald's sued a dentist who offered dental services under the name MCDENTAL, the court could conduct a similarity of marks analysis by giving predominant weight to the common use of the "MC" prefix in both the plaintiff's and the defendant's marks. *McDonald's Corp. v. Druck and Gerner, D.D.S.*, 814 F. Supp. 1127 (N.D.N.Y. 1993). In some cases, mark owners have asserted mark families in trade dress. *See, e.g., Rose Art Indus. v. Swanson*, 235 F.3d 165 (3d Cir. 2000) (alleged trade dress family in packaging for crayons and colored pencils)

The foregoing discussion of the similarity of marks factor is of particular relevance when the marks of the respective parties are not identical. If the marks *are* identical, and if the parties' respective goods or services are identical, a court may be willing to presume a likelihood of confusion. Indeed, TRIPS Art. 16(1) specifies that likelihood of confusion should be presumed in such a case.

If the result of a court's assessment of the similarity of marks factor is that the marks are dissimilar, the proper approach in the usual case is to weigh this factor strongly against the mark owner (in an infringement case), but balance this factor against the other confusion factors. *Jada Toys, Inc. v. Mattel, Inc.*, 518 F.3d 628 (9th Cir. 2008) (criticizing lower court determination of no confusion that was based on perceived dissimilarity alone). In at least one case, a court decided that the marks were so plainly dissimilar that the court could presume a lack of likelihood of confusion. *Top Tobacco, L.P. v. North Atlantic Operating Co., Inc.*, 509 F.3d 380 (7th Cir. 2007). We expect that such an analysis will be appropriate only in unusual cases.

b. Mark Strength

A mark may be "strong" for purposes of a likelihood of confusion analysis in two senses. First, a mark may be *conceptually* strong. Conceptually strong marks are marks that are accorded a high level of distinctiveness on the *Abercrombie* distinctiveness spectrum (discussed in Chapter 2). In that spectrum, marks that are arbitrary or fanciful are the most highly distinctive, and hence the most conceptually strong.

The second sense of mark strength is *market* strength. Market strength is an assessment of the degree of consumer recognition of the mark resulting from the mark owner's use of the mark. The proposition is that if a senior user's mark enjoys widespread recognition, that fact makes it more likely that consumers encountering a junior user's mark will assume that it identifies the senior user's goods and services. A related proposition is that junior users will have a greater incentive to trade off the goodwill of a senior user's mark where the senior user's mark is well-known to consumers. Market strength is an empirical determination that is not always easy to make, especially given that marks often are accompanied by other indicia, such as the mark owner's house mark. In a case involving tire trademarks, the Federal Circuit rejected the argument that the presence of the BRIDGESTONE house mark accompanying advertisements for various BRIDGESTONE tires (e.g., the POTENZA) diminished the mark strength of the POTENZA brand. *Bridgestone Americas Tire Operations, LLC v. Federal Corp.*, 673 F.3d 1330 (Fed. Cir. 2012). No such blanket rule would be appropriate, according to the court.

In the Federal Circuit's jurisprudence, which is important primarily for the confusion factors analysis carried out to determine registrability under Section 2(d), the court analyzes mark "fame." The court has sometimes said that mark fame is a "dominant factor in the likelihood of confusion analysis." *Recot, Inc. v. Becton*, 214 F.3d 1322 (Fed. Cir. 2000). Mark fame in this analysis is a matter of degree, not a simple either/or determination that a mark is either famous or not. *Coach Services, Inc. v. Triumph Learning LLC*, 668 F.3d 1356 (Fed. Cir. 2012) (explaining that, in contrast to the confusion determination, the analysis of fame for purposes of the dilution determination *is* an either/or analysis).

The fact that a registration has achieved incontestable status does not automatically indicate that the mark is strong for purposes of a likelihood of confusion analysis. *Vail Associates, Inc. v. Vend-Tel-Co., Ltd.*, 516 F.3d 853 (10th Cir. 2008). Incontestability signifies the fact that the registrant has complied with various prerequisites (some of which are procedural), and that the registrant is entitled to certain benefits, including being free from certain types of challenges. (We discuss incontestability in Chapter 5). It does not, by itself, indicate mark strength.

c. Actual Confusion

Actual confusion is merely one factor in the likelihood of confusion calculus. Accordingly, at least in theory, likelihood of confusion can be found even in the absence of any evidence of actual confusion. A showing of actual confusion is only required if the mark owner is seeking damages for past infringement. *See, e.g., Web Printing Controls Co. v. Oxy-Dry Corp.*, 906 F.2d 1202 (7th Cir. 1990).

Notwithstanding these standard statements of the law, in some instances, courts have simply not been persuaded by a mark owner's likelihood of confusion case when that case does not include evidence of actual confusion. In *Libman Co. v. Vining Indus, Inc.*, 69 F.3d 1360 (7th Cir. 1995), the court acknowledged the conventional rule regarding actual confusion, but then asserted that Libman could easily have gathered actual confusion evidence, and that it would be "pure speculation" to find a likelihood of confusion in the absence of such evidence.

The emphasis on the importance of actual confusion evidence does not carry over to the likelihood of confusion analysis in the Section 2(d) context. There, the lack of actual confusion evidence is deemed to be of little significance, especially in the context of *ex parte* examination. *In re Majestic Distilling Co.*, 315 F.3d 1311 (Fed. Cir. 2003).

When a mark owner does attempt to prove actual confusion, the evidence may take the form of testimony reporting anecdotal instances of confusion. Some courts have suggested that there is a "low bar" for showing actual confusion, and that even a relatively small number of incidents of actual confusion might suffice to raise an inference that a substantial number of consumers are likely to be confused. *Streamline Production Sys., Inc. v. Streamline Mfg., Inc.*, 851 F.3d 440 (5th Cir. 2017).

More frequently, proof of actual confusion comes in the form of survey evidence presented through expert testimony. One common form of confusion survey evidence is the so-called *Ever-Ready* survey, from

Union Carbide Corp. v. Ever-Ready, Inc., 531 F.2d 366 (7th Cir. 1976), *cert. denied* 429 U.S. 830 (1976). The mark owner sold batteries, flashlights, and bulbs under the EVEREADY brand. The defendant sold EVER-READY lamps. The survey showed respondents a picture of defendant's lamp (and mark) and asked "Who do you think puts out the lamp shown here?" and "What makes you think so?" The TTAB has endorsed this form of survey for use in assessing likelihood of confusion in the registration context. *Starbucks U.S. Brands LLC v. Ruben*, 78 U.S.P.Q.2d 1741 (TTAB 2006) (discussing the format of confusion surveys, including the *Ever-Ready* survey).

Surveys that generate 8–10% positive responses on confusion have been deemed probative of actual confusion. There is no fixed rule for assessing the quantity of confusion that will justify a finding of actual confusion. Because actual confusion is only one factor in the likelihood of confusion test, courts retain ample flexibility to give survey evidence more or less weight depending upon the percentage of positive responses.

Judges periodically express skepticism about confusion surveys. The typical complaints are that expert witnesses hired by the parties to conduct surveys are prone to bias, and surveys often fail to replicate the environment in which consumers actually encounter the marks at issue. *See, e.g., Kraft Foods Group Brands LLC v. Cracker Barrel Old Country Store, Inc.*, 735 F.3d 735 (7th Cir. 2013) (Posner, J.).

One set of cases that demonstrates the importance of the actual confusion element deals with look-alike private label goods. In a typical case, a major brand owner has established a strong consumer following for its brand and has heavily promoted the name and packaging trade dress of its product. A competitor then enters the market with a "private label" product (for example, a product that might bear the house mark of the store in which it is sold, together with a generic reference to the product—e.g., WAL-MART hand cream). Frequently, the private label product will closely emulate the product packaging trade dress, and we may assume that this is part of an intentional effort to trade off the brand owner's goodwill. In these cases, virtually all of the likelihood of confusion factors point in favor of the brand owner, except for the actual confusion factor. Although there is little caselaw to guide us, we speculate that it is generally difficult for brand owners in this scenario to make a convincing case that consumers are actually confused. This lack of persuasive actual confusion evidence appeared to doom the trademark owner's claim of infringement in *Conopco, Inc. v. May Dept. Stores*, 46 F.3d 1556 (Fed. Cir. 1994) (reversing finding of infringement). In *McNeil Nutritionals v. Heartland Sweeteners*, 511 F.3d 350 (3d Cir. 2007), involving the SPLENDA trade dress for artificial sweetener, the court rejected the argument that competing private label goods were automatically free from confusion liability. The court reversed the lower court's determination of no infringement and remanded.

d. Relatedness of Goods

Under the modern likelihood of confusion analysis, a mark owner can prevail even without showing that the alleged infringer's goods or services are identical to those of the mark owner. The likelihood of confusion test calls for an assessment of the similarity of the goods or services, and weighs the extent of similarity along with the other confusion factors.

Some early decisions on trademark liability arguably did require that the defendant's goods or services offered under the mark at issue be identical to those of the mark owner's, as the *Borden's* case (discussed above in Section A) exemplifies. However, in some prominent decisions tracing back to the early twentieth century, courts made clear that they would not insist on identity of goods in every case. In *Aunt Jemima Mills Co. v. Rigney & Co.*, 247 Fed. 407 (2d Cir. 1917), *cert. denied* 245 U.S. 672 (1918), the court pointed out that the parties' goods (pancake batter and pancake syrup) were obviously related, such that a consumer might tend to conclude that the respective products had originated from the same source, given the tendency of firms to expand into the production of related goods—that is, to "bridge the gap" between its existing goods and the related goods. In another case, *Yale Electric Corp. v. Robertson*, 26 F.2d 972 (2d Cir. 1928) (involving the marks YALE for locks and keys versus YALE for flashlights and batteries), Judge Learned Hand seemed to endorse the concept of relatedness of goods as a factor in deciding liability, although he seemed to take a more restrictive approach in some subsequent cases.

Over time, the relatedness-of-goods concept became entrenched. Courts dealing with "related goods" cases began to assess relatedness as one of several factors bearing on the likelihood of confusion. Eventually, courts largely ceased the practice of distinguishing between "identical goods" cases and "related goods" cases. Instead, they borrowed the factors analysis that had been developed in the related goods cases and applied it to all cases, arriving at the factors analysis that governs the modern cases.

In the modern cases, courts have tended to emphasize that it is the consumer's perceptions that underlie the similarity of goods factor, regardless of the trademark owner's actual plans about "bridging the gap." *See, e.g., Elvis Presley Enterprises Inc. v. Capece*, 141 F.3d 188 (5th Cir. 1998). For example, in *Scarves by Vera, Inc. v. Todo Imports Ltd.*, 544 F.2d 1167 (2d Cir. 1976), plaintiff sold women's scarves, apparel, and linens under the VERA mark; defendant introduced VERA men's cologne. The plaintiff had previously considered expanding into cosmetics and fragrances, but had not found a suitable partner, and there was no indication that the plaintiff had any intention of expanding into the fragrance market as of the time of the litigation. This was not fatal to the plaintiff's argument under the similarity of the goods factor, because the controlling question was whether consumers would perceive that the plaintiff was likely to expand into fragrances.

When the relatedness of goods factor is applied in the Section 2(d) context, it is likely that the court (or the PTO) will base its analysis on the goods or services specified in the registration document, rather than the goods or services actually sold or rendered. *Coach Services, Inc. v. Triumph Learning LLC*, 668 F.3d 1356 (Fed. Cir. 2012).

e. Other Factors: Intent; Reasonably Prudent Purchaser

As our illustrative likelihood of confusion factors test indicates (*see* Section C.1 above), there are additional factors to be assessed in typical likelihood of confusion cases. These factors warrant brief discussion here.

Intent. All likelihood of confusion tests include an intent factor. In these tests, intent does not mean intent to copy, but rather intent to trade off the senior mark owner's goodwill. In some cases, where the evidence shows that the parties' respective marks are similar and the alleged infringer was aware of the plaintiff's mark, courts are willing to presume that the alleged infringer intended to trade off the plaintiff's goodwill. *Fleischmann Distilling Corp. v. Maier Brewing Co.*, 314 F.2d 149 (9th Cir. 1963), *cert. denied* 374 U.S. 830 (1963). Guidelines such as this one are particularly important where intent is at issue, because intent can rarely be proven by direct evidence. This is as true for the likelihood of confusion test as it is in other settings.

Reasonably prudent purchaser; buyer sophistication. Courts vary significantly in articulating factors that characterize the relevant purchaser for purposes of the likelihood of confusion test. Some courts emphasize the internal characteristics of the typical purchaser, attempting to assess whether the purchaser is "sophisticated," and hence presumably more capable of recognizing deceptive practices and thus less likely to be confused by them. In many instances, courts draw conclusions about probable purchaser sophistication by considering the nature of the goods or services, the parties' tactics for marketing them, and the "reasonably prudent purchaser's" probable approach to shopping for those goods or services. The goods might be specialty goods marketed exclusively to highly sophisticated professional buyers, for example. *See, e.g., Abercrombie & Fitch Co. v. Moose Creek, Inc.*, 486 F.3d 629 (9th Cir. 2007). The goods might be luxury goods sold at a high price, leading some courts to conclude that a reasonably prudent purchaser would examine the goods closely and take time with the purchase, and thus be less prone to confusion. On the other hand, the goods might be low-cost goods marketed for impulse purchases (e.g., bubble gum marketed to children), and a court might conclude that even the reasonably prudent purchaser would pay little attention to subtleties and might be more prone to confusion. Where the class of purchasers is diverse—as might be the case where plaintiff's and defendant's goods are marketed to different audiences—it would be sensible for courts to take the least sophisticated purchaser group as the relevant purchaser for purposes of the analysis, although it is not clear that any majority approach has emerged.

D. CONFUSION AWAY FROM THE POINT OF SALE

Many discussions about likelihood of confusion envision a phenomenon that occurs at the moment when a consumer is deciding whether to purchase goods or services. The question raised by the cases in this Part is whether liability for likelihood of confusion should arise when the only likely confusion occurs prior to or after the point of purchase. Confusion occurring away from the point of sale is posited to affect *prospective* purchasers of the goods or services in question, and it may even be argued to affect the mark owner's reputation among the general public, even where the general public is composed of many individuals who are not likely to become the mark owner's customers.

Prior to 1962, Lanham Act Section 32 imposed liability for uses of registered marks that were "likely to cause confusion or mistake or to deceive *purchasers* . . . " (emphasis supplied). The 1962 amendment to Section 32 deleted the word "purchasers," among other things. Thus, the current provision does not preclude the view that confusion away from the point of sale even among the general public can give rise to liability. Nevertheless, these theories have remained controversial, for reasons that we discuss below.

Courts have recognized two types of confusion away from the point of sale: confusion prior to the point of sale, usually designated "pre-sale" or "initial interest" confusion, and confusion after the point of sale, called "post-sale" confusion. For both types of confusion, courts have invoked the standard likelihood of confusion factors analysis, sometimes without considering whether the nature of initial interest or post-sale confusion suggests modifications to individual factors. We discuss the relevant cases below.

1. INITIAL INTEREST CONFUSION

Marketers have long understood that capturing a prospective consumer's initial attention may be crucial in making a sale. It would seem to follow that new market entrants seeking to best an incumbent would be tempted to engage in the practice of confusingly emulating the incumbent's marks in advance of the point of sale, hoping to draw consumers' attention, even temporarily, to the new entrant's products or services. These are age-old tactics, bearing names like "getting a foot in the door" or (in a more derogatory sense) "bait-and-switch" tactics. Some courts have recognized that these practices could harm incumbent mark owners even if the practices do not result in an actual diversion of sales to new market entrants. In *Australian Gold, Inc. v. Hatfield*, 436 F.3d 1228 (10th Cir. 2006), the court identified three types of harm that might arise from initial interest confusion:

> (1) the original diversion of the prospective customer's interest to a source that he or she erroneously believes is authorized; (2) the

potential consequent effect of that diversion on the customer's ultimate decision whether to purchase caused by an erroneous impression that two sources of a product may be associated; and (3) the initial credibility that the would-be buyer may accord to the infringer's products-customer consideration that otherwise may be unwarranted and that may be built on the strength of the protected mark, reputation and goodwill.

Imposing liability for initial interest confusion may seem uncontroversial in view of these harms, and in some cases, the application of initial interest confusion has been relatively routine. In one case, Mobil Oil Corporation asserted that Pegasus Petroleum had caused initial interest confusion by the use of the term PEGASUS in connection with oil sales. Mobil's trademark was a flying horse symbol in the form of the Greek mythological Pegasus. Mobil successfully argued that potential purchasers were "misled into an initial interest in Pegasus" because they assumed that a petroleum firm named "Pegasus" must be affiliated with Mobil. *Mobil Oil Corp. v. Pegasus Petroleum Corp.*, 818 F.2d 254 (2d Cir. 1987).

However, in a number of other cases, initial interest confusion has received a mixed reception. In some early cases involving online advertising practices, mark owners contended that consumers were particularly susceptible to temporary distraction when navigating among Internet sites, such that the use of a competitor's mark in one's domain name or in metatags might well constitute initial interest confusion. (Metatags were being used at the time in the software that generated websites, and could be detected by search engines but were invisible to ordinary website users.) *Brookfield Communications v. West Coast Entertainment Corp.*, 174 F.3d 1036 (9th Cir. 1999) (involving Brookfield's trademark MOVIEBUFF for software and an online database, and West Coast's reservation of moviebuff.com for a website providing information about the movie industry). The court reasoned that consumers who searched for Brookfield's database via a search engine that detected West Coast's metatags, or by relying on the appearance of "moviebuff" in West Coast's domain name, would instead access West Coast's website. According to the court, "even where people realize, immediately upon accessing 'moviebuff.com,' that they have reached a site operated by West Coast and wholly unrelated to Brookfield, West Coast will still have gained a customer by appropriating the goodwill that Brookfield has developed in its 'MovieBuff' mark," and the customer might choose not to go to the trouble of continuing to search for Brookfield's website.

The Ninth Circuit applied *Brookfield* in *Playboy Enters., Inc. v. Netscape Communications Corp.*, 354 F.3d 1020 (9th Cir. 2004). Netscape required adult-oriented companies to link their advertisements to the keywords "playboy" and "playmate," both of which were Playboy's trademarks for adult entertainment. When a user entered those search terms, an unlabeled pop-up banner advertisement would appear instructing users to "click here." Users who did so would be taken to defendant's website. The court determined that there was at least a triable fact issue as to initial interest confusion; defendant was arguably taking advantage of Playboy's goodwill to induce users to click on the unlabeled banner advertisements, and Playboy could be harmed even if users quickly realized that by clicking on the advertisement, they accessed the defendant's website, not Playboy's.

These decisions generated skepticism, expressed, for example, in Judge Berzon's concurring opinion in *Playboy*. Judge Berzon pointed out that the harm identified by the majority opinion could occur even if the advertisements had been labeled, because the consumer then would still have been presented with a potentially distracting set of choices (between Playboy's website and those identified in the pop-up advertisement). Yet, being presented with distracting choices was not the same as being confused, Judge Berzon reasoned. The Ninth Circuit appeared to endorse this sentiment in *Network Automation, Inc. v. Advanced Systems Concepts, Inc.*, 638 F.3d 1137 (9th Cir. 2011).

The initial interest confusion cause of action is a variant on the traditional point-of-sale confusion cause of action, not an independent theory. Accordingly, courts have developed tests for initial interest confusion that rely upon the confusion factors but suggest some adaptations to those factors. Some adaptations would seem to be inevitable. For example, the analysis of actual confusion would call for evidence of actual confusion before the sale, evidence that standard confusion surveys might not elicit. Other adaptations might be driven more by a judicial desire to rein in allegations of initial interest confusion, especially in the Internet context. For example, in *Interstellar Starship Services, Ltd. v. Epix, Inc.*, 304 F.3d 936 (9th Cir. 2002), the court seemed skeptical that initial interest confusion would occur unless the parties' respective products were identical, asserting that "actionable initial interest confusion on the Internet is determined, in large part, by the relatedness of the goods offered and the level of care exercised by the consumer." Similarly, in *Lamparello v. Falwell*, 420 F.3d 309 (4th Cir. 2005), in which Lamparello operated a "gripe site" at fallwell.com offering views critical of the teachings of the Reverend Jerry Falwell, the court asserted that initial interest confusion could occur only if the content of Lamparello's website established that Lamparello was attempting to compete with Falwell for financial gain. Initial interest confusion could not be established merely by an analysis of the domain name alone. The court went further, noting that the Fourth Circuit had never adopted the initial interest confusion theory and calling it "relatively new and sporadically applied."

Other courts have focused on the intent factor. These courts have required a showing of deceptive intent for all initial interest confusion cases, reasoning that this is a way to ensure that initial interest confusion assertions are confined to cases that actually involve "bait-and-switch" tactics.

Designer Skin LLC v. S & L Vitamins Inc., 560 F. Supp. 2d 811 (D. Ariz. 2008).

The Ninth Circuit's decision in *Multi Time Machine, Inc. v. Amazon.com, Inc.*, 804 F.3d 930 (9th Cir. 2015), may reflect a general trend against finding initial interest confusion liability in keywording cases. Multi Time Machine ("MTM") owned a registration for MTM SPECIAL OPS used for high-end military-style watches. MTM did not sell its products through Amazon.com. Accordingly, when consumers used the search function on the Amazon.com site to search for "mtm special ops," the site displayed a search results page displaying a variety of watches from other manufacturers. MTM complained that such a display was likely to give rise to initial interest confusion. The trial court rejected this contention on summary judgment, and a divided panel of the Ninth Circuit affirmed. According to the panel majority, in keyword advertising cases involving initial interest confusion assertions, two considerations were likely to be dispositive: the degree of purchaser care (a traditional likelihood-of-confusion factor) and "the labeling and appearance of the products for sale and the surrounding context on the screen displaying the results page" (a consideration lying outside the usual factor tests). As applied here, (1) the goods at issue were expensive, suggesting that the relevant consumer was a reasonably prudent consumer accustomed to shopping online (who evidently would exercise a rather high degree of care); and (2) Amazon had "clearly labeled" products on its search results page with the product's name and manufacturer "in large, bright, bold letters," and had included a photograph of the product. Amazon was not required to state explicitly on the results page that Amazon does not sell MTM watches.

The court in *Gibson Guitar Corp. v. Paul Reed Smith Guitars, LP*, 423 F.3d 539 (6th Cir. 2005) likewise resisted what it perceived to be an attempted expansion of the initial interest confusion doctrine. The court declared that it was "unable to imagine" a set of facts that would persuade it to apply the initial interest confusion analysis to cases involving product design trade dress, although the court left open the theoretical possibility (however remote) that it might do so in some future case. Gibson had argued that defendant Paul Reed Smith had emulated the trade dress in the shape of a Gibson guitar model, such that a consumer standing in a guitar store looking at the guitar display from afar might be persuaded to take a closer look at the Paul Reed Smith guitar, temporarily believing it to be a Gibson. The panel, over a dissent, dismissed this theory. Guitar shapes included many standard, necessary elements, and so many of them might look similar when viewed from afar. Moreover, given the diversity of various store displays and consumer viewing scenarios, an inquiry into initial interest confusion would be so complicated as to be unworkable, in the court's view. Finally, recognizing initial interest confusion for product shapes would present the risk of anti-competitive effects, because it would be too easy for mark owners to raise triable issues of fact given the complexity of the inquiry, according to the court.

2. POST-SALE CONFUSION

Post-sale confusion is another theory in which confusion is assessed other than at the point of sale. In its more limited form, post-sale confusion is said to arise when there is no purchaser confusion at the point of sale, but there is subsequently confusion among potential purchasers who view the infringing mark. In a broader form, post-sale confusion arises when the subsequent, confused viewers are simply any members of the public, whether or not they are potential purchasers. Some decisions (typically older ones) have referred to post-sale confusion as "secondary" confusion and to the subsequent, confused viewers as "secondary" viewers of the mark. *See, e.g., Mastercrafters Clock & Radio Co. v. Vacheron & Constantin-Le Coultre Watches, Inc.*, 221 F.2d 464 (2d Cir. 1955), *cert. denied* 350 U.S. 832 (1955); *Academy of Motion Picture Arts & Sciences v. Creative House Promotions, Inc.*, 944 F.2d 1446 (9th Cir. 1991). Newer decisions frequently refer to post-sale confusion and invoke the 1962 Lanham Act amendments deleting the term "purchaser" as implicit statutory support for recognizing post-sale confusion.

Post-sale confusion allegations frequently arise from classic "knock-off" scenarios. For example, if a purchaser buys a fake ROLEX watch for $25 from an anonymous street vendor, there is surely no point-of-sale confusion: the purchaser knows from the price and context that the watch is a fake. But others who subsequently see the watch on the purchaser's wrist will not necessarily have any information about the context of the original purchase, and may mistakenly believe that the watch is genuine. *See, e.g., Rolex Watch, U.S.A., Inc. v. Canner*, 645 F. Supp. 484 (S.D. Fla. 1986). In such cases, the mark owner and the public may be harmed by the post-sale confusion in various ways. First, if the fake goods are inferior in quality, the mark owner's reputation for producing high quality goods may be harmed, and the mark owner's incentive to invest in maintaining high quality may be diminished. Second, the mark owner's reputation for producing limited-availability items may be damaged by the sheer proliferation of products bearing the mark, even if the products are of reasonable quality. For example, if part of the allure of driving a Ferrari sports car is the relative rarity of such vehicles, the appearance of look-alike Ferraris in every parking lot will surely make purchasing an original less desirable. *See Ferrari S.p.A. Esercizio v. Roberts*, 944 F.2d 1235 (6th Cir. 1991), *cert. denied* 505 U.S. 1219 (1992) (concluding that the maker of kit cars resembling Ferrari models was liable under a theory of post-sale confusion). Indeed, the proliferation of replica Ferraris may erode the resale value of original Ferraris, harming the owners of the originals. In cases involving replica products which are difficult to distinguish from the originals, there may be additional harm in the form of lost sales if potential purchasers come to fear that they are purchasing replicas but being charged for originals. *General Motors Corp. v. Keystone Automotive Indus., Inc.*, 453 F.3d 351 (6th Cir. 2006) (identifying this form of harm).

Harms of the type usually associated with post-sale confusion tread very close to the harms identified in the dilution cases (discussed in Chapter 8). For example, as we shall see, dilution by tarnishment may occur when a defendant applies another's mark to a shoddy product; and dilution by blurring may occur when defendants apply another's mark to a multiplicity of unrelated products, resulting in proliferation. In cases decided before the dilution cause of action became a part of the Lanham Act—that is, before the enactment of the 1995 Federal Trademark Dilution Act—courts may have used the post-sale confusion theory as a surrogate for dilution. The availability of a federal anti-dilution cause of action today may reduce the need for courts to rely on post-sale confusion.

Courts assessing post-sale confusion have generally used the likelihood of confusion factors analysis, modifying some factors so that they are properly directed to testing for confusion after the point of sale. For example, evidence of actual confusion need not be limited to the point of sale, but should take into account viewer reactions after the point of sale. The similarity of marks factors should likewise account for the post-sale context. For example, consider the *Libman* case cited above at Section C.1, involving a claim of trade dress in a colored band of bristles in a household broom. For a post-sale confusion claim, it may have been proper for a court to compare the parties' respective products without their wrappers, since that is how consumers would have encountered the trade dress post-sale. This was a potentially important point, because the alleged infringer's wrapper partially covered the colored band of bristles, possibly mitigating the similarity.

Likelihood of confusion factor tests invariably include a purchaser sophistication or purchaser care factor. The correct analysis of this factor in a post-sale confusion case should depend upon whether the alleged post-sale confusion is on the part of members of the general public who view the goods post-sale, or on the subset of potential purchasers who view the goods post-sale. If the allegation is that the general public is confused post-sale, then the level of care or sophistication of purchasers should be irrelevant. In such a case, this factor either should be dropped from the analysis altogether or directed towards the general public's level of care in viewing the goods, if that can be measured. If the allegation is that potential purchasers are confused, the factor should be adapted to address the level of care potential purchasers give when viewing the goods post-sale, not when purchasing.

Courts have not treated the purchaser care/purchaser sophistication factor(s) uniformly in the post-sale confusion context, undoubtedly reflecting the split over whether post-sale confusion should be addressed to the general public or merely to potential purchasers. In *Hermes Int. v. Lederer de Paris Fifth Ave.*, 219 F.3d 104 (2d Cir. 2000), the court concluded that the views of the general public were determinative, not the views of sophisticated purchasers of mark owner Hermes' handbags. Lederer had argued that even if members of the general public could not distinguish the Lederer bag from the genuine Hermes bag, sophisticated purchasers of Hermes bags could. In *General Motors Corp. v. Urban Gorilla, LLC*, 500 F.3d 1222 (10th Cir. 2007), involving vehicle chassis kits that allegedly replicated the plaintiff's HUMMER trade dress, the court directed its analysis of the consumer care/sophistication factor to consumers of *plaintiff's* product, finding them sufficiently sophisticated and discerning that they would not be confused by a less expensive chassis kit. In *Ferrari*, the court likewise found that the purchaser care/sophistication factor favored the defendant, although it was not clear whether the court was addressing the care and sophistication of the general public or of potential purchasers, and, in any event, other factors carried the day to establish likely post-sale confusion.

E. REVERSE CONFUSION

Thus far in this chapter, we have not distinguished between claims of "forward" and "reverse" confusion, for the simple reason that most confusion cases involve forward confusion. That is, most confusion cases rest on the claim that a junior user is seeking to trade off the goodwill of a senior user, typically by adopting a mark reminiscent of the senior user's mark. Forward confusion might arise if the two authors of this Nutshell began marketing a soft drink under the name "Coca-Cola" in an ill-fated attempt to take advantage of the Coca-Cola Company's reputation.

By contrast, in cases involving reverse confusion, the junior user is not seeking to free-ride on the senior user's reputation, but rather threatens to so saturate the market that consumers begin to associate the mark at issue with the junior user rather than the senior user. Reverse confusion might arise if the author of this Nutshell had long marketed a fruit juice drink in a few college towns (under the name "Fruition," let us say), and Coca-Cola subsequently entered the market and began selling FRUITION fruit juice drinks through a nationwide distribution chain. Coca-Cola, the junior user in this scenario, surely is not attempting to free-ride on my reputation, so consumers might not be confused in the sense of forward confusion, but they may be confused in reverse—that is, they may associate FRUITION with Coca-Cola, and may even think that I (the senior user) am actually the newcomer attempting to capitalize on Coca-Cola's reputation. For example, in *Sands, Taylor & Wood Co. v. Quaker Oats Co.*, 978 F.2d 947 (7th Cir. 1992), junior user Quaker Oats adopted the phrase GATORADE IS THIRST AID in connection with its popular GATORADE beverage. The senior user, a small Vermont-based company that owned the mark THIRST-AID for soft drinks, established that Quaker Oats' use was likely to cause reverse confusion. In *Big O Tire Dealers v. Goodyear Tire and Rubber Co.*, 561 F.2d 1365 (10th Cir. 1977), the junior user Goodyear, the world's largest tire manufacturer at the time, planned to use the mark BIGFOOT for tires, but the senior user, retail tire dealer Big O, succeeded in demonstrating reverse confusion.

Some jurisdictions recognize reverse confusion, but the concept remains controversial. On the one hand, reverse confusion may protect smaller trademark owners from being overwhelmed by larger competitors who can fund massive advertising campaigns. Without reverse confusion, large junior users might be able to appropriate the marks of smaller, senior users with impunity, eroding the senior user's incentive to invest in building up its goodwill. On the other hand, reverse confusion may protect those who have made relatively modest investments in marks at the expense of those who are prepared to make a relatively large investment in a mark. Reverse confusion might stifle innovation on the part of junior users who have established a mark in one product category and seek to carry it over to another, only to encounter a small senior user in that other product category.

When courts do recognize reverse confusion, they apply some version of the likelihood of confusion factors analysis to analyze the claim. While courts have sometimes applied the same factors analysis used for forward confusion (that is, the analysis discussed in Section D of this Chapter), the better approach is to modify the factors analysis so that it conforms sensibly to the reverse confusion concept. The court's discussion of a modified factors analysis in *A & H Sportswear, Inc. v. Victoria's Secret Stores*, 237 F.3d 198 (3d Cir. 2000) is especially helpful. *A & H* and other decisions counsel in favor of adopting the following modifications to the standard forward confusion factors test:

(1) Similarity of marks. For both forward and reverse confusion, where the marks are more similar, confusion is more likely. In a forward confusion case, the defendant's use of its own house mark in conjunction with the mark at issue, or its use of disclaimer language, would tend to reduce similarity and thus cut against confusion. In a reverse confusion case, the defendant's use of its house mark might only enhance the effect of swamping the senior user, and, accordingly, the presence of the house mark (or perhaps disclaimer language) does not necessarily reduce the likelihood of reverse confusion.

(2) Mark strength. In a forward confusion case, the greater the conceptual and market strength of the senior user's mark, the more likely is confusion. In a reverse confusion case, conceptual strength may work in the same fashion, but market strength surely does not— that is, reverse confusion is *more* likely where the *junior* user's mark is commercially strong relative to the senior user's mark. *Attrezzi LLC v. Maytag Corp.*, 436 F.3d 32 (1st Cir. 2006) (following *A & H* on this point).

(3) Intent. In a forward confusion case, evidence of the defendant's intent to trade off the plaintiff's goodwill is probative. In a reverse confusion case, by definition, the defendant is not seeking to trade off the plaintiff's reputation. Accordingly, courts should assess the defendant's intent to saturate the market in

order to strip the plaintiff of its ability to build up its own goodwill.

(4) Actual confusion. In theory, actual confusion evidence in a forward confusion case would differ from that in a reverse confusion case: in a forward confusion case, consumers would mistakenly perceive that the junior user was taking advantage of the senior user's reputation, and survey questions should be designed to test for that perception (if actual confusion is being demonstrated by survey evidence). A survey designed to test for reverse confusion would test whether consumers perceived that the senior user was actually the newcomer attempting to take advantage of the junior user's reputation. In actual practice, consumer perceptions might be difficult to predict at the outset, so a prudent mark owner might survey for both forward and reverse confusion, and such a survey might well produce evidence of both types of confusion. For example, suppose that a survey produces a substantial number of instances of reverse confusion, mainly among those who are more familiar with the junior user's mark, along with a few instances of forward confusion among the relatively small number of consumers who encountered the senior user's mark first. If the mark owner characterizes the case as a reverse confusion case, a strict rule dismissing or discounting the evidence of actual forward confusion might fail to account appropriately for the level of confusion in the marketplace. The better approach would be for the court to address

the confusion evidence flexibly in view of the factual context of the particular case.

Other factors in typical confusion tests—such as the similarity of the products/services, the similarity of channels of trade, and consumer sophistication are likely to work the same way for both forward and reverse confusion claims.

In Section C, we noted that confusion is a ground for barring registration of a mark, according to Lanham Act Section 2(d). Many Section 2(d) cases involve forward confusion, but reverse confusion has also been recognized under Section 2(d). *See, e.g., In re Shell Oil Co.*, 992 F.2d 1204 (Fed. Cir. 1993) (affirming denial of registration on ground of reverse confusion).

F. INDIRECT AND VICARIOUS THEORIES OF LIABILITY

In general tort law, it is a familiar principle that a party may be liable in tort for facilitating the torts of others. Intellectual property infringement is a tort, and so it should be expected that facilitating another's intellectual property infringement could give rise to liability. In intellectual property law, this is frequently referred to as indirect infringement. Proof of indirect infringement requires evidence of acts constituting facilitation, and evidence that the facilitation resulted in an underlying direct infringement.

The Lanham Act contains no express language establishing a cause of action for indirect trademark infringement. However, courts had appeared to endorse such an action before the passage of the Lanham Act, at least in cases in which a party intentionally induced another to engage in trademark infringement. *See, e.g., William R. Warner & Co. v. Eli Lilly & Co.*, 265 U.S. 526 (1924) (finding Warner liable where Warner induced druggists to substitute Warner's product when customers asked for Lilly's product).

In a post-Lanham Act case, the Supreme Court recognized an action for indirect infringement, labeling it contributory infringement. *Inwood Laboratories, Inc. v. Ives Laboratories, Inc.*, 456 U.S. 844 (1982). Under the *Inwood* contributory infringement standard, "if a manufacturer or distributor intentionally induces another to infringe a trademark, or if it continues to supply its product to one whom it knows or has reason to know is engaging in trademark infringement, the manufacturer or distributor is contributorially responsible for any harm done as a result of the deceit." Ives, the manufacturer of a prescription drug sold under the name CYCLOSPASMOL, sued Inwood, a firm that marketed a generic substitute for CYCLOSPASMOL. Ives sold directly to physicians, marketing to them through personal visits; Inwood sold primarily by catalog sales to hospitals and retail pharmacies, using catalogs that described the Inwood product as equivalent to Ives' product. Ives claimed that Inwood had encouraged pharmacists to substitute Inwood's product for Ives' product, asserting that consumers were not likely to detect such substitutions because pharmacists dispensed prescription medicine in pharmacists' own bottles and could easily label the bottles CYCLOSPASMOL even if they actually contained Inwood's product. The District Court rejected Ives' claim; the Court of Appeals reversed; and the Supreme Court granted certiorari. Applying its newly-articulated standard, the Supreme Court reversed and remanded.

Reviewing the District Court's findings, the Supreme Court noted that since Inwood did not market directly to physicians through personal visits, Inwood's catalogs would have been the only source of evidence of an explicit suggestion for improper substitution. But the catalogs included no such explicit suggestions. Nor was there evidence that improper substitution practices were so widespread that the equivalency statements in Inwood's catalogues could be taken as evidence of an implicit suggestion of substitution. The Court of Appeals, in finding to the contrary, had simply substituted its own view of the facts for that of the District Court, and this required reversal, according to the Supreme Court.

Inwood articulates the governing standard for contributory infringement, but reveals relatively little about how to apply the standard. Some subsequent cases, including some involving indirect infringement allegations in copyright and patent law, may provide some illumination. As for the intentional inducement prong, in a copyright case, the Supreme Court concluded that where a party distributes a product "with the object of promoting its use to infringe copyright"—that is, "where evidence goes beyond a product's characteristics or the knowledge that it may be put to infringing uses, and shows statements or actions directed to promoting infringement," the party can be liable for inducing copyright infringement. *Metro-Goldwyn-Mayer Studios Inc. v. Grokster*, 545 U.S. 913 (2005). In a patent case, *Global Tech v. SEB*, 131 S.Ct. 2060 (2011), the Court inferred that "at least some intent" is required for inducing patent infringement even though the relevant statutory provision, 35 U.S.C. § 271(b), does not expressly make reference to intent.

As to the "continued supply" prong, two principal questions have arisen. The first is whether this prong of the test should apply only to manufacturers and distributors of goods, or whether this language in the test should be treated merely as an artifact of the fact setting that happened to be before the Court in *Inwood*. This is a critical question, because most of the modern allegations of contributory trademark infringement involve service providers whose services (frequently Internet-based services) are used by customers to carry out trademark infringement. Courts have extended the *Inwood* test to this context, holding that the "continued supply" prong applies to a service provider who continues to supply a service to third parties whom the supplier knows or has reason to know are carrying out direct infringement, where the supplier exercises "[d]irect control and monitoring of the instrumentality used by a third party to infringe." *Tiffany (NJ) Inc. v. eBay Inc.*, 600 F.3d 93 (2d Cir. 2010), *cert. denied* 131 S.Ct. 647 (2010); *Lockheed Martin Corp. v. Network Solutions, Inc.*, 194 F.3d 980 (9th Cir. 1999).

The second question concerning the "continued supply" prong is how to apply the "knows or has reason to know" requirement. In *Inwood*, the Court supplied some limiting gloss to this language. In particular, the Court denied that it was creating a "watered down" standard under which contributory liability would be imposed whenever a defendant "could reasonably anticipate" an underlying direct infringement. A similar issue has arisen in contributory infringement cases involving Internet-based service providers. In *Tiffany*, it seemed evident that the defendant eBay, operator of an online bidding service, could reasonably have anticipated that some users of the eBay service were selling counterfeit merchandise bearing the TIFFANY brand. That is, eBay arguably had a general reason to know of the alleged underlying direct infringement. The Second Circuit held that this level of knowledge was not sufficient: "[f]or contributory trademark infringement liability to lie, a service provider must have more than a general knowledge or reason to know that its service is being used to sell counterfeit goods. Some contemporary knowledge of which particular listings are infringing or will infringe in the future is necessary." The Second Circuit placed weight on some comments in an important Supreme Court copyright case, *Sony Corp. of America v. Universal City Studios, Inc.*, 464 U.S. 417 (1984), which arguably distinguished between contributory liability in copyright and trademark, respectively. Those comments referred to the *Inwood* standard as a "narrow" one that called for evidence that the defendant had continued to supply "identified individuals known by it" to be engaged in infringement.

Tiffany had not satisfied this standard, according to the Second Circuit. Tiffany's "Buying Programs," in which it had purchased and inspected a quantity of supposed TIFFANY goods on eBay, had not identified particular sellers who were offering counterfeit goods. The court also appeared to be impressed with the precautions that eBay was taking. Among other things, eBay had set up a notice-and-takedown system under which IP owners could notify eBay of eBay listings containing potentially infringing goods, and eBay would (and apparently did) respond by removing the notified listing. eBay had also set up a large "Trust and Safety" department, had created a "fraud engine" that searched for potentially infringing listings, and had developed various automated warning messages, including some to sellers who listed Tiffany products. In general, this type of evidence cuts both directions. It may show that the service provider exercised appropriate diligence in its precautionary measures, but simultaneously it may show that the service provider in fact exercised a high level of direct control and monitoring.

In *Louis Vuitton Malletier, S.A. v. Akanoc Solutions, Inc.*, 658 F.3d 936 (9th Cir. 2011), in which the defendants Akanoc ran a web-hosting business and Louis Vuitton asserted that Akanoc's customers were using websites hosted on Akanoc's servers to advertise infringing goods, the court ruled that Akanoc had satisfied the contributory infringement standard. Akanoc effectively controlled the "master switch" that determined whether the customers' websites were online and available. This was sufficient evidence of control, even though Akanoc did not control the content of the individual websites. Nor could Akanoc escape liability by suggesting that it "controlled" but did not "monitor." Both were required, but the evidence was sufficient to show monitoring. Similarly, in *Rosetta Stone Ltd. v. Google, Inc.*, 676 F.3d 144 (4th Cir. 2012), the evidence was sufficient for Rosetta Stone to raise a triable issue of fact as to contributory infringement. Rosetta Stone alleged that it had notified Google of approximately 200 instances in which a website associated with a keyword-triggered "sponsored link" was advertising counterfeit Rosetta Stone products, and that Google had allowed the same advertisers to continue to use Rosetta Stone's marks, albeit for sponsored links connected with other websites controlled by the same advertisers. The court distinguished *eBay*, noting that *eBay* had not been decided on summary judgment.

In cases involving the "knows or has reason to know" analysis, the mark owner is likely to offer an alternative argument that the alleged contributory infringer intentionally shielded itself from knowledge of the underlying infringement, and should therefore be deemed to know or have reason to know. This is the familiar argument of willful blindness. In *Tiffany*, the court stated that a service provider is not permitted to indulge in willful blindness and thus escape a charge of contributory infringement. However, it found no willful blindness on eBay's part on the basis of the evidence in the record. The willful blindness argument is likely to continue to arise in these cases, especially after the Supreme Court relied on it in a patent case involving induced patent infringement, *Global-Tech Appliances, Inc. v. SEB S.A.*, 131 S.Ct. 2060 (2011). There, the Court concluded that the alleged inducer had been willfully blind to the existence of the relevant patent rights, and set forth two requirements for a showing of willful blindness that will undoubtedly be invoked in trademark cases involving contributory trademark infringement: (1) the defendant must subjectively believe that there is a high probability that a fact exists and (2) the defendant must take deliberate actions to avoid learning of that fact.

Contributory infringement is the most common indirect infringement claim discussed in U.S. trademark cases, but is it not the sole route to indirect infringement liability. Courts have discussed the possibility of applying common law vicarious liability concepts to trademark infringement. In *Hard Rock Cafe Licensing Corp. v. Concession Servs., Inc.*, 955 F.2d 1143 (7th Cir. 1992), the court appeared to suggest that vicarious liability for another's trademark infringement could apply where the defendant and direct infringer have an apparent or actual partnership, the authority to bind one another in transactions with third parties, or authority to exercise joint ownership or control over the infringing product. Where the defendant and direct infringer can be shown to be in a principal/agent relationship, liability might also conceivably arise as a matter of agency law.

In some cases, questions may arise about the liability of printers or publishers for carrying out trademark infringement by printing advertisements or the like at the behest of customers. In such cases, the customers may face exposure to liability as potential contributory infringers under the rules discussed above, while the printers and publishers may be deemed the underlying direct infringers. Notably, the Lanham Act limits liability for various printers and publishers who can establish that their actions were "innocent." Lanham Act Section 32(2)(A) provides that under those circumstances, the mark owner is entitled only to injunctive relief against future printing.

CHAPTER 8

NON-CONFUSION-BASED CLAIMS: DILUTION, CYBERSQUATTING, AND COUNTERFEITING

This chapter deals with a diverse array of Lanham Act claims. The common connection between these claims is that they are not based on a theory of likely consumer confusion. Instead, they depart from that formulation in various ways, to solve particular problems. The anti-dilution claim seeks to remedy the diminution of a mark's value that may occur when a mark is used without authorization in a manner that does not cause confusion but nonetheless triggers an association with the mark owner. *See* Section A. The anti-cybersquatting claim seeks a remedy against parties who register domain names that incorporate others' trademarks, as discussed in Section B. The anti-counterfeiting claim seeks to strike down acts of unauthorized duplication of marks under specified circumstances. This is the topic of Section C.

A. DILUTION

The trademark dilution theory is based on the premise that some types of unauthorized acts that do not give rise to confusion may nonetheless harm a trademark owner. For example, suppose that a firm uses KODAK in connection with shoes. Consumers might not believe that the famous film and camera manufacturer manufactures the shoes—that is, consumers might not be confused as to the source of the shoes. Nonetheless, the unique connection in consumers' minds between the term "Kodak" and the products of the camera manufacturer may be impaired. Consumers may begin to associate the term "Kodak" with a variety of products emanating from a variety of different producers. Similarly, if a firm uses KODAK in connection with drug paraphernalia, the camera manufacturer's image may be harmed even if consumers do not mistakenly believe that the manufacturer is the source of the goods. Dilution theory posits that trademark owners should be entitled to enjoin unauthorized activities that are likely to give rise to harms of these types, under specified conditions.

1. ORIGINS AND EVOLUTION OF THE DILUTION THEORY

The law of dilution in the U.S. traces back to a proposal in an influential law review article. Frank I. Schechter, *The Rational Basis of Trademark Protection*, 40 HARV. L. REV. 813 (1927). Schechter proposed that *any* unauthorized use of a "unique" mark necessarily reduced the mark's uniqueness, and should give rise to liability. The harm resulting from this "whittling away" of the mark's hold on the public—and not the harm resulting from confusion—was the only "rational basis" for protecting trademarks, according to Schechter.

The Schechter model is difficult to harmonize with traditional models of the trademark right because Schechter's proposal would have afforded absolute property rights (property rights in gross) to trademark owners. Perhaps for this reason, a proposal as extensive as Schechter's has never been adopted either in state or federal law. However, a number of states did enact less expansive anti-dilution statutes during the twentieth century. These statutes typically prohibited the use of a mark that created a "likelihood of dilution" of the mark's distinctive quality, leaving it to the courts to define what "dilution" meant. *See, e.g.*, N.Y Gen. Bus. Law § 360–1. One influential approach to defining and evaluating dilution originated in Judge Sweet's concurring opinion in *Mead Data Cent., Inc. v. Toyota Motor Sales U.S.A., Inc.*, 875 F.2d 1026 (2d Cir. 1989). Judge Sweet proposed that the following factors be used to test for dilution: (1) similarity of the marks; (2) similarity of the products covered by the marks; (3) sophistication of consumers; (4) predatory intent; (5) renown of the senior mark; and (6) renown of the junior mark. This test was used for assertions of dilution by blurring, a form of dilution that is discussed in more detail below.

The anti-dilution cause of action remained exclusively the province of state law until 1995. At that point, Congress incorporated an anti-dilution provision into the Lanham Act, as discussed below.

2. DILUTION UNDER THE LANHAM ACT

At the end of 1995, Congress passed the Federal Trademark Dilution Act ("FTDA"), which was codified in various sections of the Lanham Act, primarily in Section 43(c). Section 43(c) provided an injunction against specified acts that "cause[d] dilution of the distinctive quality of the mark" at issue. It limited the anti-dilution action to "famous" marks and provided a multi-factor test for assessing fame. It also included a definition of dilution in Section 45, which specified that dilution referred to "the lessening of the capacity of a famous mark to identify and distinguish goods or services, regardless of the presence or absence of (1) competition between the owner of the famous mark and other parties; or (2) likelihood of confusion, mistake, or deception." The legislation also specified acts that would not be actionable, such as fair use of the mark at issue in comparative commercial advertising. Section 43(c)(4). Finally, the legislation specified that dilution could be a basis for opposing or cancelling a registration.

The FTDA was in effect until 2006, when Congress passed the Trademark Dilution Revision Act ("TDRA"). The TDRA changed much of the language quoted above. It established a likelihood of dilution standard, eliminated the definition of dilution (and substituted tests for "dilution by tarnishment" and "dilution by blurring") and changed the fair use exclusion, among other things, although it left intact the concept of dilution as a basis for challenging registrations. The discussion below explains these changes in more detail, and also explains the extent to which cases decided under the FTDA may remain relevant.

Elements of anti-dilution claims—§ 43(c)(1). Section 43(c)(1), as amended in 2006, provides protection against dilution when the following elements are satisfied: (1) the mark at issue is famous, as defined in Section 43(c)(2)(A); (2) the defendant commenced use of the mark at issue after the mark became famous; (3) the defendant's use is likely to cause dilution by blurring or dilution by tarnishment of the mark (as defined in Sections 43(c)(2)(B) and (C), respectively), "regardless of the presence or absence of actual or likely confusion, of competition, or of actual economic injury." If these elements are met, the owner of the famous mark is entitled to injunctive relief (subject to various exclusions set out in Section 43(c)(3)), and may be entitled to damages if the violation was willful (under the conditions specified in Section 43(c)(5)).

One of the most important aspects of Section 43(c)(1) is its adoption of the "likelihood of dilution" standard. The statute employs a forward-looking "likelihood of" standard (comparable to likelihood of confusion) rather than an actual dilution standard that would require the plaintiff to show consummated, past acts of dilution. The likelihood of dilution standard is one of the key features that distinguishes the current version of Section 43(c) from the FTDA (1995) version. The 1995 version of Section 43(c) provided that the owner of a famous mark was entitled to injunctive relief against another person's commercial use of a mark or trade name if that use "causes dilution of the distinctive quality" of the famous mark. The lower courts had split over whether that language required a showing of actual dilution, or merely a showing of likelihood of dilution. In *Moseley v. V Secret Catalogue, Inc.*, 537 U.S. 418 (2003), the U.S. Supreme Court construed the language of the 1995 FTDA as requiring a showing of actual dilution. However, in 2006, Congress legislatively overruled *Moseley,* adopting the "likelihood of" language that appears in the current version of Section 43(c)(1).

Types of marks subject to anti-dilution protection— § 43(c)(1); § 43(c)(4). Section 43(c) extends to both registered and unregistered marks (as is the case for other Section 43 causes of action), as long as the marks are distinctive. Section 43(c)(1) does not limit the dilution cause of action to *inherently* distinctive marks, but rather extends it to both inherently distinctive marks and marks that have acquired distinctiveness. In this regard, the current provision overrules *TCPIP Holding Co., Inc. v. Haar Comm., Inc.*, 244 F.3d 88 (2d Cir. 2001), which had construed the 1995 dilution provision as extending only to inherently distinctive marks.

On its face, Section 43(c)(1) extends both to word marks and to non-verbal marks such as trade dress. Section 43(c)(4) implicitly confirms this reading. It specifies that in actions for dilution of unregistered trade dress, the trade dress owner has the burden of establishing that the claimed trade dress is not functional, is famous, and that such fame is "separate and apart from" any fame that may attach to registered marks that may form part of the unregistered trade dress. Some cases decided under the 1995 provision, such as *I.P. Lund Trading ApS v. Kohler Co.*, 163 F.3d 27 (1st Cir. 1998), included dicta questioning whether extending the dilution cause of action to product design trade dress would create the equivalent of a perpetual patent right, and consequently would violate the Intellectual Property Clause of the U.S. Constitution (Art. I, Sec. 8, cl. 8), which provides that patent rights may only be granted for "limited times."

Fame requirement—§ 43(c)(1), § 43(c)(2)(A). Section 43(c)(1) extends the dilution cause of action only to "famous" marks, and specifies that only activities commencing after a mark has become famous can be alleged to constitute dilution. Section 43(c)(2)(A) defines the concept of fame, stating that a mark is famous "if it is widely recognized by the general consuming public of the United States as a designation of source of the goods or services of the mark's owner," and providing an illustrative list of factors that courts may use in assessing fame (including factors such as the duration and geographic reach of advertising of the mark, the amount and geographic extent of sales of goods or services offered under the mark, and the extent of actual recognition of the mark).

The Federal Circuit has held that the fame requirement for Section 43(c) is difficult to satisfy. *Coach Services, Inc. v. Triumph Learning LLC*, 668 F.3d 1356 (Fed. Cir. 2012) (concluding that COACH for luxury goods had not been proven famous); *see also Toro Co. v. ToroHead Inc.*, 61 U.S.P.Q.2d 1164 (TTAB 2001). Some courts call for a showing that the mark has become a "household name." *Coach Services*, 668 F.3d at 1373; *Nissan Motor Co. v. Nissan Computer Corp.*, 378 F.3d 1002 (9th Cir.

2004); *Thane Int'l, Inc. v. Trek Bicycle Corp.*, 305 F.3d 894 (9th Cir. 2002).

In two specific respects, the fame requirement as currently defined appears to be stricter than the fame requirement found in the 1995 version of Section 43(c). First, it appears unlikely that a mark that is merely regionally famous satisfies the fame requirement under the current statute, in view of the statutory language requiring that the mark be recognized by the general consuming public "of the United States." On the other hand, the statute leaves room for some argument here, in that the geographic extent of advertising and sales are both factors to be considered in assessing fame. Section 43(c)(2)(A)(i), (ii). Second, it appears that fame established only in a niche market is insufficient under the current statute (which refers to "the general consuming public"). *Top Tobacco, L.P. v. North Atlantic Operating Co., Inc.*, 509 F.3d 380 (7th Cir. 2007).

Fame requirement and time of defendant's first use—§ 43(c)(1). The statute also imposes a timing requirement for fame. A party incurs liability under Section 43(c) only by "commencing use" of the mark at issue "at any time after the . . . mark has become famous." Mark fame for purposes of Section 43(c) is measured as of the time when the defendant adopted and began use. *Rosetta Stone Ltd. v. Google, Inc.*, 676 F.3d 144 (4th Cir. 2012). If the defendant's adoption and use occurred before the mark at issue became famous, then Section 43(c) does not reach the defendant's activity, and the fact that the mark at issue later became famous should not convert the defendant's formerly legal activity into illegal activity.

Nature of defendant's use—§ 43(c)(1), § 43(c)(3). Section 43(c)(1) specifies that a defendant may be subject to liability for dilution if the defendant "commences use of a mark or trade name in commerce" that is likely to cause dilution, if the other elements of the statute are met. According to one view, this language calls for the plaintiff to show that the defendant's use is an actionable use (also referred to as a "trademark use") in order for the plaintiff to make out a *prima facie* case. *National Business Forms & Printing, Inc. v. Ford Motor Co.*, 671 F.3d 526 (5th Cir. 2012). (As we discussed in Chapter 7, "actionable use" means that the defendant is using the mark at issue to identify the defendant's own goods and services.) Other courts adhere to the contrary view that no such actionable use requirement is included as an element of the plaintiff's prima facie case. *Rosetta Stone Ltd. v. Google, Inc.*, 676 F.3d 144 (4th Cir. 2012). The court in *Rosetta Stone* pointed out that Section 43(c)(3) excludes from liability any fair use "other than as a designation of source for the [defendant's] own goods or services," suggesting that the defendant bears the burden of establishing, as an element of its fair use defense, that its use is not a trademark use.

Dilution by blurring—§ 43(c)(2)(B). Under the current statute, Section 43(c)(2)(B) defines dilution by blurring as the "association arising from the similarity between a mark or trade name and a famous mark that impairs the distinctiveness of the famous mark." The statute proceeds to authorize courts to consider "all relevant factors" in assessing blurring, and specifically lists the following factors:

(i) The degree of similarity between the mark or trade name and the famous mark.

(ii) The degree of inherent or acquired distinctiveness of the famous mark.

(iii) The extent to which the owner of the famous mark is engaging in substantially exclusive use of the mark.

(iv) The degree of recognition of the famous mark.

(v) Whether the user of the mark or trade name intended to create an association with the famous mark.

(vi) Any actual association between the mark or trade name and the famous mark.

The statutory factors for blurring are reminiscent of the "Sweet" factors for dilution by blurring under New York state anti-dilution law that appeared in Judge Sweet's concurring opinion in *Mead Data Cent. v. Toyota Motor Sales U.S.A., Inc.*, 875 F.2d 1026 (2d Cir. 1989) (Sweet, J., concurring), discussed above in A.2.

The canonical example of blurring is the use of a famous mark in connection with products or services that are quite remote from those offered by the famous mark owner—as in COCA-COLA for surgical equipment. *But cf. Hugunin v. Land O' Lakes, Inc.*,

815 F.3d 1064 (7th Cir. 2016) (questioning whether the use of LAND O' LAKES for fishing tackle could dilute the mark LAND O' LAKES for dairy products because "the products of the two companies are too different"). The premise of dilution by blurring is that such a use may cause marketplace clutter that diminishes the unique connection between the mark and the products of the famous mark owner. Put another way, dilution by blurring gives rise to a "multiplication of meanings" for the mark, a phenomenon which is said to constitute "the essence of dilution by blurring." *Visa Int'l Service Assoc. v. JSL Corp.*, 610 F.3d 1088 (9th Cir. 2010). In *Visa*, involving the famous mark VISA for credit card services, the court observed that the defendant's use of "eVisa" for an online "multilingual education and information business" was likely to cause such a multiplication of meanings. By contrast, ordinary references to the word "visa" to denote travel visas would elicit in the hearer's mind only the standard dictionary definition of "visa." There would be no harm to the famous mark owner in such circumstances, and no dilution by blurring.

Courts analyze blurring claims by balancing the statutory factors set forth in Section 43(c)(2)(B). In this regard, the form of the analysis is reminiscent of the likelihood of confusion analysis. As with that analysis, it is helpful to elaborate some rules of thumb for assessing the individual factors. We offer some guidance in the following paragraphs.

Similarity factor—§ 43(c)(2)(B)(i). Factor (i) calls for an assessment of the "degree" of similarity. It would be inconsistent with this language to require that the famous and accused marks be identical. Pre-2006 cases that appeared to impose a threshold identity requirement are no longer good law. *See Levi Strauss & Co. v. Abercrombie & Fitch Trading Co.*, 633 F.3d 1158 (9th Cir. 2011). Moreover, the statutory language calls into question whether there is even a requirement that the famous and accused marks be "substantially similar." The court discarded the substantial similarity requirement in *Starbucks Corp. v. Wolfe's Borough Coffee, Inc.*, 588 F.3d 97 (2d Cir. 2009). The TTAB follows the same approach when assessing dilution in the context of opposition or cancellation proceedings. *See, e.g., Rolex Watch U.S.A., Inc. v. AFP Imaging Corp.*, 101 U.S.P.Q.2d 1188 (TTAB 2011) (stating that "the test we employ is the *degree* of similarity or dissimilarity of the marks in their entireties" and rejecting any requirement for identity or for substantial similarity). However, even without an elevated requirement for identity or substantial similarity, the similarity of marks assessment is still meaningful. In *Starbuck's*, after remand of the 2009 decision and another appeal, the Second Circuit upheld the trial court's determination that the STARBUCKS marks were only minimally similar to the defendant's CHARBUCKS BLEND and MISTER CHARBUCK'S marks when the defendant's marks were viewed in the context of their actual uses on defendant's packaging and its website. *Starbucks Corp. v. Wolfe's Borough Coffee, Inc.*, 736 F.3d 198 (2d Cir. 2013).

Where the famous mark and the defendant's mark were effectively identical, and the famous mark was widely recognized, these facts were sufficient to uphold a grant of summary judgment in favor of the famous mark owner on the likelihood of dilution by blurring. *Visa Int'l Service Assoc. v. JSL Corp.*, 610 F.3d 1088 (9th Cir. 2010).

"Strength" factors—§ 43(c)(2)(B)(ii)–(iv). Factors (ii), (iii), and (iv) of the blurring test all pertain to various aspects of mark strength, and accordingly may conveniently be grouped together. Evidence of a mark's conceptual strength is relevant to factor (ii), and evidence of a mark's market strength is pertinent to all of these factors. The same evidence that is offered to support the fame requirement will also be useful in proving blurring factors (ii)–(iv).

Intent factor—§ 43(c)(2)(B)(v). In an ordinary case, courts are likely to hold that the stronger the plaintiff's showing under any of the factors, the more probable is the conclusion of blurring. Thus, a strong showing of intent to create an association, or a strong showing of actual association, would ordinarily cut in favor of blurring. However, in *Louis Vuitton Malletier S.A. v. Haute Diggity Dog, LLC*, 507 F.3d 252 (4th Cir. 2007), the court concluded that a showing that the famous mark enjoys a high degree of distinctiveness or recognition might actually cut against dilution by blurring in cases of allegedly parodic use of a famous mark, on the ground that the parodic use might itself contribute to making the famous mark an icon. Likewise, the fact that the defendant's use was a successful parody affected the court's analysis of the intent factor (intent to parody is not intent to create an association) and the similarity factor (a high degree of similarity is expected when the challenged use is a parody). In the case, discussed in more detail in Chapter 9, defendant made dog chew toys bearing the label CHEWY VUITON using trade dress that was arguably reminiscent of that used by Louis Vuitton on high-end handbags.

Intent to create an association is not synonymous with bad faith. That is, one might have the requisite intent even if one did not act in bad faith. *Starbucks Corp. v. Wolfe's Borough Coffee, Inc.*, 588 F.3d 97 (2d Cir. 2009). Intent to create an association is a separate factor from actual association, and a finding of intent does not give rise to a presumption of actual association, according to the Second Circuit in *Starbucks Corp. v. Wolfe's Borough Coffee, Inc.*, 736 F.3d 198 (2d Cir. 2013).

Actual association factor—§ 43(c)(2)(B)(vi). Survey evidence is not required in order to establish a likelihood of dilution. *Visa Int'l Service Assoc. v. JSL Corp.*, 610 F.3d 1088 (9th Cir. 2010) ("[A] plaintiff seeking to establish a likelihood of dilution is not required to go to the expense of producing expert testimony or market surveys; it may rely entirely on the characteristics of the marks at issue."). Nonetheless, the blurring test does include an actual association factor, and survey evidence is likely to be useful in proving actual association. In the CHARBUCKS case, the survey evidence offered by Starbucks showed that 30.5% of surveyed consumers responded that "Starbucks" came to mind when they heard "Charbucks," and 3.1% of surveyed consumers stated that Starbucks was the possible source of a product called Charbucks. However, the record apparently contained no evidence that "Charbucks" ever appeared to consumers in isolation. Because the survey had presented the defendant's marks outside of their ordinary marketplace context, the trial court had not erred in treating the survey as weighing only minimally in favor of actual association. *Starbucks Corp. v. Wolfe's Borough Coffee, Inc.*, 736 F.3d 198 (2d Cir. 2013).

For a discussion of actual association evidence in the context of opposition and cancellation proceedings, *see Rolex Watch U.S.A., Inc. v. AFP Imaging Corp.*, 101 U.S.P.Q.2d 1188 (TTAB 2011).

Other blurring factors. The list of statutory blurring factors in Section 43(c)(2)(B) is open-ended. However, the courts and the TTAB have not, to date, tended to rely on additional factors beyond those explicitly listed. For example, if the allegedly diluting mark is owned by a small business, and the allegedly diluted mark is owned by a multinational company, should this factor be given weight in a blurring analysis? In *Nike, Inc. v. Maher*, 100 U.S.P.Q.2d 1018 (TTAB 2011), Maher (the owner of the registration being challenged) asserted that the TTAB should recognize as a separate factor in the blurring analysis the disparity in size between the famous mark owner's business (a large multinational company) and the Maher's business (allegedly a "very small company"). The TTAB seemed to suggest that the existence of numerous small players in the market enhanced the prospect of dilution, such that, if it recognized size disparity as a factor, it would weigh in favor of the famous mark owner.

Dilution by tarnishment—§ 43(c)(2)(C). Section 43(c)(1) identifies two forms of dilution that may give rise to liability: dilution by blurring and dilution by tarnishment. As noted above, pre-2006 dilution law recognized both blurring and tarnishment, but neither was the subject of a definitive test.

Section 43(c)(2)(C) specifically recognizes a theory of dilution by tarnishment. This is significant, because the Supreme Court in *Moseley* had questioned whether dilution by tarnishment was cognizable under the pre-2006 version of Section 43(c). The statute now defines dilution by tarnishment as "association arising from the similarity between a mark or trade name and a famous mark that harms the reputation of the famous mark." In pre-2006 dilution cases, courts tended to find dilution by tarnishment where the defendant associated the plaintiff's mark with activities deemed illicit or immoral—such as associating a variant of plaintiff's famous toy store brand (TOYS 'R US) with a pornographic website. *Toys "R" Us, Inc. v. Akkaoui*, 40 U.S.P.Q.2d 1836 (N.D. Cal. 1996). The statutory concept of harm to reputation does not lend itself to precise definition and will need to be developed by courts over time.

In *V Secret Catalogue, Inc. v. Moseley*, 605 F.3d 382 (6th Cir. 2010), the court opined that if the defendant's mark is used to sell "sex-related products," there should be a "very strong inference" that the defendant's mark is likely to tarnish the plaintiff's famous mark, assuming that there is a semantic association between the two. The panel majority ruled that the effect of this strong inference would be to actually place the burden on the defendant of going forward with evidence rebutting a likelihood of dilution. The dissenting judge took the view that the statute does not support such a burden shift, such that the burden to show likelihood of dilution by tarnishment remains with the famous mark owner. The dissenting judge's view reflects the more plausible view of the legislative history, and it is reasonable to expect that it will prevail.

Tarnishment allegations are also common where the defendant's use gives rise to other types of connotations deemed to be negative, or where defendant's products and services are shown to be of low quality. Such arguments failed to persuade the court in *Starbucks Corp. v. Wolfe's Borough Coffee, Inc.*, 588 F.3d 97 (2d Cir. 2009), where the court considered whether defendant's use of CHARBUCKS BLEND and MISTER CHARBUCKS in connection with dark roasted coffee caused a likelihood of dilution by tarnishment of plaintiff's STARBUCKS mark. In *Louis Vuitton Malletier S.A. v. Haute Diggity Dog, LLC*, 507 F.3d 252 (4th Cir. 2007), the court dismissed a dilution by tarnishment claim with little discussion, finding that the claim was based on speculation that defendant's CHEWY VUITON dog toy (which sold for $10) must be inferior in quality to plaintiff's LOUIS VUITTON handbags (which sold for more than $1,000). As we discuss in Chapter 9, the court was persuaded that the defendant's use was parodic, and this may have played a role in the court's tarnishment analysis.

Exclusions—§ 43(c)(3). Because anti-dilution protection confers potentially powerful rights on trademark owners, the limitations on (and exclusions to) such protection are critically important. Section 43(c)(3) specifically excludes the following three classes of activities from dilution liability: fair uses as defined in Section 43(c)(3)(A); "[a]ll forms of news reporting and news commentary" as specified in Section 43(c)(3)(B); and "[a]ny noncommercial use of a mark" as specified in Section 43(c)(3)(C). Of particular interest is the fair use provision. On the one hand, some parts of the provision seem to signal an intent to give fair use a broad scope. The provision shields from dilution liability "any" fair use (including both nominative and descriptive fair use, terms which we define in Chapter 9), and defines fair use to include uses in connection with parodies as well as comparative advertisements. The provision also shields parties who facilitate the fair uses of others. On the other hand, the provision only encompasses fair uses in which the defendant is using the famous mark "other than as a designation of source" for the defendant's own goods or services. Thus, for example, in *Louis Vuitton Malletier S.A. v. Haute Diggity Dog L.L.C.*, 507 F.3d 252 (4th Cir. 2007), the court held that defendant's use of CHEWY VUITON in connection with its dog chew toys was not a shielded fair use under Section 43(c)(3)(A) because defendant was using the CHEWY VUITON designation to identify its own goods. However, as discussed above, the court still found no liability for dilution by blurring. The reader should consult Chapter 9 for a full discussion of fair use doctrines as they apply to both confusion and dilution claims.

Remedies—§ 43(c)(5). The primary remedy for dilution claims is injunctive relief, and mark owners may also be entitled to additional remedies where dilution is shown to be willful. Regarding injunctive relief, Section 43(c)(1) specifies that the owner of a famous mark is entitled to injunctive relief against dilution if the conditions delineated in Section 43(c) are met, and Section 43(c)(5) echoes this rule, adding that the injunctive relief is to be awarded as set forth in Lanham Act Section 34, one of the Lanham Act's general remedies provisions. The relevant provisions in Section 34 specify fairly routine procedural obligations. *See* Lanham Act §§ 34(a)–(c). *See* Chapter 12 for a discussion of equitable remedies generally in Lanham Act cases.

Regarding additional remedies for willful violations, Section 43(c)(5) sets out two threshold requirements. Section 43(c)(5)(A) specifies that these remedies are only available where the defendant's mark at issue was first used in commerce after the date of enactment of the 2006 TDRA. Section 43(c)(5)(B) sets out willfulness requirements for dilution by blurring claims (in 43(c)(5)(B)(i)) and dilution by tarnishment claims (in 43(c)(5)(B)(ii)). If these requirements are met, the mark owner is entitled to the award of certain monetary remedies (specified in Section 35(a)) and an order for destruction of defendant's goods at issue (specified in Section 36).

Federal registration as a bar—§ 43(c)(6). The Lanham Act does not preempt state law anti-dilution causes of action. However, it does limit state law by providing that ownership of a federal registration on the principal register is a complete bar to a statutory or common law state cause of action for dilution by blurring or dilution by tarnishment with respect to the use of the registered mark. Lanham Act § 43(c)(6)(A). In addition, ownership of a federal registration is likewise a bar against "any claim of actual or likely damage or harm to the distinctiveness or reputation of a mark, label, or form of advertisement." Lanham Act § 43(c)(6)(B).

3. DILUTION IN THE REGISTRATION CONTEXT

Lanham Act Section 2(f) specifies that dilution is a ground for opposing or cancelling a registration. For example, when a firm sought to register ROLL-X for medical and dental x-ray tables, the owner of the mark ROLEX for watches petitioned to oppose the registration on the ground that the registration would be likely to cause dilution by blurring of the ROLEX mark. *Rolex Watch U.S.A., Inc. v. AFP Imaging Corp.*, 101 U.S.P.Q.2d 1188 (TTAB 2011) (dismissing the petition).

The dilution language in Section 2(f), as amended in 2006, adopts a likelihood of dilution standard, specifying that "[a] mark which would be likely to cause dilution by blurring or dilution by tarnishment under section 43(c)" may be refused registration in an opposition proceeding under Lanham Act Section 13, or, if the mark is registered, the registration may be cancelled in a cancellation proceeding under Lanham Act Section 14. By virtue of its reference to Section 43(c), Section 2(f) incorporates relevant aspects of the dilution law as developed in the litigation context. The discussion of dilution rules in the preceding section (with the exception of the discussion on remedies) is relevant to analyzing dilution in the Section 2(f) context.

B. CYBERSQUATTING

The practice that has now become known as "cybersquatting" originated in the 1990s. At that time, anyone could reserve a domain name through a first-come, first-served process that took no account of trademark rights. A person having no connection to the makers of COORS beer might simply reserve the domain name coors.com before the Coors Brewing Co. thought to do so, intending to sell the domain name to Coors for a substantial sum later.

It was not clear that the U.S. trademark law of the 1990s afforded a remedy for this behavior. Merely holding a domain name without even associating it with a website would not cause likely confusion, at least in any traditional sense. Accordingly, mark owners turned to the anti-dilution remedy. In *Panavision Int'l v. Toeppen*, 141 F.3d 1316 (9th Cir. 1998), the court accepted the argument that the defendant's behavior constituted a new form of dilution under Section 43(c), "dilution by cybersquatting," and awarded injunctive relief. (The case arose under the 1995 version of the dilution provisions, which did not define blurring and tarnishment as the sole forms of dilution.) However, even if courts were to accept a novel dilution theory, it seemed evident that it would be difficult for mark owners to obtain jurisdiction over cybersquatters and enforce judgments against them.

Mark owners pursued two avenues of recourse concurrently, and ultimately succeeded in both. In 1999, Congress passed the Anticybersquatting Consumer Protection Act (ACPA), now codified principally in Lanham Act Section 43(d). Also in 1999, in consultation with the World Intellectual Property Organization (WIPO), the Internet Corporation for Assigned Names and Numbers (ICANN) promulgated an administrative dispute resolution policy, the Uniform Domain Name Dispute Resolution Policy (UDRP). Mark owners have used both mechanisms, although they have relied much more heavily on the UDRP.

1. ANTICYBERSQUATTING CONSUMER PROTECTION ACT (ACPA): LANHAM ACT SECTION 43(d)

Lanham Act Section 43(d) creates two related causes of action: (1) an action *in personam* against the cybersquatter, grounded in bad faith registration or use of the domain name (Section 43(d)(1)); and (2) an action *in rem* against the domain name itself (Section 43(d)(2)). We discuss the two causes of action separately below.

In personam *action under Section 43(d)(1).* The Section 43(d)(1) *in personam* cause of action calls for a showing that a person (1) has a bad faith intent to profit from the mark at issue (Section 43(d)(1)(A)(i)); and (2) "registers, traffics in, or uses a domain name" that is "identical or confusingly similar to" the mark at issue (in the case of a distinctive mark) (Section 43(d)(1)(A)(ii)(I)) or that is "identical or confusingly similar to or dilutive of" the mark at issue (in the case of a famous mark) (Section 43(d)(1)(A)(ii)(II)). The statute lays out a lengthy set of factors for determining bad faith intent to profit (Section 43(d)(1)(B)(i)(I)–(IX)), and specifies that bad faith intent "shall not be found in any case in which the court determines that the person believed and had reasonable grounds to believe that the use of the domain name was a fair use or otherwise lawful." Section 43(d)(1)(B)(ii). Courts have stressed that Section 43(d)(1)(B)(ii)'s safe harbor should be used "very sparingly and only in the most unusual cases." *GoPets Ltd. v. Hise*, 657 F.3d 1024 (9th Cir. 2011). The statute also defines "traffics in" generously. *See* Section 43(d)(1)(E).

In analyzing the bad faith intent element, courts are likely to find bad faith intent with little analysis when the facts appear to fit the standard cybersquatting narrative recounted at the beginning of this Section. A number of reported decisions deal with behavior that does not resemble that of the standard narrative. The court found bad faith in another case in which the cybersquatter had reserved the domain name with the objective of entering into competition with the mark owner and blocking the mark owner from reserving the domain name. *Sporty's Farm L.L.C. v. Sportsman's Market, Inc.*, 202 F.3d 489 (2d Cir. 2000), *cert. denied* 530 U.S. 1262 (2000). By contrast, where an individual (Lamparello) reserved the domain name www.fallwell.com and associated it with a website critical of the teachings of the Reverend Jerry Falwell, the court declined to find bad faith intent. *Lamparello v. Falwell*, 420 F.3d 309 (4th Cir. 2005), *cert. denied* 547 U.S. 1069 (2006) (relying, inter alia, on statutory factor IV, which counsels against bad faith intent where the domain name is used for purposes of comment and criticism). In *DSPT Int'l, Inc. v. Nahum*, 624 F.3d 1213 (9th Cir. 2010), the court held that holding a domain name "for ransom" could qualify as bad faith intent under Section 43(d). In that case, the defendant, a former employee of the plaintiff, had blocked access to the content of the plaintiff's website as leverage to bargain with the plaintiff for money that the plaintiff allegedly owed him. And, in *Newport News Holdings Corp. v. Virtual City Vision, Inc.*, 650 F.3d 423 (4th Cir. 2011), defendant Virtual City had a bad faith intent to profit in the sense of Section 43(d). Virtual City had registered newportnews.com and initially associated it with a website that provided information about the city of Newport News, Virginia, but later transformed it into a website that predominantly advertised women's clothing. The plaintiff owned a number of trademark registrations for NEWPORT NEWS for clothing.

Courts have tended to construe the bad faith requirement flexibly, looking to the totality of the circumstances. The Ninth Circuit declined to tether bad faith evidence to a particular time frame, holding that bad faith may be proven based on evidence that dates after the time the domain name was reserved. *Lahoti v. VeriCheck, Inc.*, 586 F.3d 1190 (9th Cir. 2009).

When analyzing the second element, in which the court may need to consider whether the domain name is "confusingly similar" to the mark at issue, courts have tended to conclude that the traditional likelihood of confusion factors analysis is a "poor fit" for the ACPA "confusingly similar" inquiry. *DSPT Int'l, Inc. v. Nahum*, 624 F.3d 1213 (9th Cir. 2010); *Northern Light Tech., Inc. v. Northern Lights Club*, 236 F.3d 57 (1st Cir. 2001) (describing the ACPA inquiry as narrower); *see also Coca-Cola Co. v. Purdy*, 382 F.3d 774 (8th Cir. 2004) (same). To be sure, the ACPA provides for liability "without regard to the goods or services of the parties," § 1125(d)(1)(A), so resorting to the factors per se would seem to be inappropriate. However, the courts have not substituted an alternative test, seeming instead to indulge in conclusory assertions about similarity.

Section 43(d) provides an array of remedies for violations of Section 43(d)(1). Section 43(d)(1)(C) specifies that a court may order the forfeiture or cancellation of the domain name, or the transfer of the domain name to the owner of the mark at issue. In addition, the court may order other forms of injunctive relief under Lanham Act Section 34(a). The plaintiff may also seek compensatory damages, electing either actual damages under Lanham Act

Section 35(a), or statutory damages under Section 35(d) (which sets forth statutory damages applicable exclusively to Section 43(d)(1) violations).

Section 43(d)(1)(D) specifies that liability under Section 43(d)(1) is limited to domain name registrants or their licensees. The Ninth Circuit has concluded that Section 43(d) forecloses the possibility of a claim for contributory cybersquatting. *Petroliam Nasional Berhad v. GoDaddy.com, Inc.*, 737 F.3d 546 (9th Cir. 2013).

In rem *action under Section 43(d)(2).* Section 43(d)(2) creates an *in rem* cause of action—a civil action against the domain name itself—under prescribed circumstances. There are two primary elements: (1) the domain name violates "any right of the owner registered" in the U.S. Patent and Trademark Office, or protected under Sections 43(a) or (c) (Section 43(d)(2)(A)(i)); and (2) the court finds that the mark owner was not able to obtain *in personam* jurisdiction over the person who reserved the domain name, or through diligence (including taking specified actions) the mark owner was not able to find the person who would have been the defendant in the action. (Section 43(d)(2)(A)(ii)(I), (II)). In such a circumstance, the mark owner can bring an *in rem* civil action against the domain name in the judicial district where the domain name registrar, registry, or other authority that registered the domain name is located. Section 43(d) further specifies how to determine the situs of the domain name. Section 43(d)(2)(C). The remedies in an *in rem* action are limited to the forfeiture or cancellation of the domain name, or its transfer to the mark owner, as specified in Section 43(d)(2)(D).

In *Harrods Ltd. v. Sixty Internet Domain Names*, 302 F.3d 214 (4th Cir. 2002), the court determined that the *in rem* remedy under Section 43(d)(2) is not limited to instances of cybersquatting, but extends to claims under Sections 43(a) and (c). The court focused on the language in Section 43(d)(2) indicating that the claim is applicable to "any right . . . registered" in the PTO, "*or* protected under" Sections 43(a) or (c) (emphasis supplied).

2. ICANN UNIFORM DOMAIN NAME DISPUTE RESOLUTION POLICY (UDRP)

The UDRP was adopted in 1999 as another response to the problem of cybersquatting. The text of the policy is reproduced online at http://www.icann.org/resources/pages/help/dndr/udrp-en. The premise of the UDRP is to use an alternative dispute resolution mechanism tied to the domain name registration process as a means for addressing cybersquatting.

Under the UDRP, anyone who registers a domain name agrees to submit to an administrative proceeding before an alternative dispute resolution provider (selected from an approved list maintained by ICANN) if a dispute arises. An applicable dispute arises when a complainant asserts that the registered domain name is identical or confusingly similar to a trademark or service mark in which the complainant has rights; the domain name registrant has no rights or legitimate interests in respect of the domain name; and the domain name has been registered and is being used in bad faith. UDRP ¶ 4a. The UDRP sets out a series of factors for assessing bad faith. UDRP ¶ 4b. It also sets out circumstances that demonstrate that the domain name registrant has "rights or legitimate interests" in the domain name. UDRP ¶ 4c. Finally, the UDRP specifies that the only remedies available in a UDRP proceeding are the cancellation of the domain name or the transfer of the domain name to the complainant. UDRP ¶ 4i.

As we have noted, in a typical case of cybersquatting, the alleged cybersquatter may hold a domain name without ever associating it with a website. In *World Wrestling Federation Ent. Inc. v. Bosman*, WIPO Case No. D1999–0001 (WIPO Arb. & Med. Center 2000), the Panel made clear that such activity sufficed to demonstrate that the domain name was in fact being "used" as called for in UDRP ¶ 4a(iii) (which requires that the domain name "has been registered and is being used in bad faith"). Similarly, passive holding of a domain name was considered to be evidence that the domain name was being used in bad faith in the circumstances presented in *Telstra Corp. Ltd. v. Nuclear Marshmallows*, WIPO Case No. D2000–0003 (WIPO Arb. & Med. Center 2000) (listing as relevant circumstances the facts that complainant's trademark was widely known; that respondent had shown no evidence of contemplated good faith use; and that the respondent had taken active steps to conceal its identity and had provided false contact information).

3. THE RELATIONSHIP BETWEEN THE UDRP AND ACPA

Paragraph 4k of the UDRP specifies that the UDRP does not purport to displace court proceedings concerning the domain name, such as proceedings under the ACPA. Paragraph 4k also indicates that ICANN will defer to judicial decisions on disputed domain names.

The primary source of litigation over the relationship between the ACPA and UDRP has concerned the opposite problem: whether a court should give binding effect to a prior UDRP decision. In *Barcelona.com v. Excelentisimo Ayuntamiento de Barcelona*, 330 F.3d 617 (4th Cir. 2003), the City Council of Barcelona had prevailed in a UDRP proceeding against Barcelona.com, Inc., in which the panelist had applied Spanish law. Barcelona.com then sought declaratory relief under a provision of the ACPA, Section 43(2)(D)(v), which provides that a domain name holder whose domain name has been transferred may seek a declaration that the registration or use of the domain name was not unlawful (and thus should not have been transferred). (An erroneous transfer of a domain name under such circumstances is sometimes referred to as "reverse domain name hijacking.") In *Barcelona.com*, the court held that it owed no deference to the decision in the UDRP proceeding, and that the ACPA required that the court apply the Lanham Act, not foreign law. The ACPA requires a showing that the mark owner in fact holds valid trademark rights, a determination whose outcome might depend upon whether the court applies the Lanham Act or the law of some other jurisdiction.

C. COUNTERFEITING

A number of provisions in the Lanham Act and elsewhere deal with trademark "counterfeiting." In common parlance, counterfeiting usually refers to the unauthorized use of an identical copy of a mark owner's mark on similar goods or services, but the definitions in these various statutes of "counterfeit" and the activities that constitute "counterfeiting" are not so limited. In considering rules of counterfeiting, then, it is critical to understand these definitions, and how they relate to the variety of remedies that the various statutes impose.

There are three sources of rules on trademark counterfeiting at the federal level: the Lanham Act, which imposes civil liability; the federal criminal law; and the Tariff Act, which empowers U.S. Customs to seize counterfeit imports. We discuss each below.

1. CIVIL LIABILITY FOR COUNTERFEITING

Lanham Act § 32(1)(a), the Act's main infringement provision for registered marks, refers to the use of counterfeit marks as one of the types of unauthorized activities that gives rise to infringement liability. As we have discussed (*see* Chapter 7), Section 32(1)(a) provides a civil remedy upon a showing that a person has, without the registrant's consent, used in commerce "any reproduction, *counterfeit*, copy, or colorable imitation of a registered mark." (emphasis supplied). Lanham Act § 45, in turn, defines a "counterfeit" as follows:

> A "counterfeit" is a spurious mark which is identical with, or substantially indistinguishable from, a registered mark.

Viewed through the prism of these provisions, trademark counterfeiting may seem to amount to little more than a relatively blatant form of trademark infringement that may warrant correspondingly more severe penalties as compared to the ordinary trademark infringement case. That is one way to understand the current Lanham Act approach to trademark counterfeiting, although it is not entirely satisfying, for several reasons. First, whereas civil liability for trademark infringement rests upon a showing of likelihood of confusion, it might be incorrect to describe trademark counterfeiting as merely an extreme and crude instance of causing likely confusion. If a street vendor is selling a watch that is marked with an exact replica of the ROLEX mark, but the watch is priced at $10 and is obviously made from inferior materials, it is unlikely that a consumer at the point of sale would be confused. One might call this post-sale confusion (*see* the discussion in Chapter 7), or perhaps one might call it trademark dilution, or perhaps it would be more sensible to define an independent, non-confusion-based offense of "counterfeiting."

Second, it is not clear how to measure whether an allegedly counterfeit mark is "substantially indistinguishable from" the original mark at issue.

Perhaps one should measure it by assessing likely confusion, although Congress could have said as much in the statute had Congress intended for that analysis to be used. Perhaps, instead, Congress meant to define some other concept that is unique to counterfeiting. This, too, is problematic, because the "substantially indistinguishable from" language only helps define what a counterfeit is; in theory, the mark owner still must show that the counterfeit gives rise to likely confusion according to the language of Section 32(1)(a). The courts have not explored these puzzles.

Instead, civil litigation in counterfeiting cases tends to focus on the available remedies rather than the existence of liability. The remedies are more severe than those available in civil trademark infringement actions. In addition to standard forms of injunctive relief after trial, Section 34(d) provides that in a counterfeiting action, the mark owner may obtain an *ex parte* order for seizure of the counterfeit goods. Section 34(d) prescribes in great detail the required contents of the mark owner's application, the conditions for granting the order, and contents of the order. Section 34(d) also incorporates procedural safeguards and provides a remedy in the event of wrongful seizures.

Trademark owners may also seek compensatory damages for trademark counterfeiting. There are two alternative avenues for monetary relief. First, the trademark owner may invoke the regular damages provision, Section 35(a), and prove actual damages. (*See* Chapter 12 for additional discussion of Section

35(a)). In this case, Section 35(b) provides that the court shall, unless "extenuating circumstances" apply, award the mark owner three times the actual damages, and a reasonable attorney's fee, if the counterfeiting was intentional as defined in Sections 35(b)(1) and (2).

Second, in the alternative to actual damages, the trademark owner in a trademark counterfeiting case may elect statutory damages under Section 35(c). The statute provides for damages ranging from $1,000 to $200,000 per counterfeit mark per type of goods sold for non-willful counterfeiting; and up to $2,000,000 per counterfeit mark per type of goods sold for willful counterfeiting. The courts have confirmed that these amounts are assessed against each *type* of goods sold, not against each individual good sold. *Gabbanelli Accordions & Imports, LLC v. Ditta Gabbanelli Ubaldo di Elio Gabbanelli*, 575 F.3d 693 (7th Cir. 2009). In addition, the Second Circuit has held that where the trademark owner elects statutory damages under Section 35(c), the owner may also seek attorney's fees even though Section 35(c) makes no express reference to such fees. *Louis Vuitton Malletier S.A. v. LY USA, Inc.*, 676 F.3d 83 (2d Cir. 2012) (reasoning that the mark owner should be entitled to attorney's fees if the case is exceptional, in accordance with the rule in Section 35(a) that applies to civil trademark infringement actions generally). Section 35(c) statutory damages are not limited to cases of direct infringement; they also can be elected in counterfeiting cases in which the defendant is a contributory infringer. *Louis Vuitton*

Malletier S.A. v. Akanoc Solutions, Inc., 658 F.3d 936 (9th Cir. 2011).

2. CRIMINAL LIABILITY FOR COUNTERFEITING

In 1984, Congress enacted federal criminal penalties for trademark counterfeiting. The primary provision is found in 18 U.S.C. § 2320, which pertains to the criminal offense of trafficking in counterfeit goods and services. As amended in 2011, Section 2320 defines three types of intentional trafficking: (1) trafficking in goods or services, where the defendant knowingly uses a counterfeit mark on or in connection with those services; (2) trafficking in labels and the like, where the defendant knows that a counterfeit mark has been applied thereto, the use of which is likely to cause confusion; and (3) trafficking in counterfeit military goods or services, under prescribed conditions. Attempted trafficking and conspiracy to traffic are also punishable. A conviction under Section 2320(a) may subject the defendant to substantial fines and/or imprisonment. 18 U.S.C. § 2320(b). All "defenses, affirmative defenses, and limitations on remedies that would be applicable in an action under the Lanham Act" also apply in Section 2320 prosecutions. 18 U.S.C. § 2320(d). Although this would certainly include the first sale doctrine, the statute makes that limitation explicit, precluding Section 2320 prosecutions for "the repackaging of genuine goods or services not intended to deceive or confuse." 18 U.S.C. § 2320(g).

Section 2320 also includes a complex definition of "counterfeit." 18 U.S.C. § 2320(f)(1)(A). In some respects, the definition is comparable to the Lanham Act Section 45 definition: both refer to a "spurious mark" (18 U.S.C. § 2320(f)(1)(A)) that is "identical with, or substantially indistinguishable from," a registered mark (18 U.S.C. § 2320(f)(1)(A)(ii)). In *United States v. Chong Lam*, 677 F.3d 190 (4th Cir. 2012), the court concluded that the defendant's mark (a plaid background and equestrian knight overlay) was identical to or substantially indistinguishable from Burberry's registered "Check" mark, even though the registration did not include an equestrian knight overlay. The evidence showed that Burberry often sold goods displaying the Check mark with a knight overlay.

The Section 2320 definition also adds the requirement that the use of the mark is likely to cause confusion. 18 U.S.C. § 2320(f)(1)(A)(iv). The confusion element of the Section 2320 definition does not require a showing that consumers at the point of sale were confused by the counterfeits. For example, in *United States v. Foote*, 413 F.3d 1240 (10th Cir. 2005), the defendant operated a business called "Replicas" that openly advertised to consumers that the goods offered for sale were reproductions of brand-name products. When charged under Section 2320, Foote argued that the marks did not satisfy the statutory definition of "counterfeit" because his use of the marks was not likely to cause confusion. The court rejected this argument, reasoning that a showing of likely post-sale confusion sufficed under the statute.

In *United States v. Diallo*, 575 F.3d 252 (3d Cir. 2009), the Third Circuit upheld the defendant's conviction under Section 2320. During a traffic stop, the police discovered that Diallo's van contained numerous sealed bags containing handbags marked with the Louis Vuitton "LV" mark. Diallo had admitted all of the elements of Section 2320 counterfeiting, except that he argued that the prosecution had not proven that he had "used" the counterfeit marks in connection with goods, because they were not being displayed for sale at the time of the traffic stop. The court rejected this argument. The bags were destined for Diallo's store in Indianapolis, and they were thus part of his inventory at the time of the stop. This was sufficient to show "use" in the sense of Section 2320.

Congress amended Section 2320 in 2011, increasing the severity of the penalties and expressly including conspiracy to traffic in counterfeits as a prohibited act. 18 U.S.C. § 2320(a). The conspiracy language is significant because it does not include a requirement for the co-conspirator to have carried out any overt act in furtherance of the conspiracy. Accordingly, planning a conspiracy could constitute a criminal offense even if the conspiracy never comes to fruition.

Federal law also separately provides criminal penalties for knowingly trafficking in counterfeit labels on particular types of goods, such as copies of software, motion pictures, or sound recordings. 18 U.S.C. § 2318.

3. PROTECTION AGAINST COUNTERFEIT IMPORTS

Owners of U.S. trademarks may also invoke the assistance of the U.S. Customs Service in dealing with counterfeiting. Regarding registered marks, Lanham Act Section 42 prohibits the importation of goods that "copy or simulate" federally registered trademarks. As for unregistered marks, Lanham Act Section 43(b) forbids the importation of "goods marked or labeled in contravention of" Section 43(a). The remedy that U.S. Customs will enforce on behalf of the trademark owner depends upon (1) whether the mark is registered; (2) whether the mark is recorded with the Customs Service; and (3) whether the imported goods bear a "counterfeit" mark or a "confusingly similar" mark. "Counterfeit" is defined in accordance with Lanham Act Section 45 (a "spurious" mark that is "identical with, or substantially indistinguishable from," a registered mark). One court has held that there is no requirement that the alleged counterfeiter's goods be identical to those of the mark owner. *United States v. Able Time*, 545 F.3d 824 (9th Cir. 2008).

The following chart summarizes the most relevant rules.

Registered?	Recorded?	Counterfeit?	Remedy
Y	Y	Y	Mandatory seizure—19 U.S.C. § 1526(e)
Y	N	Y	Subject to possible seizure—19 U.S.C. § 1595a(c)(2)(C)
Y	Y	N, but confusingly similar	Subject to possible seizure—19 U.S.C. § 1595a(c)
N	N	Y	Subject to possible seizure—19 U.S.C. § 1595a(c)
Y	N	N, but confusingly similar	Not subject to seizure
N	N	N, but confusingly similar	Not subject to seizure

Several of these rules are discussed in *Ross Cosmetics Dist. Ctr. v. United States*, 18 C.I.T. 979 (C.I.T. 1994).

CHAPTER 9
PERMISSIBLE USES OF ANOTHER'S TRADEMARK

In a number of circumstances, the trademark law permits one party to use another's trademarks without the other's permission. Some of these permissible uses are types of uses that typically would not give rise to a likelihood of confusion or dilution in any event. Other permissible uses do pose some threat of confusion or dilution, yet are excluded from liability in order to safeguard competition or to protect speech values. A number of loosely related doctrines, developed primarily in the courts, may be invoked to support a claim of permissible use of another's trademark. In Section A, we consider the doctrine of trademark fair use (itself a collection of doctrines). In Section B, we then turn to cases involving the use of another's trademark on genuine goods, where the "first sale" doctrine and related rules are relevant. We conclude in Section C with an analysis of parody and free speech claims involving trademarks.

A. FAIR USE OF ANOTHER'S TRADEMARK

At common law, courts long ago developed the principle that even if a common English word became the subject of trademark rights, those rights did not extend to the use of the word in its ordinary sense to convey its original meaning. In the absence of such a limitation, trademark owners might deprive others of the use of fundamental elements of the language, and, in many cases, such uses did not give rise to a likelihood of confusion among consumers in any event. *KP Permanent Make-Up, Inc. v. Lasting Impression I, Inc.*, 543 U.S. 111 (2004); *Delaware & Hudson Canal Co. v. Clark*, 80 U.S. 311 (1872). Eventually, this principle came to be referred to as the "fair use" defense to trademark liability.

The Lanham Act incorporates at least some aspects of the common law fair use doctrine. Lanham Act Section 33(b)(4) provides that one of the preserved defenses against incontestable registrations is

> **(4)** That the use of the name, term, or device charged to be an infringement is a use, otherwise than as a mark, of the party's individual name in his own business, or of the individual name of anyone in privity with such party, or of a term or device which is descriptive of and used fairly and in good faith only to describe the goods or services of such party, or their geographic origin . . . .

Some courts have concluded that the common law principle of fair use is codified in Section 33(b)(4). *Car-Freshner Corp. v. S.C. Johnson & Son, Inc.*, 70 F.3d 267 (2d Cir. 1995). Accordingly, some courts may look to Section 33(b)(4) to define the elements of a fair use defense not only in cases involving incontestable registrations, but also in all other cases. *See, e.g., King-Size, Inc. v. Frank's King Size Clothes, Inc.*, 547 F. Supp. 1138 (S.D. Tex. 1982) (involving a registered mark that was not yet incontestable); *Wonder Labs, Inc. v. Procter &*

Gamble Co., 728 F. Supp. 1058 (S.D.N.Y. 1990) (involving an unregistered mark).

Trademark fair use should not be confused with the more widely-known copyright law doctrine of fair use. Copyright fair use, codified at 17 U.S.C. § 107, is the primary defense to liability in the copyright system and has been the subject of countless court decisions. Fair use under the Copyright Act revolves around four statutory factors, including not only inquiries into the characteristics of the defendant's use (factor #1), but also "the effect of the use upon the potential market for or value of the copyrighted work." (factor #4). Trademark fair use, by contrast, has not been as commonly invoked as its copyright counterpart, and operates in accord with different principles, and under different tests. Below we discuss the commonly-identified fair use doctrines—descriptive fair use and nominative fair use, describing how they have been applied in typical infringement actions. Separately, we discuss the fair use doctrines available under the dilution provision, Section 43(c).

1. DESCRIPTIVE ("CLASSIC") FAIR USE

"Descriptive" fair use arises when firm *A* uses firm *B*'s trademark in the course of describing firm *A*'s own products or services. For example, where Ocean Spray advertised the flavor of its cranberry juice as "sweet-tart," the court concluded that the use was a descriptive fair use and hence did not violate Sunmark's rights in the mark SWEETART for candies. *Sunmark, Inc. v. Ocean Spray Cranberries,*

Inc., 64 F.3d 1055 (7th Cir. 1995). Some courts have tended to call this form of fair use "classic" fair use. *Cairns v. Franklin Mint Co.*, 292 F.3d 1139 (9th Cir. 2002).

Courts recognized this form of fair use long before the existence of the Lanham Act. *See, e.g., William R. Warner & Co. v. Eli Lilly & Co.*, 265 U.S. 526 (1924). However, for a number of years, the relationship between the fair use doctrine and theories of liability (such as likelihood of confusion) was unclear. Courts invoked fair use in a number of cases without consistently labeling the principle a defense to liability. Moreover, in a series of decisions, courts held that if a mark owner could prove that a defendant's use of a mark was likely to cause confusion, the defendant was foreclosed from arguing that the use was a descriptive fair use. In *KP Permanent Make-Up, Inc. v. Lasting Impression I, Inc.*, 543 U.S. 111 (2004), the Court overruled those cases. The Court held that the burden of proving likelihood of confusion lies with the mark owner, and it was error to adopt a test for fair use under Section 33(b)(4) that purported to place an independent burden on the defendant to prove the lack of likelihood of confusion. However, the Court did not rule out likely confusion as potentially relevant to the fair use inquiry. Instead, the Court explicitly left the door open for courts to consider likely confusion and other factors in adjudicating descriptive fair use claims.

Courts have not settled on a standard methodology for identifying the elements of descriptive fair use, even when they accept the language of Section 33(b)(4) as governing the inquiry. At a minimum, Section 33(b)(4) sets forth two elements for the descriptive fair use defense: (1) a descriptiveness prong; and (2) a good faith prong. The descriptiveness prong, as we have identified it, requires a showing that the mark was used only to describe the user's goods and services, and was used otherwise than as a mark. One Ninth Circuit decision subdivides the descriptiveness prong into two, calling for separate showings that the use was only for description and was "otherwise than as a mark." *Fortune Dynamic, Inc. v. Victoria's Secret Stores Brand Mgmt., Inc.*, 618 F.3d 1025 (9th Cir. 2010). We find it more sensible to discuss these concepts under the heading of descriptiveness, as we have done below.

Descriptiveness. As noted, the descriptiveness prong is satisfied by showing that the defendant's use is only to describe the defendant's goods or services and is "otherwise than as a mark." A use is only for descriptive purposes if it is either (1) a use of the defendant's individual name in his or her business; or (2) a use that describes the goods or services, or describes their geographic origin. A use is otherwise than as a mark if the use does not associate the mark with a particular manufacturer, does not seek to attract public attention via the mark, or if the user included labeling that minimizes the risk that the mark will be perceived as a source identifier. *Fortune Dynamic, Inc. v. Victoria's Secret Stores Brand Mgmt., Inc.*, 618 F.3d 1025 (9th Cir. 2010).

In some relatively straightforward cases, a defendant's use is "descriptive" in the sense of the fair use test because the use literally describes qualities of the defendant's goods or services. For example, where plaintiff owned the mark DENTISTS' CHOICE for toothbrushes, and defendant's advertising referred to its CREST toothpaste product as "the dentists' choice for fighting cavities" on its toothpaste package, defendant's use of the phrase "dentists' choice" is literally descriptive of the (alleged) qualities of the defendant's product, and the descriptiveness element of the fair use defense is met. *Wonder Labs, Inc. v. Procter & Gamble Co.*, 728 F. Supp. 1058 (S.D.N.Y. 1990). Note that the analysis does not require that the plaintiff's mark fall into the "merely descriptive" category of the *Abercrombie* framework (discussed in Chapter 2). The mark APPLE for computers would presumably be categorized as arbitrary under the *Abercrombie* framework, yet it is easy to imagine descriptive uses of that word (for example, "Our auto paint is apple red.")

In other cases, courts find that a defendant is using a term "in a descriptive sense" even if the use does not literally describe qualities of the products or services. For example, a court found fair use where plaintiff owned the mark SEALED WITH A KISS for lip gloss and defendant marketed its COLOR SPLASH lipstick using a promotional display that invited consumers to place a lipstick imprint on a postcard and mail it "to the one you love." The words "Seal it with a Kiss!!" appeared next to the postcards. The court concluded that the defendant's display used the words in their descriptive sense because they characterized the instruction being given to users of defendant's post cards (even though the words obviously did not describe the defendant's product in literal terms). *Cosmetically Sealed Industries, Inc. v. Chesebrough-Pond's USA Co.*, 125 F.3d 28 (2d Cir. 1997). Similarly, defendant ABC's use of the phrase "What's your problem?" in advertisements featuring the stars of its fictional lawyer drama was a use in a descriptive sense in that it was a reference generally to lawyers addressing legal problems. *Arnold v. ABC, Inc.*, 2007 WL 210330 (S.D.N.Y. 2007). Courts may need to invoke similar reasoning when deciding whether non-verbal indicia are being used in their descriptive sense. In *Car-Freshner Corp. v. S.C. Johnson & Son, Inc.*, 70 F.3d 267 (2d Cir. 1995), Car-Freshner claimed rights in the shape of its pine-tree cardboard air freshener. S.C. Johnson used a pine-tree-shaped plug-in for its home air freshener line of products during the Christmas holiday season. That was a descriptive use, according to the court, because the pine-tree shape indicated the product's pine scent, and indicated its connection with the Christmas season.

On remand from the Supreme Court in the *KP Permanent* case, the Ninth Circuit set out a list of factors pertinent to the descriptiveness inquiry. These include "the degree of likely confusion, the strength of the trademark, the descriptive nature of the term for the product or service being offered by [the defendant] and the availability of alternate descriptive terms, the extent of the use of the term prior to the registration of the trademark, and any differences among the times and contexts in which [the defendant] has used the term." *KP Permanent Make-Up, Inc. v. Lasting Impression I, Inc.*, 408 F.3d 596 (9th Cir. 2005).

Some courts treat descriptiveness as a matter of degree. In *Fortune Dynamic, Inc. v. Victoria's Secret Stores Brand Mgmt., Inc.*, 618 F.3d 1025 (9th Cir. 2010), the court questioned whether defendant's use of DELICIOUS on a tank top was *sufficiently* descriptive to justify the defense. The court stated that its assessment of the descriptiveness prong would depend upon the "descriptive purity" of the use at issue. The defense would be more difficult to make out as the defendant's use became less and less purely descriptive.

As Section 33(b)(4) of the Lanham Act indicates, a term may be deemed descriptive of the geographic origin of products or services, even if the term does not otherwise describe the qualities of those goods or services. Suppose that a party adopts the term WALTHAM for watches made in Waltham, Massachusetts, and, over time, the term acquires secondary meaning. A competing manufacturer of watches also located in Waltham, Massachusetts should be precluded from advertising its watches as "Waltham Watches" because the use of the term in this fashion does not merely describe the geographic origin of the competitor's goods, but also invokes the mark owner's goodwill. On the other hand, advertising text such as "Timely Brand Watches made in Waltham, Mass.," presumably exemplifies the use of the term "Waltham" to describe the geographic source of the goods, and should presumably be allowed if undertaken in good faith. In *American Waltham Watch Co. v. United States Watch Co.*, 53 N.E. 141 (Mass. 1899), Oliver Wendell Holmes, Jr., then Justice of the Massachusetts Supreme Court, acknowledged the difficulty of striking an appropriate balance between the mark owner and the competitor in such a case. One solution in close cases is to find the competitor's use not descriptive (i.e., to reject the fair use defense) but to limit the mark owner's injunctive relief so that the competitor has a fair opportunity to identify truthfully the geographic origin of its goods using appropriate explanatory text or disclaimers.

Of course, some cases may be resolved without reaching the fair use doctrine at all. For example, two competing wine producers operated in Michigan's Leelanau peninsula area, a senior producer using LEELANAU CELLARS and a junior producer using CHATEAU DE LEELANAU VINEYARD AND WINERY, for wines. Based on a likelihood-of-confusion factors analysis, the court concluded that there was no likely confusion even though both marks referred to "Leelanau." *Leelanau Wine Cellars Ltd. v. Black & Red Inc.*, 502 F.3d 504 (6th Cir. 2007).

Section 33(b)(4) also identifies the use of one's personal name in connection with one's business as a descriptive use. Some early cases seemed to establish an absolute right to the use of one's name in one's business. Such a rule might lead to some troubling results—for example, an individual who happened to have the surname "Hilton" might open a "Hilton

Hotel," confusing consumers who associated the hotel with the famous HILTON chain—although a strong bad faith rule would presumably address this behavior. Current cases reject any such absolute "right" to use one's name, but attempt to strike a balance to accommodate the legitimate desires of business owners to identify themselves with their businesses. As we observed above in the discussion of geographic marks, fair use is one among several mechanisms that might be used to strike an appropriate balance. In *L.E. Waterman Co. v. Modern Pen Co.*, 235 U.S. 88 (1914), L.E. Waterman, owner of the mark WATERMAN for pens, asserted that its competitor Modern Pen should be enjoined from using the name "A.A. Waterman" on its fountain pens, despite Modern Pen's allegation that an individual named Arthur A. Waterman had been affiliated with its business. The Supreme Court upheld a qualified injunction: Modern Pen was not absolutely enjoined from the use of the designation "Waterman," but was required to spell out the individual's first name (i.e., ARTHUR A. WATERMAN) and was also required to include a disclaimer ("not connected with the L.E. Waterman Co."). Similarly, a court is likely to use its equitable discretion to shape injunctive relief in cases in which the founder of a business sells the business and then establishes a competing business. In a leading case, *Levitt Corp. v. Levitt*, 593 F.2d 463 (2d Cir. 1979), William J. Levitt's firm developed the real estate development LEVITTOWN; Levitt thereafter sold the business and its trademark rights. Some time later, the eventual successor, Levitt Corp., objected when William J. Levitt started a new construction venture near Orlando under the name LEVITTOWN FLORIDA. The Second Circuit upheld a rather broad injunction precluding the use of the name LEVITTOWN and precluding various references to the role of William J. Levitt in the new development.

Good faith. Many courts have analyzed good faith for fair use purposes by duplicating the "intent" factor from the likelihood of confusion analysis—that is, by asking whether the alleged fair user intended to trade off the goodwill of the trademark owner. *International Stamp Art, Inc. v. United States Postal Service*, 456 F.3d 1270 (11th Cir. 2006); *EMI Catalogue P'ship v. Hill, Holiday, Connors, & Cosmopulos, Inc.*, 228 F.3d 56 (2d Cir. 2000). Courts may consider a number of factors in determining whether the evidence establishes intent to trade off the mark owner's goodwill. Where the alleged fair user displays its own marks in proximity to the challenged term, this may cut against a conclusion that the fair user intended to trade off the trademark owner's goodwill in the term. *Cosmetically Sealed Industries, Inc. v. Chesebrough-Pond's USA Co.*, 125 F.3d 28 (2d Cir. 1997). Where the evidence shows that the alleged fair user could have used a non-infringing alternative, some courts have found that this raises at least a fact issue as to good faith. *Institute for Scientific Info., Inc. v. Gordon & Breach, Science Publishers, Inc.*, 931 F.2d 1002 (3d Cir. 1991); *Sierra On-Line, Inc. v. Phoenix Software, Inc.*, 739 F.2d 1415 (9th Cir. 1984). However, proceeding to use a term despite one's knowledge that a registration exists does not alone establish bad faith. *Packman v.*

Chicago Tribune Co., 267 F.3d 628 (7th Cir. 2001). Nor does one's awareness of a registration trigger an affirmative duty to obtain a formal clearance opinion from counsel in order to satisfy the requirement of good faith. *Car-Freshner Corp. v. S.C. Johnson & Son, Inc.*, 70 F.3d 267 (2d Cir. 1995).

2. NOMINATIVE FAIR USE

In many settings, both commercial and non-commercial, one party may wish to refer to another party, or that party's products or services, by using that party's mark. For example, this book refers to marks by name on practically every page, as might an editorial writer criticizing a mark owner's products, a retailer advertising that it sells the mark owner's goods, or a competitor referring to its rivals' products in a comparative advertisement (for example, a Coca-Cola ad proclaiming that "COKE is better than PEPSI").

None of these scenarios fit neatly into the framework of descriptive fair use that we have defined above, because none involve a party who uses another's marks to describe the party's own products. Instead, the scenarios involve nominative uses—a party using another's mark to identify the other or the others' goods or services. If such uses, or some subset of such uses, are to be deemed fair uses, then it may be helpful to recognize a second form of fair use—"nominative" fair use.

Section 33(b)(4), excerpted above, does not use the phrase "nominative fair use." However, some courts have recognized the doctrine. The Ninth Circuit's opinion in *Cairns v. Franklin Mint Co.*, 292 F.3d 1139 (9th Cir. 2002) explained that "[t]he nominative fair use analysis is appropriate where a defendant has used the plaintiff's mark to describe the plaintiff's product, even if the defendant's ultimate goal is to describe his own product." The Ninth Circuit had adopted a test for nominative fair use in *New Kids on the Block v. News Am. Publ'g Inc.*, 971 F.2d 302 (9th Cir. 1992). Under the *New Kids* test, a defendant asserting nominative fair use must prove: "(1) that the product or service in question is one not readily identifiable without use of the trademark; (2) that only so much of the mark or marks is used as is reasonably necessary to identify the product or service; and (3) that the user did nothing that would, in conjunction with the mark, suggest sponsorship or endorsement by the trademark holder." In *Century 21 Real Estate Corp. v. Lendingtree, Inc.*, 425 F.3d 211 (3d Cir. 2005), the Third Circuit adopted a modified form of the *New Kids* test, requiring the defendant to prove "(1) that the use of plaintiff's mark is necessary to describe both the plaintiff's product or service and the defendant's product or service; (2) that the defendant uses only so much of the plaintiff's mark as is necessary to describe plaintiff's product; and (3) that the defendant's conduct or language reflect the true and accurate relationship between plaintiff and defendant's products or services."

The seemingly modest difference between prong (3) of the respective *New Kids* and *Century 21* tests derives from a quite significant difference among the circuits concerning the proper relationship between likelihood of confusion and the nominative fair use doctrine. In a series of cases, the Ninth Circuit held that its *New Kids* test for nominative fair use "replaces" the likelihood of confusion test. *See, e.g., Playboy Ent. v. Welles*, 279 F.3d 796 (9th Cir. 2002). Some of these cases also stood for the proposition that the defendant bears the burden of establishing nominative fair use. *See, e.g., Brother Records, Inc. v. Jardine*, 318 F.3d 900 (9th Cir. 2003). However, the cases assigning the burden of proof preceded the Supreme Court's *KP Permanent* decision. Reviewing the burden of proof issue in a nominative fair use case after *KP Permanent*, the Ninth Circuit decided that *KP Permanent* had effectively overruled cases that assigned the burden of proving nominative fair use to the defendant. *Toyota Motor Sales U.S.A., Inc. v. Tabari*, 610 F.3d 1171 (9th Cir. 2010). According to *Tabari*, a defendant seeking to invoke nominative fair use need only show that it used the mark to refer to a trademarked product or service. The burden then shifts to the mark owner to show likelihood of confusion under the *New Kids* test—essentially a requirement that the mark owner show that the defendant's use is *not* nominative. In *Tabari*, the defendant had used plaintiff's LEXUS marks in domain names, such as buy-a-lexus.com, to promote an auto brokerage business in which the defendant contacted authorized LEXUS automobile dealers to arrange for auto purchases for customers. The district court had enjoined the defendant from using any domain name that included "Lexus." The Ninth Circuit vacated and remanded. The Ninth Circuit reasoned that there were many domain names that would include the term "Lexus" but would still pass muster under the test for nominative fair use, including some domain names that expressly disavowed a connection with Toyota (such as we-are-definitely-not-lexus.com), but not limited to such domain names. Accordingly, the use of buy-a-lexus.com might constitute nominative fair use, and the court remanded for a further assessment under the *New Kids* test.

In *Century 21*, the Third Circuit adopted a different approach, one that also attempts to take account of *KP Permanent*. According to the Third Circuit, the traditional likelihood-of-confusion factors test does not adequately accommodate cases in which the allegedly infringing use is arguably a nominative one, because some of the confusion factors do not seem apt in such a context. For example, the similarity of marks factor would invariably favor the plaintiff in a case of nominative use because the defendant would ordinarily be using the plaintiff's identical mark; the *Century 21* court considered this problematic. Consequently, the court advocated a modified likelihood-of-confusion test designed particularly for nominative uses, in which likelihood of confusion is analyzed on the basis of only four factors: (1) consumer care; (2) "the length of time the defendant has used the mark without evidence of actual confusion" (3) defendant's intent; and (4) actual confusion. Under the court's approach, if the plaintiff succeeds in meeting the burden of demonstrating likelihood of confusion under the modified test, the defendant must then take up the burden of showing that the use is a nominative fair use. One may wonder whether the court's modified factors test unduly privileges intent evidence, which may play a lesser role in full-fledged factors tests for confusion.

In contrast with the Ninth and Third Circuits, the Sixth Circuit seems to have rejected the nominative fair use doctrine altogether. Under the Sixth Circuit's approach, courts should apparently apply the standard likelihood of confusion test. *PACCAR Inc. v. Telescan Techs., L.L.C.*, 319 F.3d 243 (6th Cir. 2003). Uses that are characterized as nominative fair uses under tests from other circuits might be deemed nonconfusing under the Sixth Circuit's test, but it is also possible that the different tests would produce different outcomes, with the Sixth Circuit's test being more likely to result in liability for the defendant. Because the Supreme Court's *KP Permanent* opinion seems supportive of fair use generally, the Sixth Circuit's approach to nominative fair use may need to be reexamined.

Yet another view of nominative fair use appears to prevail in the Second Circuit. In *International Information Systems Security Certification Consortium, Inc. v. Security University, LLC*, 823 F.3d 153 (2d Cir. 2016), the court concluded that the text of Lanham Act Section 33(b)(4) does not support an affirmative defense of nominative fair use. However, this refusal to recognize nominative fair use *as an affirmative defense* did not rule out consideration of nominative fair use as part of the likelihood-of-confusion analysis. According to the court, in nominative use cases, district courts should supplement their likelihood of confusion factors analyses with some consideration of nominative fair use factors, drawing those factors from the Ninth and Third Circuits' tests. The court also specified that when analyzing the third nominative fair use factor (whether the user did anything that might trigger confusion), courts should not restrict themselves to considering source confusion, but should also consider arguments pertaining to affiliation, sponsorship, or endorsement.

As mentioned above, one common example of a nominative fair use is comparative advertising—a statement in a defendant's advertisement that uses a plaintiff's mark to reference the plaintiff's product, in order to compare it with the defendant's product. For many years, courts protected these comparative statements against claims of trademark liability, but without necessarily invoking nominative fair use or even fair use at all. Thus, some authorities speak of a "comparative advertising" defense, but the cases can be understood as fair use cases, and they may perhaps fit best into the framework of nominative fair use. In a leading early case, Justice Holmes concluded that the defendant should be permitted to advertise that its "bitter water" was an attempt to reproduce plaintiff's HUNYADI JANOS spring water. *Saxlehner v. Wagner*, 216 U.S. 375 (1910). Justice Holmes reasoned that defendants had "a right to tell the public what they are doing, and to get whatever share they can in the popularity of the water by advertising that they are trying to make the same article, and that they think they can succeed." Similarly, in *Smith v. Chanel, Inc.*, 402 F.2d 562 (9th Cir. 1968), the court permitted defendant's comparative advertisements containing references to plaintiff's CHANEL NO. 5 mark for perfume. For example, one advertisement included the statement "We dare you to try to detect any difference between Chanel #5 ($25.00) and [defendant's product] Ta'Ron's 2d Chance ($7.00)." Without the ability to communicate this truthful comparison, the defendant's "right to copy" plaintiff's unpatented perfume formula might be jeopardized, the court asserted. Of course, if the defendant's comparative statements were false, that would raise a separate issue of defendant's potential liability for false advertising under Section 43(a)(1)(B), discussed in Chapter 10.

3. FAIR USE DEFENSES TO DILUTION

The policies that support the recognition of a fair use defense to infringement apply with equal (or perhaps even greater) force in the context of dilution. Recall from Chapter 8 that dilution is a type of harm that is thought to be caused as a result of "blurring" or "tarnishment" of a protected mark, as those concepts are now defined in Lanham Act Section 43(c). The current version of Section 43(c), amended in 2006, contains the following provision on fair use and related concepts:

> **(3)** Exclusions. The following shall not be actionable as dilution by blurring or dilution by tarnishment under this subsection:
>
> **(A)** Any fair use, including a nominative or descriptive fair use, or facilitation of such fair use, of a famous mark by another person other

than as a designation of source for the person's own goods or services, including use in connection with—

(i) advertising or promotion that permits consumers to compare goods or services; or

(ii) identifying and parodying, criticizing, or commenting upon the famous mark owner or the goods or services of the famous mark owner.

Unlike Section 33(b)(4), the dilution provision recited above explicitly references descriptive and nominative fair use. Note that the provision also extends the exclusion to those who allegedly facilitate another's fair use. However, the provision also seems to add an important qualifier: the alleged descriptive or nominative fair use must be a use "other than as a designation of source for the person's own goods or services." As we have seen, Section 33(b)(4) contains the phrase "otherwise than as a mark," but courts have not provided any definitive construction of that phrase, much less explored in any depth the similarities and differences between it and the language of Section 43(c)(3).

In one leading case, the Fourth Circuit confronted the tasks of determining (1) whether a defendant's alleged parodic fair use was in fact a use as a designation of source for the defendant's own products, and (2) if so, whether this meant that the defendant could not claim the fair use exclusion to dilution. *Louis Vuitton Malletier S.A. v. Haute Diggity Dog, LLC*, 507 F.3d 252 (4th Cir. 2007).

There, the plaintiff used the mark LOUIS VUITTON and various logos on expensive handbags, and the defendant sold dog chew toys, some resembling small handbags, under the name CHEWY VUITON. The court concluded that the defendant was using CHEWY VUITON as a designation of source for its own products (equating this to use "as a trademark"), and then decided that the statute's "plain language" compelled the court to conclude that the defendant therefore could not rely on the fair use defense. However, the court proceeded to conclude that the parodic nature of the defendant's use was still relevant, and ultimately supported the determination of no liability for dilution by blurring. (In Section C below, other aspects of the decision relevant to the parody claim concerning both confusion and dilution are analyzed.) By contrast, in *Louis Vuitton Malletier, S.A. v. My Other Bag, Inc.*, 156 F. Supp. 3d 425 (S.D.N.Y. 2016), the defendant's use of cartoon-like renditions of plaintiff's trade dress on one side of a canvas tote bag, accompanied by the phrase "My Other Bag." on the other side of the tote bag, fell within the Section 43(c) parody exclusion, the court ruled. The defendant was not using the plaintiff's trade dress as a designation of source for its tote bag. Rather, the whole point of the defendant's parody was to suggest that the tote bag owner's other bag was a Louis Vuitton bag, not that the tote bag was affiliated with Louis Vuittion. *Id.* at 438.

The Fourth Circuit applied the Section 43(c) exclusions again in *Radiance Foundation, Inc. v. National Assoc. for the Advancement of Colored*

People, 786 F.3d 316 (4th Cir. 2015). The dispute arose when the Radiance Foundation's websites made a reference to the "National Association for the Abortion of Colored People" in the title of an article criticizing the NAACP's position on abortion. The district court had concluded that Radiance's uses had diluted the NAACP's marks by tarnishment. The Fourth Circuit reversed, ruling that the uses constituted nominative fair uses undertaken for the purpose of criticizing or commenting on the famous mark owner. The uses thus clearly fell within Section 43(c)(3)(A)(ii), according to the court. The uses also appeared to fall within the Section 43(c)(C) exclusion for non-commercial use, the court added.

Section 43(c)(3) provides a fair use *defense* to dilution. Once a trademark owner establishes a prima facie case of dilution by blurring or tarnishment, the burden is on the defendant to establish the elements of Section 43(c)(3). *Rosetta Stone Ltd. v. Google, Inc.*, 676 F.3d 144 (4th Cir. 2012). It was error for a district court to require the mark owner to show, as part of the *prima facie* case of dilution, that the defendant was using the mark owner's mark as a source identifier for the defendant's own products or services.

As noted in Chapter 8, a dilution allegation may arise under Section 2(f), but the Section 43(c)(3)(A) defense should have no application in that context. For example, suppose that Acme, a maker of hair care products seeks to register NIKE in connection with those goods, and Nike, the athletic goods manufacturer, opposes the registration on the grounds that Acme's use of NIKE for hair care products would be likely to dilute Nike's marks. Based simply on the fact that Acme is seeking to register the mark, Acme should be precluded from claiming that it is using NIKE "other than as a designation of source for [Acme's] own goods or services" under Section 43(c)(3)(A). *Research in Motion, Ltd. v. Defining Presence Marketing Group, Inc.*, 2012 WL 893481 (TTAB 2012) (applicant seeking to register CRACKBERRY for a website concerning mobile phone services could not claim entitlement to Section 43(c)(3)(A) in response to an opposition petition filed by owners of the BLACKBERRY mark for mobile phones).

B. USE OF ANOTHER'S TRADEMARK ON GENUINE GOODS

Suppose that a firm B is in the business of purchasing and reselling goods that were originally put on the market by firm A, and bear firm A's trademark. There are three common scenarios in which B's resale activity could raise issues under the trademark laws. First, where the goods are new, but B has altered them, or refurbished the goods, B may incur trademark liability under some circumstances. Second, where the goods are used, and B has purportedly refurbished them, B may be liable in some cases. Third, if the goods were originally manufactured for overseas markets, and B has imported them for resale without A's authorization, B may risk either trademark liability or trademark-related penalties imposed under the authority of customs officials. We explore all three scenarios in the following paragraphs.

Repackaged new goods. A leading decision on the trademark liability of a reseller who has altered and resold genuine trademarked goods is *Prestonettes, Inc. v. Coty*, 264 U.S. 359 (1924). Prestonettes had repackaged and resold genuine Coty perfumes and powders (in the case of the powders, also adding a binder and subjecting the powders to pressure). The labels on the repackaged products indicated that Prestonettes was not affiliated with Coty, that Prestonettes had independently repackaged the product, and also truthfully identified the constituents of the products, naming Coty as the original source. Justice Holmes concluded that Prestonettes had not infringed Coty's trademarks, because Prestonettes' mere "collateral" references to Coty's trademarks were truthful statements that would not have tended to deceive consumers.

The rule from *Prestonettes* bears some resemblance to the general principle in U.S. intellectual property law that the authorized, unconditional "first sale" of an intellectual-property-protected product "exhausts" the seller's intellectual property rights in the sold product, such that the buyer can resell the product without the intellectual property owner's permission. Some modern courts applying *Prestonettes* to resale cases frame their analyses in terms of the "first sale" doctrine. *Brilliance Audio, Inc. v. Haights Cross Comm'ns, Inc.*, 474 F.3d 365 (6th Cir. 2007). In other areas of intellectual property, courts sometimes use the term "exhaustion" doctrine as a synonym for the first sale doctrine.

Courts have identified two related situations in which the *Prestonettes* first sale rule does not shield the defendant from liability. First, some courts have recognized a "quality control" exception to the *Prestonettes* rule. The argument in favor of an exception is that even where a reseller labels the resold goods with a *Prestonettes*-style label, there may still be a danger of deceiving consumers if the reseller has failed to conform to the original trademark owner's quality control standards, especially where the reseller's failure gives rise to a potential defect that the consumer could not readily detect. For example, a petroleum reseller could not invoke the protection of the *Prestonettes* rule for reselling oil under Shell Oil trademarks where the reseller had failed to conform to Shell's tank and pump cleaning requirements, a failure that consumers would have been unable to detect. *Shell Oil Co. v. Commercial Petroleum, Inc.*, 928 F.2d 104 (4th Cir. 1991). The court here said that the first sale doctrine only applies to the sale of "genuine" trademarked goods, and goods that do not comport with the trademark owner's quality controls are not genuine. By contrast, in another first sale case, defendant Costco was allowed to repackage plaintiff's PRECIOUS MOMENTS porcelain figures for resale in clear, blister-pack packaging, even though Costco's packaging might inadequately protect the figurines from breaking or chipping. On these facts, a *Prestonettes*-style label would adequately inform consumers that Costco was the likely source of the chipping, and so there was no need to invoke a quality-control exception to the *Prestonettes* rule. *Enesco v. Price/Costco Inc.*, 146 F.3d 1083 (9th Cir. 1998).

In a second, related situation, courts have also carved out an exception from the *Prestonettes* rule: where the alleged infringer resells trademarked goods which are "materially different" from the original goods sold by the trademark owner. *See, e.g., Davidoff & CIE, SA v. PLD Int'l Corp.*, 263 F.3d 1297 (11th Cir. 2001) (concluding that the resold goods were materially different because the reseller had removed batch code information from the originally-sold bottles). The "material differences" test arises in the related context of trademark liability for transactions involving grey market goods, described later in this Section.

Reconditioned goods. While the cases discussed thus far deal with the resale of new goods, a related line of cases concerns the resale of used goods. In the leading case, *Champion Spark Plug Co. v. Sanders*, 331 U.S. 125 (1947), Sanders collected, reconditioned, and resold used spark plugs bearing the plaintiff's CHAMPION mark. Sanders had stamped the used plugs with the word "Renewed" (though not always legibly), and the packaging included some references to the fact that the plugs had been "renewed." The lower courts found infringement but split on the remedy. The trial court had ordered Sanders to remove the CHAMPION mark from the used plugs, but the Court of Appeals had eliminated that part of the order. The Supreme

Court agreed with the Court of Appeals on the point. According to Justice Douglas, the rule from *Prestonettes* merely required the second-hand dealer to give full disclosure to customers, in such a way that the original manufacturer was not identified with the "inferior qualities" of the product that may have resulted from the reconditioning or wear and tear. Customers expected second-hand articles to be inferior in some respects, especially when the articles were sold at a discount. Under those circumstances, assuming that the articles were clearly marked as "used" or "repaired," customers would not likely be misled into thinking that they were purchasing new items. Justice Douglas acknowledged that this approach resulted in the second-hand dealer getting some advantage from the mark, but did not seem to find this troubling.

On the other hand, Justice Douglas did note that in some cases, the reconditioning might be so "extensive" or "basic" that merely disclosing that the article was reconditioned might be inadequate to escape infringement. The reconditioning of the spark plugs did not alter important design features such as the size of the threads. It did affect the plug's thermal characteristics, but inferiority in that regard would have come as no surprise to consumers.

Courts applying *Champion* have frequently explored this question of the allowable degree of alteration of the resold goods. The Ninth Circuit has borrowed from patent law's "permissible repair" doctrine to develop a list of factors to consider in determining whether alterations were overly extensive under the *Champion* rule. *Karl Storz Endoscopy-America, Inc. v. Surgical Technologies, Inc.*, 285 F.3d 848 (9th Cir. 2002) (identifying as factors "the nature and extent of the alterations, the nature of the device and how it is designed (whether some components have a shorter useful life than the whole), whether a market has developed for service and spare parts . . . and, most importantly, whether end users of the product are likely to be misled as to the party responsible for the composition of the product."). In *Nitro Leisure Prods., L.L.C. v. Acushnet Co.*, 341 F.3d 1356 (Fed. Cir. 2003), the Federal Circuit concluded, over a dissent, that a reseller of refurbished, used golf balls had remained within the bounds of allowable alteration. Nitro's refurbishing process involved retrieving scuffed ACUSHNET golf balls, removing the base coat of paint, the clear coat, and the trademark and model markings, then repainting the balls, adding a clear coat, and re-applying the ACUSHNET trademark. Nitro also stamped the balls with a legend indicating that the balls were used and had been refurbished by firms associated with Nitro, and included additional labels in its packaging that alluded to the refurbishing steps and disclaimed any connection with the original trademark owner. On the contrary, in *Rolex Watch, U.S.A., Inc. v. Michel*, 179 F.3d 704 (9th Cir. 1999), where the reseller refurbished the Rolex watch dial (sometimes adding diamonds), made changes to the watch bracelet, and sometimes replaced the watch bezel, these alterations were so extensive that it would have been deceptive to consumers to allow the reseller to sell the watches under the ROLEX trademark.

Grey market goods. The rules discussed above apply where the defendant's resale activities occurred within the United States. Another line of cases—resting on similar principles of first sale and its qualifications—applies where the defendant's activities cross national boundaries. A canonical example is the distribution of so-called grey market goods (also called "parallel imports"). A grey market good is a genuine trademarked good that is sold outside its authorized distribution channels. For example, suppose that a U.S. trademark owner manufacturers a consumer product (say, shampoo) for the overseas market, and then a buyer purchases the trademarked products overseas and ships them into the U.S. for resale. The products have been the subject of an authorized sale, which counsels in favor of applying the first sale doctrine, but there may also be a danger of consumer deception and erosion of the U.S. mark owner's goodwill if, for example, the products destined for the overseas market differ from those marketed domestically (say, because manufacturer formulates the shampoo a bit differently in different countries). Note that these considerations apply in the same way whether the goods are actually manufactured overseas, or are manufactured domestically but designed for an overseas market. *See Bourdeau Bros., Inc. v. I.T.C.*, 444 F.3d 1317 (Fed. Cir. 2006) (involving goods that were manufactured in the U.S. but sold overseas).

Whether distributors of grey market goods should be liable under domestic intellectual property laws has been the subject of intense debate in international intellectual property negotiations, perhaps because the issue may also be viewed as implicating the principle that trademarks are traditionally territorial. (*See* Chapter 6 for a discussion.) The grey market goods issue is particularly sensitive in Europe, where encouraging the free movement of goods across national boundaries to facilitate Community-wide competition is a central tenet of the new European economy. Reflecting the sensitivity of the issue, the TRIPS agreement does not establish any mandate for rules on exhaustion in any area of intellectual property law. TRIPS Article 6 expressly permits WTO member states to adopt a rule of international exhaustion (i.e., an authorized sale of an intellectual property-protected good anywhere in the world exhausts domestic intellectual property rights) or national exhaustion (i.e., only an authorized domestic sale exhausts domestic intellectual property rights).

United States trademark law initially embraced international exhaustion, but has since moved to a regime of national exhaustion rules. At the turn of the twentieth century, U.S. courts had adopted a notion of the universality of trademarks, meaning that if the mark owner had authorized the placement of its mark on genuine goods, the trademark was legitimate universally, irrespective of where the goods were bought or sold. It followed that the sale of marked goods overseas exhausted the mark owner's rights just as a domestic sale would exhaust them. However, in *A. Bourjois & Co., Inc. v. Katzel*, 260 U.S. 689 (1923), the Court concluded that the domestic trademark owner's rights had not been exhausted by the sale overseas of genuine goods. Some commentators have read *Bourjois* as a rejection of the principle of universality in favor of the principle of territoriality—i.e., the principle that trademark rights have an independent, separate existence in each country. But it was not clear that *Bourjois* embraced a strict notion of territoriality, under which rights would never be exhausted by an overseas sale even if the products sold overseas were identical to the domestically marketed products. *Bourjois* involved trademarked face powder, and there were differences (color, for example) between the powder marketed domestically and the grey market powder imported by the defendant. That fact seemed significant to the Court, and provides a rationale for limiting the holding of *Bourjois* to cases in which the imported products differ materially from the domestic products.

The modern U.S. approach to regulating the distribution of trademarked grey goods accepts the principle of territoriality but diverges from it in some circumstances. *See generally American Circuit Breaker Corp. v. Oregon Breakers Inc.*, 406 F.3d 577 (9th Cir. 2005). Litigation over grey goods arises either in the context of an infringement action, or as a matter of Customs enforcement. Concurrently with the Court's decision in *Bourjois*, Congress passed tariff legislation, now codified at 19 U.S.C. § 1526(a), which prohibits the importing "into the United States any merchandise of foreign manufacture if such merchandise ... bears a trademark owned by a citizen of, or by a corporation or association created or organized within, the United States, and registered in the Patent and Trademark Office by a person domiciled in the United States ..., unless written consent of the owner of such trademark is produced at the time of making entry."

In addition, Lanham Act Section 42 authorizes U.S. Customs to deny entry to goods bearing marks which "copy or simulate" a registered trademark, or bearing marks "calculated to induce the public to believe that the article is manufactured in the United States" or in a location other than its genuine location of manufacture. Accordingly, modern grey market goods cases involving trademarked goods typically arise when Customs denies entry to an importer's goods under either the relevant Tariff Act or Lanham Act provision, and litigation ensues over whether the goods are prohibited grey market goods, or, by contrast, goods as to which the mark owner's rights have been exhausted. The analysis in such cases centers around *Bourjois* and its progeny, and has primarily focused on two issues: the "affiliate exception" and the test for "material differences," though the latter issue dominates today.

Starting in the 1930s, the Customs Service had adopted an "affiliate exception" to both the Lanham Act provision (now Section 42) and the Tariff Act provision (now 15 U.S.C. § 1526). Under the Customs approach, if the overseas sale originated from a firm affiliated with the U.S. mark owner, then the overseas sale should exhaust rights because there was a reasonable likelihood that the affiliate was adhering to the U.S. mark owner's quality control standards. In response to a challenge that the Custom Service's regulation was inconsistent with 15 U.S.C. § 1526, the Supreme Court upheld the regulation but did not reach the question of whether the regulation also comported with Lanham Act § 42. *K Mart Corp. v. Cartier, Inc.*, 486 U.S. 281 (1988). In *Lever Brothers Co. v. United States of America*, 877 F.2d 101 (D.C. Cir. 1989), *later proceeding* 981 F.2d 1330 (D.C. Cir. 1993), the court struck down the affiliate exception, holding that Section 42 "bars foreign goods bearing a trademark identical to a valid US trademark but physically different, regardless of the trademark's genuine character abroad or affiliation between the producing firms," because if physically different goods were marketed under identical trademarks, confusion could result.

The *Lever Bros.* approach to Section 42 has been accepted, and, accordingly, the Section 42 grey market goods cases have centered around whether the grey market goods were materially different from the corresponding domestic goods. As the Federal Circuit has described it, "[t]he courts have applied a low threshold of materiality, requiring no more than showing that consumers would be likely to consider the differences between the foreign and domestic products to be significant when purchasing the product, for such differences would suffice to erode the goodwill of the domestic source." *Gamut Trading Co. v. U.S.I.T.C.*, 200 F.3d 775 (Fed. Cir. 1999). Materiality is most easily satisfied where the imported products differ significantly in their physical attributes from the corresponding trademarked domestic products, but a showing of physical differences is not required. *SKF USA Inc. v. I.T.C.*, 423 F.3d 1307 (Fed. Cir. 2005). Differences in labeling, and in the availability of repair services and parts, have been deemed material. In *Gamut Trading Co.,* instructional and warning labels on grey market tractors were in Japanese rather than English, and repair services and parts for grey market tractors could not be obtained through authorized U.S. dealers. These differences were material—though it should be noted that the grey market tractors also differed structurally from the U.S. models in significant ways. For example, the imported tractors at issue had weaker front and rear axles, and a number of other weaker structural parts, than the corresponding U.S. models. In *Original Appalachian Artworks v. Granada Electronics*, 816 F.2d 68 (2d Cir. 1987), grey market "Cabbage Patch" dolls materially differed from those authorized for the domestic market because the instructions and adoption papers for the grey market dolls were in Spanish.

Differences that are readily apparent to consumers may nevertheless be material under this test on the rationale that the existences of the differences may still erode the mark owner's goodwill, even if they do not deceive consumers. *Martin's Herend Imports, Inc. v. Diamond & Gem Trading USA, Co.*, 112 F.3d 1296 (5th Cir. 1997) (grey market "Herend" porcelain figures materially differed in color, pattern and shape from corresponding U.S. models). In addition, courts have applied the material differences test whether the grey market goods are new or used, reasoning that consumer deception and the potential erosion of the mark owner's goodwill are the ultimate considerations to be assessed in either case. *Gamut Trading Co. v. U.S.I.T.C.*, 200 F.3d 775 (Fed. Cir. 1999); *Red Baron-Franklin Park, Inc. v. Taito Corp.*, 883 F.2d 275 (4th Cir. 1989).

C. USE OF ANOTHER'S TRADEMARK IN PARODY, ART, OR SPEECH

Trademarks have become so prominent in the cultural environment that it is no surprise to discover them being used in public discourse of all kinds, as well as in artistic works. Because these usages are frequently unauthorized, and often may portray marks in an unflattering or controversial context, trademark owners may feel compelled to assert Lanham Act violations in an effort to limit or enjoin such uses. While doctrines such as nominative fair use (discussed *supra* in A) may provide some measure of protection for these uses, courts have not relied solely on the fair use doctrine in setting the limits on Lanham Act liability. Instead, courts have formulated a variety of other approaches in an attempt to strike an appropriate balance between the public interest in upholding First Amendment guarantees of free expression and the public interest in avoiding consumer confusion.

Traditionally, speech interests have come into issue in trademark cases in which a trademark owner sues an unauthorized user and the user claims that the use should be shielded from liability as a parody or other artistic use. There is no universally accepted definition of parody for purposes of trademark law, but in general, a parody of a trademark is one that evokes the original mark while simultaneously conveying that it is in fact not the original mark. That is, a parody communicates both the "idealized image" associated with the original mark and an irreverent or mocking representation of that idealized image for purposes of humor or social commentary. *Louis Vuitton Malletier S.A. v. Haute Diggity Dog, L.L.C.*, 507 F.3d 252 (4th Cir. 2007). Courts in trademark cases sometimes also refer to the Supreme Court's characterization of parody in the copyright context, in *Campbell v. Acuff-Rose Music, Inc.*, 510 U.S. 569 (1994), in which the Court emphasizes that parody targets the original for comment and ridicule, and hence must borrow from the original.

Although a substantial body of caselaw exists, courts have recognized that "[t]here is no simple, mechanical rule by which courts can determine when a potentially confusing parody falls within the First Amendment's protective reach." *Anheuser-Busch, Inc. v. Balducci Publications*, 28 F.3d 769 (8th Cir. 1994). Several general approaches can be seen in the cases.

One approach treats parody as a threshold inquiry independent of the likelihood of confusion (or dilution) inquiries. Whether the defendant's use is determined to be a successful parody has a significant influence on the likelihood of confusion (or dilution) analysis. For example, in *Louis Vuitton*, defendant sold dog chew toys under the name

CHEWY VUITON, using logos and trade dress that resembled those of Louis Vuitton's handbags. The court concluded that the defendant's use was a successful parody: defendant was evoking the upscale, elegant image associated with the Louis Vuitton marks, incorporated into an inexpensive product made to be chewed by a dog—thus achieving the sort of juxtaposition of contrary images that characterizes parody. Having so concluded, the court then turned to the confusion factors analysis, which depended heavily on the conclusion that the defendant's use was a successful parody. Plaintiff's marks were strong, but in the context of a successful parody, mark strength merely made it more likely that consumers would recognize defendant's use as parodic—so mark strength did not cut in favor of confusion. As to the similarity of marks, the court reasoned that since it had already determined that defendant's use was a successful parody, it had already impliedly concluded that the defendant's marks were only similar enough to the plaintiff's to enable consumers to recognize the target of the parody, yet were simultaneously dissimilar enough to enable consumers to recognize that defendant was distinguishing itself from plaintiff. As to the defendant's intent, since the court had already determined that defendant's use was a successful parody, the court had already absolved defendant of any bad intent.

The *Louis Vuitton* court proceeded similarly in its analysis of the likelihood of dilution by blurring. That is, the threshold determination of successful parody significantly affected the blurring factors analysis, in numerous ways: (1) it suggested a negative answer to the overall question of whether the defendant's use was likely to impair the mark's distinctiveness; (2) it indicated that factor (v)—defendant's intent to create an association, and factor (vi)—actual association—cut in defendant's favor; (3) it indicated that factors (i), (ii), and (iv) (the degree of similarity between the two marks, the degree of distinctiveness of the famous mark, and its recognizability) all favored defendant. As to these last factors, the court went so far as to suggest that "by making the famous mark an object of the parody, a successful parody might actually enhance the famous mark's distinctiveness by making it an icon." Under the *Louis Vuitton* approach, it would seem that the threshold determination of parody largely dictates the outcome of the remaining confusion and dilution analyses, at least when that determination is that defendant's use is a successful parody.

The Fourth Circuit advocated the use of an additional threshold analysis for dealing with expressive uses in *Radiance Foundation, Inc. v. National Assoc. for the Advancement of Colored People*, 786 F.3d 316 (4th Cir. 2015). In particular, the court invoked the requirement from Lanham Act Section 32 (largely reiterated in Section 43(a)) that the alleged infringer's use be "in connection with the sale, offering for sale, distribution, or advertising" of goods or services. According to the court, this language did not merely restate the jurisdictional requirement that the defendant's use be "in commerce." Instead, the language provided a threshold "commercial use" requirement that ought to be informed by First Amendment commercial speech doctrine. That doctrine calls for courts to consider whether speech "does no more than propose a commercial transaction," which might entail inquiring into whether the speech is an advertisement, whether the speech references a particular good or service, and whether the speaker has demonstrated an economic motivation for the speech. *United States v. United Foods, Inc.*, 533 U.S. 405 (2001); *Bolger v. Youngs Drug Prods. Corp.*, 463 U.S. 60 (1983). Where the alleged infringer in a trademark matter was using the mark as a source identifier for its own goods or services, the "in connection with" requirement would clearly be met, the court suggested.

Applying these concepts to the Radiance Foundation's use of the NAACP marks, the court could find no sufficient nexus between Radiance's uses and any goods or services that Radiance provided. While Radiance was an advocacy organization that solicited donations, these fundraising activities were not tied closely enough to the particular uses being challenged.

Another approach (the "confusion" approach) includes no explicit threshold determination of parody, but instead treats the existence of a parody as a matter to be determined within the trademark owner's likelihood of confusion (or dilution) case. In *Elvis Presley Ent., Inc. v. Capece*, 141 F.3d 188 (5th Cir. 1998) (denying a claim of parody made on behalf of an Elvis-themed bar), the court ruled that "parody is not a defense to trademark infringement, but rather another factor to be considered, which weighs against a finding of a likelihood of confusion." In *Lyons Partnership v. Giannoulas*, 179 F.3d 384 (5th Cir. 1999) (upholding a claim of parody brought on behalf of the "San Diego Chicken" character in response to a suit brought by the owners of trademark rights in the BARNEY the dinosaur character), the court clarified that its rule from *Elvis* meant that parody was to be blended together with an analysis of the confusion factors as a whole; it did not mean that parody was to be analyzed in isolation as a separate element. As the *Louis Vuitton* opinion illustrates, parody may affect many of the confusion factors, particularly the intent factor. At bottom, although courts dutifully recite the confusion factors in such cases, it appears that some courts simply doubt that typical parodic or artistic uses are likely to result in consumer confusion. *See, e.g., Davis v. Walt Disney Co.*, 430 F.3d 901 (8th Cir. 2005) (involving the use of a trademark in connection with a fanciful villain in a Disney movie).

Other approaches treat parody (or related artistic or other expressive uses) as a defense that turns on an interest-balancing analysis. Prominent among these approaches is the "artistic relevance" test from *Rogers v. Grimaldi*, 875 F.2d 994 (2d Cir. 1989). There, defendant had produced a movie entitled "Fred and Ginger," and the actress Ginger Rogers sued under the Lanham Act. The court concluded that the use of the title ordinarily would not violate the Lanham Act. If the title had no "artistic relevance" to the underlying work, or, if the title did have "artistic relevance" but explicitly mislead consumers as to the source or content of the work, then the Lanham Act might be violated. In two cases involving Mattel's BARBIE mark for dolls, the Ninth Circuit applied the artistic relevance test to shield unauthorized artistic uses of the plaintiff's mark (*Mattel, Inc. v. MCA Records*, 296 F.3d 894 (9th Cir. 2002) (use of the phrase "Barbie Girl" as the title of an allegedly parodic song); *Mattel, Inc. v. Walking Mountain Prods.*, 353 F.3d 792 (9th Cir. 2003) (use of "Barbie" in titles of photographs depicting BARBIE dolls in various absurd and suggestive positions)). In another case, the Ninth Circuit emphasized that the level of artistic relevance must merely be "above zero" in order for a defendant to secure the protection of the *Rogers v. Grimaldi* test. *E.S.S. Ent. 2000, Inc. v. Rock Star Videos, Inc.*, 547 F.3d 1095 (9th Cir. 2008). In *E.S.S.*, a video game maker had depicted a strip club in its video game product, and, in doing so, had used marks and trade dress that were strongly reminiscent of plaintiff's marks and trade dress from its actual strip club. Although the video game was not "about" the strip club, the strip club still had some artistic relevance to video game maker's objective of recreating scenes that reminded the video game player of East Los Angeles. This sufficed under the first prong of the *Rogers* test. Because the video game also did not explicitly mislead as to the source or content of the work (no reasonable consumer would have thought that the strip club operator was affiliated with the video game maker or had been responsible for producing the video game), the second prong of the *Rogers* test was also satisfied.

The defendant in *The University of Alabama Bd. of Trustees v. New Life Art, Inc.*, 683 F.3d 1266 (11th Cir. 2012) also satisfied the *Rogers v. Grimaldi* test. An artist, Moore, painted scenes depicting the University of Alabama's football players, necessarily including the university's uniforms, helmet designs, and colors. The court concluded that the use of the University's marks and trade dress in Moore's paintings themselves (and prints and calendars) was artistically relevant to Moore's objective of depicting famous scenes from Alabama football history. In addition, the court determined that Moore had never explicitly marketed any items as being endorsed or sponsored by the University. Even if some consumers drew the incorrect inference that the University had some involvement with Moore's paintings, the interest in facilitating artistic expression outweighed concerns about confusion, and this sufficed for the second prong of the *Rogers* analysis.

In *Parks v. LaFace Records,* 329 F.3d 437 (6th Cir. 2003), the court rejected both the confusion test (as being insufficiently speech-protective) and the alternative avenues test (as being too likely to entangle the court in artistic judgments about titles of creative works), and applied the artistic relevance test. Under that test, the court found a triable issue of fact where defendant (the rap group Outkast) used "Rosa Parks" as the title for a rap song whose lyrics did not mention Rosa Parks or the civil rights movement, and included only a brief, oblique reference to people moving "to the back of the bus." In *ETW Corp. v. Jireh Publ'g, Inc.*, 332 F.3d 915 (6th

Cir. 2003), involving a painting depicting golfer Tiger Woods, the court adopted a similar analysis.

While most of the cases above deal with alleged parodic or artistic uses of others' trademarks, trademarks may also be employed for many other expressive purposes that may facilitate important speech interests even if those uses are not undertaken as parodies in the strictest sense, or as matters of artistic expression. For example, a group's use of the term GAY OLYMPICS, at issue in *San Francisco Arts & Athletics, Inc. v. United States Olympic Committee,* 483 U.S. 522 (1987), may constitute a form of political speech that must be analyzed by balancing relevant interests in accord with general First Amendment jurisprudence. *See id.* (upholding injunction in a case involving special legislation affording protection to Olympics-related terms without a need for a showing of confusion).

CHAPTER 10
FALSE ADVERTISING

This chapter deals with actions for false advertising under the Lanham Act. The false advertising cause of action may apply to a wide variety of false representations in advertising, not limited to false representations involving trademarks. Accordingly, false advertising is a cause of action distinct from the trademark infringement or false designation of origin causes of action discussed in Chapter 7, though false advertising is closely related to those theories.

This chapter traces the evolution of false advertising claims (Section A); identifies and discusses two types of threshold issues in modern false advertising cases (Section B); analyzes the elements of a modern false advertising claim (Section C); and briefly discusses remedies for false advertising (Section D).

A. THE EVOLUTION OF SECTION 43(a) FALSE ADVERTISING CLAIMS

1. PREDECESSORS TO THE MODERN SECTION 43(a) FALSE ADVERTISING CLAIM

At common law, courts recognized a tort of false advertising. As articulated in the Restatement (First) of Torts § 761 (1939), the false advertising tort was quite narrow compared to its modern incarnation. It applied only to an advertiser's false representations about the ingredients or qualities of its *own* goods—

false statements about a competitor's goods were not actionable. Moreover, it was premised on a showing that the advertiser's false representations had caused economic loss by actually diverting trade away from the competitor. Some courts recognized a "single source" prerequisite, holding that a competitor could not possibly show that false advertising actually diverted trade if there were multiple alternative sources for the falsely advertised product.

When the Lanham Act came into being in 1946, it did not contain an explicit false advertising provision. However, it did contain Section 43(a), prompting claims that false advertisements constituted one type of false representation that Section 43(a) prohibited. Initially, some courts construed Section 43(a) so narrowly as to preclude it from serving as a meaningful vehicle for false advertising claims, holding that false advertising was a viable claim under Section 43(a) only if the advertiser were making the false statement in order to pass off its goods as those of the competitor. *Chamberlain v. Columbia Pictures Corp.*, 186 F.2d 923 (9th Cir. 1951). Later, other courts began to advocate a broader interpretation, holding that a false advertising claim under Section 43(a) did not require a showing of passing off, *L'Aiglon Apparel v. Lana Lobell, Inc.*, 214 F.2d 649 (3d Cir. 1954), and that Section 43(a) did not incorporate the common law single-source prerequisite. *Johnson & Johnson v. Carter-Wallace, Inc.*, 631 F.2d 186 (2d Cir. 1980).

As courts took up this more generous view of Section 43(a) as a vehicle for false advertising claims, many courts adopted a five-factor test for Section 43(a) false advertising first enunciated in *Skil Corp. v. Rockwell Int'l Corp.*, 375 F. Supp. 777 (N.D. Ill. 1974). Under the *Skil Corp.* test, a successful claim of false advertising required a showing that (1) defendant made false statements of fact about its own product in its advertisements; (2) the advertisements actually deceived or had the tendency to deceive a substantial segment of their audience; (3) the deception was material, meaning that it was likely to influence the purchasing decision; (4) defendant caused its falsely advertised goods to enter interstate commerce; and (5) plaintiff was or was likely to be injured as a result of the false statements, either by a direct diversion of sales from itself to defendant, or by lessening the goodwill which its products enjoy with consumers. While the *Skil Corp.* test no longer governs false advertising claims under the post-1988 Section 43(a)(1)(B), the modern false advertising test resembles it in many respects. Notably, the *Skil Corp.* test retained the common law restriction that the advertiser's statements were actionable only when directed to the advertiser's own goods or services.

2. POST-1988 SECTION 43(a)(1)(B)

In the 1988 Trademark Law Revision Act, Congress amended Section 43(a) to incorporate an explicit false advertising provision. The amended provision split Section 43(a) into a subsection that provided a basis for false designation of origin and other causes of action (designated Section 43(a)(1)(A)) and another subsection specifically devoted to false advertising claims (designated Section 43(a)(1)(B)). Section 43(a)(1)(B) specifies that liability results when a party's commercial advertising or promotion makes misrepresentations about the party's own goods, services, or commercial activities, *or* those of another. Relevant misrepresentations are those concerning the "nature, characteristics, qualities, or geographic origin" of the goods, services, or activities at issue. The provision parts from the common law, and from interpretations of the pre-1988 Section 43(a), in that it specifically extends to misrepresentations about others' goods, services, or commercial activities.

Section 43(a)(1)(B) intersects with many other federal and state laws that regulate product labels. In *Pom Wonderful LLC v. Coca-Cola Co.*, 134 S.Ct. 2228 (2014), the Court held that the existence of food labeling restrictions under the Federal Food, Drug, and Cosmetic Act, which are enforced via the Food and Drug Administration, do not preclude private parties from initiating Section 43(a)(1)(B) false advertising actions directed against allegedly false statements in those food labels.

B. THRESHOLD ISSUES IN SECTION 43(a)(1)(B) FALSE ADVERTISING CLAIMS

For purposes of discussion, it is useful to designate two issues in Section 43(a)(1)(B) false advertising cases as threshold issues, although courts do not always segregate these issues carefully from others.

The first threshold issue is standing, a controversial issue in Section 43(a)(1)(B) cases. The second threshold issue is the requirement that the allegedly false representations occur in "commercial advertising or promotion."

1. STANDING

Section 43(a)(1)(B) specifies that "any person who believes that he or she is likely to be damaged" by false advertising may sue under Section 43(a)(1)(B). However, this language must be understood in view of two background limitations. First, Article III imposes minimum constitutional requirements for standing (injury-in-fact, causation, and redressability). Generally, allegations of lost sales and/or damage to business reputation will suffice for Article III constitutional standing in a Lanham Act case. Second, the Lanham Act is understood to impose additional statutory restrictions on standing, deriving from the Act's statement of Congressional intent found in Lanham Act Section 45. In *Lexmark Int'l, Inc. v. Static Control Components, Inc.*, 134 S.Ct. 1377 (2014), the Court ruled that statutory standing under the Lanham Act requires an additional two-part showing: that the plaintiff falls "within the class of plaintiffs whom Congress has authorized to sue" under whichever Lanham Act provision the plaintiff invokes (the "zone of interests" inquiry), and that the defendant's acts proximately caused the plaintiff's injury. *Lexmark*, 134 S.Ct. at 1387. To fall within the zone of interests in a false advertising suit under Section 43(a)(1)(B), a plaintiff must allege "an injury to a commercial interest in reputation or sales," the Court held. *Id.* at 1390. To satisfy the proximate-cause inquiry, a false advertising plaintiff "ordinarily must show economic or reputational injury flowing directly from the deception wrought by the defendant's advertising; and that that occurs when deception of consumers causes them to withhold trade from the plaintiff." Merely showing that a deceptive advertisement injures another commercial actor, in turn affecting the plaintiff, usually is not sufficient.

In adopting the zone of interest and proximate cause inquiries, the Court rejected all three of the tests that had developed in the circuits. In particular, the Court rejected (1) a test that required a showing that the alleged false advertiser was a direct competitor of the plaintiff; (2) a test that had inquired into the reasonableness of the plaintiff's interest and basis for believing that the interest was likely to be damaged—rather than asking what the statute provided; and (3) a multifactor balancing test from *Conte Bros. Automotive, Inc. v. Quaker State-Slick 50, Inc.*, 165 F.3d 221, 225 (3d Cir. 1998), because, *inter alia*, it was unpredictable in application, it treated the zone of interest and proximate cause as mere factors to be weighed rather than requirements in every case, and it permitted courts to deny standing based on the difficulty of quantifying damages, even though the plaintiff might conceivably be entitled to various forms of equitable relief.

Applying the two-part standard, the Court concluded that Static Control had standing to challenge Lexmark's allegedly false commercial representations that had disparaged Static Control's product. Lexmark sold laser printers containing toner cartridges, and used license restrictions and a microchip in each cartridge to discourage consumers from buying replacement cartridges from third parties. Static Control had developed a chip that mimicked the functions of Lexmark's chip. Static Control sold its chips to third-party refurbishers who placed them in refurbished Lexmark cartridges, which it then sold to consumers. Hence, Static Control was not a direct competitor of Lexmark in the laser printer market. Nonetheless, Static Control satisfied the test for standing. It had alleged that it had lost sales and suffered damage to its business reputation (and thus fell within the protected "zone of interests"); and it had alleged that Lexmark had directly disparaged its product in a manner that might cause a drop in the sales of refurbished cartridges, in turn causing Static Control to lose chip sales (thus establishing the proximate cause element).

Under the *Lexmark* standard, consumers lack standing to sue for Section 43(a)(1)(B) false advertising because the "zone of interests" test requires a showing of some impact on sales or commercial reputation. This had been the prevailing rule prior to *Lexmark*. *Serbin v. Ziebart Int'l Corp.*, 11 F.3d 1163 (3d Cir. 1993). By contrast, trade associations are likely to be able to establish statutory standing under the *Lexmark* standard even though they may not be direct competitors of the alleged false advertiser. Some courts had arrived at this result pre-*Lexmark*. *Camel Hair & Cashmere*

Inst., Inc. v. Associated Dry Goods Corp., 799 F.2d 6 (1st Cir. 1986).

2. "COMMERCIAL ADVERTISING OR PROMOTION"

Section 43(a)(1)(B) specifies that only misrepresentations that are made "in commercial advertising or promotion" may trigger false advertising liability. In *Gordon & Breach Science Publishers, S.A. v. American Inst. of Physics*, 859 F. Supp. 1521 (S.D.N.Y. 1994), the court held that misrepresentations constitute commercial advertising or promotion if they are: (1) commercial speech; (2) by a defendant who is in commercial competition with plaintiff; (3) for the purpose of influencing consumers to buy defendant's goods or services; and (4) disseminated sufficiently to the relevant purchasing public to constitute advertising or promotion within that industry. Some courts have accepted the *Gordon & Breach* test. *Sports Unlimited, Inc. v. Lankford Enter., Inc.*, 275 F.3d 996 (10th Cir. 2002); Coastal Abstract Serv., Inc. v. First Am. Tit. Ins. Co., 173 F.3d 725 (9th Cir. 1999); *Seven-Up Co. v. Coca-Cola Co.*, 86 F.3d 1379 (5th Cir. 1996). By contrast, Judge Easterbrook sharply criticized the test in *First Health Group Corp. v. BCE Emergis Corp.*, 269 F.3d 800 (7th Cir. 2001). His critique focused on the First Amendment overtones of the "commercial speech" factor. According to Judge Easterbrook, the language "commercial advertising or promotion" suggests that Congress sought to distinguish between types of commercial speech, not that Congress sought to distinguish between commercial speech and political speech. Commercial advertising is a subset of commercial speech that involves the dissemination of promotional materials to anonymous recipients.

In *Fashion Boutique of Short Hills, Inc. v. Fendi USA, Inc.*, 314 F.3d 48 (2d Cir. 2002), the court expressed some discomfort with the *Gordon & Breach* test, but also criticized Judge Easterbrook's analysis in *First Health*. As for the *Gordon & Breach* test, the Second Circuit accepted element (1) (though it agreed that Section 43(a)(1)(B) could not encompass the entire universe of commercial speech); accepted elements (3) and (4); but questioned whether the text of Section 43(a)(1)(B) supported element (2). In the Second Circuit's view, the touchstone of the inquiry into whether misrepresentations were made "in commercial advertising or promotion" was whether the misrepresentations were part of an "organized campaign to penetrate the market," which normally called for a showing of "widespread dissemination within the relevant industry." Within this framework, "advertising" could be understood as "widespread communication through print or broadcast media," while "promotion" might include other forms of publicity, such as sales displays or other presentations to buyers. The court faulted *First Health* for failing to distinguish between advertising and promotion. Applying its approach, the Second Circuit concluded that where employees at one store "bad-mouthed" a competing store (asserting that the competitor sold bogus or inferior merchandise), these acts alone constituted neither advertising nor promotion.

Without referring to these prior debates, the Eleventh Circuit in *Tobinick v. Novella*, 848 F.3d 935 (11th Cir. 2017) used commercial speech doctrine as the basis for its conclusion that the defendant's blog posts criticizing plaintiff's medical treatment practices did not constitute commercial advertising or promotion for Lanham Act purposes.

C. ELEMENTS OF THE SECTION 43(a)(1)(B) FALSE ADVERTISING CLAIM

Courts typically require a plaintiff in a § 43(a)(1)(B) false advertising case to prove the following elements: "(1) a false statement of fact by the defendant in a commercial advertisement about its own or another's product; (2) the statement actually deceived or has the tendency to deceive a substantial segment of its audience; (3) the deception is material, in that it is likely to influence the purchasing decision; (4) the defendant caused its false statement to enter interstate commerce; and (5) the plaintiff has been or is likely to be injured as a result of the false statement, either by direct diversion of sales from itself to defendant or by a loss of goodwill associated with its products." *Southland Sod Farms v. Stover Seed Co.*, 108 F.3d 1134 (9th Cir.1997). Much of the law has developed around the falsity element (element 1) and the deception element (element 2).

Most false advertising cases involve claims by the allegedly harmed party directly against the alleged false advertiser. However, courts have not ruled out the possibility of claims for contributory false advertising—i.e., claims by the allegedly harmed party against one who facilitates another's false advertisements. In *Duty Free Americas, Inc. v. Estee Lauder Cos., Inc.*, 797 F.3d 1248, 1278–79 (11th Cir. 2015), the court endorsed a doctrine of contributory false advertising, ruling that the proponent of such a claim would need to establish "that a third party in fact directly engaged in false advertising that injured the plaintiff" and that "the defendant contributed to that conduct either by knowingly inducing or causing the conduct, or by materially participating in it." Plaintiff Duty Free had merely alleged an ordinary business relationship between defendant Estee Lauder and the alleged false advertiser, which did not suffice by itself to state a claim for contributory false advertising, the court ruled.

1. FALSITY AND DECEPTION

In applying the first element of the test for Lanham Act false advertising, courts have identified two classes of actionable false statements: (1) statements that are literally false; and (2) statements that are literally true but nonetheless likely to mislead consumers. *Castrol, Inc. v. Pennzoil Co.*, 987 F.2d 939 (3d Cir. 1993). The distinction is critical. If the plaintiff proves that the challenged statement is literally false, most courts presume that consumers were actually deceived (element 2 of the test). *United Indus. Corp. v. Clorox Co.*, 140 F.3d 1175 (8th Cir. 1998). This is an important presumption. Without it, the plaintiff must gather evidence of public reaction—often in the form of survey evidence—to attempt to satisfy element 2, the deception element.

To determine whether a statement is literally false, courts consider the advertisement's explicit, unambiguous statements. For example, a firm's advertisement claiming that its golf ball was the "longest ball on tour" was declared literally false in view of evidence that other balls traveled further under different testing conditions. *Callaway Golf Co. v. Slazenger*, 384 F. Supp. 2d 735 (D. Del. 2005). Where the advertisement claims that the advertised goods or services are superior, without offering any basis for that claim, a challenger probably must do more than merely point out the lack of substantiation in order to show literal falsity. Where the advertisement claims that "tests prove" superiority, a challenger might succeed in showing literal falsity by showing that the tests were not sufficiently reliable to support the claim of superiority, although the determination is highly context-specific. *United Indus. Corp. v. Clorox Co.*, 140 F.3d 1175 (8th Cir. 1998).

Some courts have extended the concept of literal falsity beyond *express* literal falsity. That is, even if the advertisement's explicit statements are not literally false, the court may still find literal falsity if the message that the advertisement conveys by necessary implication is false. *Novartis Consumer Health, Inc. v. Johnson & Johnson-Merck Consumer Pharm. Co.*, 290 F.3d 578 (3d Cir. 2002). An advertiser's claim is said to be literally false by necessary implication "when, considering the advertisement in its entirety, the audience would recognize the claim as readily as if it had been explicitly stated." *Clorox Co. Puerto Rico v. Proctor & Gamble Comm. Co.*, 228 F.3d 24 (1st Cir. 2000). For example, Robot-Coupe's advertisement for its food processors claimed "Robo-Coupe 21. Cuisinart 0," accompanied by a statement that twenty-one of the three-star restaurants in France's Michelin Guide chose "the same professional model food processor." The court found that the statements necessarily implied that the Robot-Coupe and Cuisinart food processors were competing alternatives, when in fact Cuisinart did not make a professional grade model of food processor. *Cuisinarts, Inc. v. Robot-Coupe Int'l Corp.*, 1982 WL 121559 (S.D.N.Y. 1982). In another case involving an advertisement that featured actor William Shatner in his role as Captain Kirk (from the well-known science fiction television series "Star Trek"), Shatner's line praising the "amazing picture clarity of DIRECTV HD" followed by his statement that "settling for cable would be illogical," necessarily implied that cable's HD television picture quality was inferior to that of DIRECTV. The Second Circuit upheld a finding that the statements were literally false by necessary implication. *Time Warner Cable, Inc. v. DIRECTV, Inc.*, 497 F.3d 144 (2d Cir. 2007).

As noted, if a statement is not literally false, it may still be actionable if it is likely to mislead consumers. Where an advertisement contains claims that are attenuated, merely suggestive, or balanced between several plausible meanings, courts should decline to find literal falsity, but may still find that the statements are likely to mislead or deceive. *Clorox*

Co. Puerto Rico v. Proctor & Gamble Comm. Co., 228 F.3d 24 (1st Cir. 2000). The inquiry may require proof of *likely* deception, or it may require proof of *actual* deception. Some courts require proof of actual consumer deception if the plaintiff seeks damages, but only proof of a tendency to deceive consumers if the plaintiff seeks only injunctive relief. *Pizza Hut, Inc. v. Papa John's Int'l, Inc.*, 227 F.3d 489 (5th Cir. 2000). Deception is likely to be proven by survey evidence. In an unusual case, *Pernod Ricard USA, LLC v. Bacardi U.S.A., Inc.*, 653 F.3d 241 (3d Cir. 2011), the Third Circuit concluded that the unambiguously truthful language of the advertisement at issue trumped the plaintiff's survey evidence. Defendant's HAVANA CLUB rum was labeled "Puerto Rican Rum," and the label also (truthfully) stated that the rum was "distilled and crafted in Puerto Rico." Plaintiff Pernod submitted survey evidence allegedly showing that some consumers believed that the rum originated in Havana notwithstanding the references to Puerto Rico on the label. The court concluded that this was a rare case in which no reasonable person could be misled by the advertisement, and determined that it was therefore proper to disregard the survey evidence under these circumstances. The court warned that, in most cases, survey evidence about consumers' reactions to advertisements could not so readily be disregarded. On the other hand, in *Merck Eprova AG v. Gnosis S.p.A.*, 760 F.3d 247 (2d Cir. 2014), the court indicated that in cases of implied falsity where there is also evidence of the advertiser's intent to deceive, the court may presume consumer deception and shift to the advertiser the burden of overcoming this presumption with evidence showing that the advertisement does not deceive consumers.

In a number of cases, courts distinguish between actionable false statements of fact and non-actionable "puffery." Although there are doubtlessly many varieties of statements that might qualify as puffery, courts have frequently encountered two types: (1) a boastful statement so plainly exaggerated that no reasonable consumer would rely on it; and (2) a claim of superiority so general or vague that reasonable consumers would construe it as a mere expression of opinion rather than an empirically verifiable statement. For example, one court concluded that a pizza restaurant's advertising slogan, "Better Ingredients. Better Pizza." was non-actionable puffery. *Pizza Hut, Inc. v. Papa John's Int'l, Inc.*, 227 F.3d 489 (5th Cir. 2000). In another case, the court determined that a grass seed company's advertising claim that "Less is More" was puffery, but its claim that grass grown from the seed required "50% less mowing" was not puffery, but rather was a specific and measurable claim of superiority. *Southland Sod Farms v. Stover Seed Co.*, 108 F.3d 1134 (9th Cir. 1997).

The burden of proving falsity lies with the proponent of the false advertising theory. However, the Third Circuit has recognized an exception: "a court may find that a completely unsubstantiated advertising claim by the defendant is *per se* false without additional evidence from the plaintiff to that effect." *Novartis Consumer Health, Inc. v. Johnson &*

Johnson-Merck Consumer Pharm. Co., 290 F.3d 578, 90 (3d Cir. 2002). The court alluded to the *Novartis* exception in *Groupe SEB USA, Inc. v. Euro-Pro Operating LLC*, 774 F.3d 192 (3d Cir. 2014). There, the defendant advertiser had offered an expert report in support of the truth of its advertising statements, and had argued that in view of the report, the advertising claim could not be deemed to be "unsubstantiated." The court disagreed, concluding that the expert report did not address the falsity of certain claims regarding the power of steam irons measured in grams per shot, even though it did address power measured by calculating the kinetic energy of a steam burst. The *Novartis* exception would appear to add further complexity to an already-complex falsity analysis.

2. MATERIALITY

Courts also generally require false advertising plaintiffs to prove that the deception arising from the allegedly false statements is material. Materiality means that the deception is likely to influence the purchase decision. *Apotex Inc. v. Acorda Therapeutics, Inc.*, 823 F.3d 51 (2d Cir. 2016). Presumably, the rules for proving materiality for purposes of showing that a mark should be excluded from registration for deceptiveness under Lanham Act § 2(a) would also be useful in proving materiality in a false advertising case.

Some jurisdictions have adopted presumptions that relieve the false advertising plaintiff from affirmatively proving materiality under some circumstances. For example, in some jurisdictions, evidence that a statement is literally false triggers a presumption of materiality. *Pizza Hut, Inc. v. Papa John's Int'l, Inc.*, 227 F.3d 489 (5th Cir. 2000). In some jurisdictions, evidence that the false or misleading statement relates to an inherent quality or characteristic of the product gives rise to a presumption of materiality. *National Basketball Ass'n v. Motorola, Inc.*, 105 F.3d 841 (2d Cir. 1997); *Samson Crane Corp. v. Union Nat'l Sales, Inc.*, 87 F. Supp. 218 (D. Mass. 1949).

Plaintiffs in false advertising cases are not limited to any particular form of proof in demonstrating materiality. Survey evidence may often be needed, although courts sometimes accept anecdotal evidence such as consumer declarations or evidence of communications from dissatisfied customers. *Skydive Arizona, Inc. v. Quattrocchi*, 673 F.3d 1105 (9th Cir. 2012).

3. CAUSATION AND INJURY

Under the final two elements of the typical false advertising test, the false advertising plaintiff must prove causation and past or prospective injury. In some circuits, courts presume causation where the evidence shows that the advertiser intentionally set out to deceive consumers by statements in advertising. *Porous Media Corp. v. Pall Corp.*, 110 F.3d 1329 (8th Cir. 1997).

Cognizable injury in a false advertising case may take many forms. The false advertising might divert sales away from the plaintiff to the defendant. In such a case, the plaintiff's lost profits on the diverted sales may constitute the injury. *BASF Corp. v. Old World Trading Co.*, 41 F.3d 1081 (7th Cir. 1994). The false advertising may cause the plaintiff to incur the costs of producing its own advertising that corrects the falsehoods in the defendant's advertising. Both past and anticipated future costs associated with corrective advertising may constitute injury in a false advertising case.

In *Cashmere & Camel Hair Mfrs. Inst. v. Saks Fifth Avenue*, 284 F.3d 302 (1st Cir. 2002), defendant Harve Benard's advertisements represented that its blazers contained 70% cashmere, when there was evidence to suggest that the blazers contained no cashmere. Plaintiff offered evidence to show that Harve Benard paid $5 less per yard for its material, allowing it to undersell members of plaintiff's organization, resulting in lost sales. This evidence was sufficient proof of causation to withstand defendant's motion for summary judgment.

By contrast, the plaintiff failed to show causation and injury in *Verisign, Inc. v. XYZ.COM LLC*, 848 F.3d 292 (4th Cir. 2017). Plaintiff Verisign, which sold internet domain names using the .com and .net top level domains, complained of various representations made by defendant XYZ.COM, made in the course of promoting domain names ending in the .xyz top level domain. Some such statements (referred to in the opinion as the "self-promoting" statements) touted the popularity of the .xyz top level domain, claiming that it had registered a large number of domain names. Verisign asserted that these statements had diverted registrations away from its own .net registry, offering an expert report showing a drop in Verisign's sales during the relevant time period. However, the report did not survive a *Daubert* challenge, and, in any event, the report merely demonstrated a temporal correlation between XYZ.COM's activities and Verisign's sales drop-off; it did not establish that those activities caused each lost registration, the court reasoned.

D. REMEDIES

The plaintiff in a Section 43(a)(1)(B) false advertising case is entitled to the same range of remedies that would be available to plaintiffs asserting other types of Section 43(a) causes of action. Accordingly, remedies in the form of both injunctive relief and damages may be available. To assess the plaintiff's entitlement to injunctive relief, the court in *PBM Prods., LLC v. Mead Johnson & Co.*, 639 F.3d 111 (4th Cir. 2011) applied the multi-factor test from *eBay Inc. v. MercExchange, L.L.C.*, 547 U.S. 388 (2006) (requiring the plaintiff to show (1) that it has suffered an irreparable injury; (2) that remedies available at law, such as monetary damages, are inadequate to compensate for that injury; (3) that, considering the balance of hardships between the plaintiff and defendant, a remedy in equity is warranted; and (4) that the public interest would not be disserved by a permanent injunction). Courts applying the *eBay* test are likely to decline any categorical rule presuming irreparable harm upon a showing of likelihood of success on the merits.

See, e.g., Groupe SEB USA, Inc. v. Euro-Pro Operating LLC, 774 F.3d 192 (3d Cir. 2014).

Permanent injunctive relief in a false advertising case must be calculated to compel the advertiser to discontinue the false statements, while leaving the advertiser free to engage in truthful commercial advertising. As in other matters of equity, the trial courts have broad discretion to fashion injunctive relief that is appropriate in scope.

It should be rare that permanent injunctions in false advertising cases implicate First Amendment concerns, because false or misleading commercial statements fall outside the reach of First Amendment protections. *Central Hudson Gas & Elec. Corp. v. Public Serv. Comm'n of N.Y.*, 447 U.S. 557 (1980). However, where the deceptive statements are intermingled with truthful commercial speech, a court may find it difficult to tailor an injunction so that it only precludes the deceptive statements, and First Amendment concerns might arise. In *TrafficSchool.com, Inc. v. Edriver, Inc.*, 653 F.3d 820 (9th Cir. 2011), the court discussed these concerns in reviewing an injunction that required the defendant to use a disclaimer in the form of a "splash screen" that was presented to every visitor to defendant's website. The splash screen warned visitors that the defendant's website (a for-profit website located at dmv.org) was not affiliated with any government department of motor vehicles, and required visitors to press a "continue" button in order to proceed to defendant's website. The Ninth Circuit remanded the case, instructing the trial court to consider how long to require the defendant to use the splash screen and the conditions that the defendant needed to satisfy in order to remove the splash screen, for example.

The standard Lanham Act provisions on damages for trademark infringement matters also apply to false advertising claims. *See* Chapter 12 for a full treatment of Lanham Act remedies, including an explanation of the damages provisions. Compensatory damages for acts of false advertising may be calculated in various ways. In cases involving false comparisons between competitive products, an award of the defendant's lost profits may be relatively easy to prove. *TrafficSchool.com, Inc. v. Edriver, Inc.*, 653 F.3d 820 (9th Cir. 2011) (asserting that in such cases "it would be reasonable to presume that every dollar defendant makes has come directly out of plaintiff's pocket"). In cases involving a defendant's misrepresentations about its own products, it may be much more difficult to determine the portion of defendant's profits that is attributable to the false statements and necessary to compensate the plaintiff. *Harper House, Inc. v. Thomas Nelson, Inc.*, 889 F.2d 197 (9th Cir. 1989).

CHAPTER 11
ENDORSEMENT, ATTRIBUTION, AND THE RIGHT OF PUBLICITY

This chapter covers causes of action that relate to aspects of personal identity—one's name, likeness, or other attributes. When a personal characteristic such as one's name is used commercially, in connection with goods or services, it takes on the attributes of a mark. In some cases, celebrities and others who have developed commercial value in their personal identities have sought to invoke the Lanham Act to secure that value against unauthorized uses. While the plaintiffs have prevailed in some such cases, the Supreme Court's 2003 decision in *Dastar* has dramatically reduced the prospect of success. We discuss the relevant cases in Section A.

The commercial value of a person's identity may also be protected under state law in most states, through the right of publicity. Right of publicity laws provide in-gross property rights in personal identity with no requirement for registration or other formalities. While publicity rights can therefore be quite powerful, the fact that they exist only as a matter of state law reduces their effectiveness for many celebrities, whose notoriety usually extends beyond the borders of any individual state. We discuss the right of publicity in Section B.

A. SECTION 43(a) FALSE AFFILIATION THEORIES

We have seen that Section 43(a) imposes liability for the use, in connection with goods and services, of "any word, term, name, symbol, or device, or any combination thereof, or any false designation of origin, false or misleading description of fact, or false or misleading representation of fact," assuming that the additional elements found in either 43(a)(1)(A) or (B) are met. In cases that were decided prior to *Dastar Corp. v. Twentieth Century Fox Film Corp.*, 539 U.S. 23 (2003), some courts found that the quoted language could support claims of false attribution, affiliation, or endorsement. These were all essentially claims involving false representations about personal identity.

The pertinent cases fell into two groups. The first group involved allegations of unwanted attribution ("over-attribution"), in which a person's identity was used without permission in connection with another's product or service. These cases could be conceived of as being similar to ordinary "passing off" cases requiring an analysis of likelihood of confusion, if personal identity or some aspect of it could be considered analogous to a mark. The second group involved alleged omissions of attribution ("under-attribution"). Cases in this latter group tended to be more controversial. They were analogous to reverse passing off cases—that is, cases in which the defendant sells the mark owner's goods without the mark owner's mark. (This is passing off in reverse because the defendant is passing off the *mark owner's* goods as originating from the *defendant*.) As the Court pointed out in the *Dastar* case, allegations of reverse passing off in cases involving false omissions about personal identity (particularly omissions of authorship credit) may appear to be problematic to the extent that they might be used to circumvent the limitations of copyright law. We discuss these issues in the following subsections.

1. FALSE OVER-ATTRIBUTION

In some decisions in the 1990s, the Ninth Circuit recognized claims for "false endorsement" based on Section 43(a). In *Waits v. Frito-Lay, Inc.*, 978 F.2d 1093 (9th Cir. 1992), *cert. denied* 506 U.S. 1080 (1993), the court upheld a jury's determination that Frito-Lay's use of a Tom Waits sound-alike in a commercial constituted a "false endorsement" under Section 43(a). (At the time, Tom Waits was a well-known recording artist.) In *Abdul-Jabbar v. General Motors Corp.*, 75 F.3d 1391 (9th Cir. 1996), *amended on denial of rehearing* 85 F.3d 407 (9th Cir. 1996), the court found at least a triable fact issue on a false endorsement claim involving a General Motors automobile advertisement that mentioned the name of basketball player Lew Alcindor (who later changed his name to Kareem Abdul-Jabbar). In both cases, the court analyzed the Section 43(a) claim by applying the likelihood of confusion factors. In *Facenda v. NFL Films, Inc.*, 542 F.3d 1007 (3d Cir. 2008), the court suggested that the likelihood of confusion factors analysis be adapted for Section 43(a) cases involving personal identity, *citing Downing v. Abercrombie & Fitch*, 265 F.3d 994 (9th

Cir. 2001). In particular, the court suggested replacing the similarity of marks factor with an analysis of "the similarity of the likeness used by the defendant to the actual plaintiff." The court also suggested analyzing the plaintiff's "level of recognition" among the consumers of defendant's goods, and the "relatedness of the fame or success of the plaintiff to the defendant's product," in addition to a number of the other traditional confusion factors. *See also Fifty-Six Hope Road Music, Ltd. v. A.V.E.L.A., Inc.*, 778 F.3d 1059 (9th Cir. 2015) (applying the tailored likelihood of confusion factors and upholding the determination that the defendant's unauthorized use of a Bob Marley image on t-shirts and other merchandise constituted a false endorsement in violation of Section 43(a)).

By contrast, the court in *ETW Corp. v. Jireh Publ'g, Inc.*, 332 F.3d 915 (6th Cir. 2003) refused to analogize attribution claims to trademark claims. The court held that "as a general rule, a person's image or likeness cannot function as a trademark" because images and likenesses of a person "do not distinguish the source of goods." The case involved images of the professional golfer Tiger Woods, and the court reasoned that images of Woods were so ubiquitous in various forms of media that "[n]o reasonable person could believe that merely because these photographs or paintings contain Woods's likeness or image, they all originated with Woods." This strikes us as an unverified empirical assumption that surely should not be extrapolated to invalidate any claim of Lanham Act protection for a personal likeness.

In other cases involving claims of false over-attribution, courts had relied on the false advertising prong of Section 43(a)—that is, Section 43(a)(1)(B) (discussed in Chapter 10). *King v. Innovation Books*, 976 F.2d 824 (2d Cir. 1992) (involving allegations that movie credits for the movie *The Lawnmower Man* falsely exaggerated author Stephen King's involvement in the movie production process). The false advertising theory was problematic in some cases, particularly in the Ninth Circuit, because Section 43(a)(1)(B) imposes standing requirements that call for the existence of a "competitive" injury—i.e., one that is harmful to the plaintiff's ability to compete with the defendant. *Jack Russell Terrier Network of Northern California v. American Kennel Club, Inc.*, 407 F.3d 1027 (9th Cir. 2005). By contrast, there is no analogous competitive injury requirement for a likelihood of confusion theory under Section 43(a)(1)(A).

2. FALSE UNDER-ATTRIBUTION ("REVERSE PASSING OFF")

In a few cases involving claims of false under-attribution (reverse passing off), the Ninth Circuit had held that when the defendant removes the plaintiff's name from the plaintiff's own work and passes that identical work off as the defendant's own, a reverse passing off claim is made out. *Shaw v. Lindheim*, 919 F.2d 1353 (9th Cir. 1990). It was not sufficient to show that the defendant's work was substantially similar to plaintiff's (because the copyright law provided an adequate remedy in those cases); instead, the plaintiff had to show "bodily appropriation." *See also Cleary v. News Corp.*, 30 F.3d 1255 (9th Cir. 1994) (concluding that the "bodily appropriation" test was not satisfied despite many similarities between the works at issue).

The Supreme Court did away with the "bodily appropriation" test, and substantially limited reverse passing off claims, in *Dastar Corp. v. Twentieth Century Fox Film Corp.*, 539 U.S. 23 (2003). Plaintiff Fox asserted a Lanham Act reverse passing off theory against Dastar. Fox was distributing a set of videotapes derived from a television series about World War II. Fox had owned the copyright in the television series but had failed to renew it, and the copyright had expired. Dastar had copied and edited tapes of the same television series and was also distributing a videotape set. Dastar's packaging omitted crediting the original television series, and Fox argued that this amounted to reverse passing off because it created the false impression that Dastar was the origin of the content of the videotapes. In an unpublished opinion, the Ninth Circuit had concluded that Fox had satisfied the "bodily appropriation" test, and that the test relieved Fox of the need to show likelihood of confusion. The Supreme Court granted *certiorari* and reversed. The Court acknowledged the existence of a reverse passing off cause of action under Lanham Act Section 43(a), but narrowed the cause of action substantially. The Court concluded that "origin" as used in Section 43(a) "refers to the producer of the tangible goods that are offered for sale, and not to the author of any idea, concept, or communication embodied in those goods." Thus, a reverse passing off claim could survive if, for example, defendant tore the cover off plaintiff's book and substituted a cover that falsely suggested that the defendant had printed the book, because this would be a cognizable allegation about the manufacturing origin of the goods. By contrast, a reverse passing off claim based on allegedly false representations about the authorship of the creative content of a work would not form the basis for a claim under Lanham Act Section 43(a), because there would be no false representation about manufacturing origin. According to the Court, a contrary result would convert Lanham Act protections into "a mutant form of copyright."

The Court determined that Fox's allegations were of the latter variety. Dastar had manufactured the videotapes that it was distributing. The only allegedly false representation was about the origin of the creative content of the tapes, and so the Lanham Act reverse passing off claim could not survive.

In succeeding years, the courts have applied *Dastar* in a wide variety of settings, striking down false attribution claims in virtually every instance. For example, in *Zyla v. Wadsworth*, 360 F.3d 243 (1st Cir. 2004), plaintiff Zyla sued book publisher Wadsworth on a Section 43(a) reverse passing off theory based on the fact that the fourth edition of book published by Wadsworth omitted mention of Zyla's contributions to prior editions. The court applied *Dastar* and dismissed the claim, identifying it as a claim about allegedly false representations about creative content, not about manufacturing origin. In *Bretford Mfg. Inc. v. Smith Sys. Mfg. Corp.*,

419 F.3d 576 (7th Cir. 2005), *Dastar* precluded a claim by a furniture manufacturer, Bretford, against its competitor Smith System. Smith System had incorporated some of Bretford's table leg assemblies into a sample table and showed the sample to a purchaser without crediting Bretford. *See also Kehoe Component Sales, Inc. v. Best Lighting Prods., Inc.*, 796 F.3d 576 (6th Cir. 2015) (*Dastar* precluded a claim of reverse passing off where a supplier filled orders for a first customer and then used the same tooling to make a separate batch of the same product for other customers without revealing the connection to the first customer's product).

In *Syngenta Seeds v. Delta Cotton Co-operative, Inc.*, 457 F.3d 1269 (Fed. Cir. 2006), the Federal Circuit dismissed a reverse passing off claim even though the claim did seem to relate to the manufacturing origin of the goods. Defendant Delta, operator of a grain elevator, had allegedly sold feed wheat in bags marked DELTA COTTON CO-OPERATIVE and FEED WHEAT. Some of the bags contained plaintiff Syngenta's COKER wheat seed (probably because farmers who had sold wheat to the elevator had grown COKER seed).

These facts surely fit the typical pattern for express reverse passing off cases: Delta was applying its own mark to products that had not originated with it. The jury found Delta liable under that theory, but the Federal Circuit overturned the verdict. The Federal Circuit found no sufficient evidence of reputational injury to Syngenta because purchasers from Delta "could never know" that they had purchased a product containing Syngenta seed. Such reasoning seems to do away with the reverse passing off cause of action altogether, although the court did not purport to be doing that.

In the wake of *Dastar*, it has been very difficult-perhaps impossible—to prevail on personal identity claims when they are framed as Lanham Act Section 43(a) claims for under-attribution in the form of reverse passing off. Courts have also tended to reject alternative claims based on Section 43(a)(1)(B) false advertising, sometimes on grounds that the plaintiff lacks a competitive injury and hence lacks standing. As a consequence, right of publicity regimes are especially important at this time for claims of the unauthorized commercial use of personal identity.

B. THE RIGHT OF PUBLICITY

Traditional trademark law provides only limited protection for aspects of a person's identity. One's name and likeness can function to indicate the source of particular goods or services, and so is the type of subject matter that could qualify for trademark protection under the rules discussed above in Chapters 2–5. Lanham Act Sections 2(c) and 2(a) (through its "false connection" clause), prevent applicants from registering another's name as a trademark without the other's consent. *See* Chapter 5. Lanham Act Section 43(a) may provide limited rights against false affiliation as discussed above, although the protection is minimal after *Dastar*. And Lanham Act Section 47 provides liability where a person registers a domain name consisting of the name of another person, if specified conditions are met.

However, neither the Lanham Act nor other federal intellectual property statutes contain right-of-publicity provisions—that is, provisions providing rights to control the commercial exploitation of an individual's personal identity. The right of publicity is strictly a creature of state law. In about twenty states, the right of publicity has been codified, although statutes tend to vary considerably from state to state. Examples include statutes in Indiana (IC 32–36–1–1 et seq.); California (CA § 3344.1); New York (NY Civ. R §§ 50–51) and Tennessee (TN 47–25–1104). In the remaining states, the right of publicity is a matter of state common law (or state law is silent as to whether the right of publicity is recognized).

1. ORIGINS; JUSTIFICATIONS; RELATIONSHIP WITH RIGHT OF PRIVACY

The notion of a "right of publicity" in U.S. law is usually traced to Judge Frank's opinion in *Haelan Labs., Inc. v. Topps Chewing Gum, Inc.*, 202 F.2d 866 (2d Cir. 1953). In prior cases involving claims that one party had misappropriated the identity of another for commercial purposes, courts had attempted to address the claims under the law of privacy rights. Privacy rights were conceived of as personal rights, actionable because their violation gave rise to psychic damage. But privacy rights were a poor fit for typical cases in which the likenesses of well-known athletes or performers were appropriated without consent for commercial gain. The celebrities were thought to have waived their privacy interests to some degree merely by virtue of their celebrity status, and, in any event, the damage complained of was primarily commercial damage, not psychic damage. In *Haelan*, Judge Frank reasoned that in addition to a right of privacy, there should be a "right of publicity," that it should be actionable because its violation gives rise to commercial damage, and that it should be freely alienable like any other in gross property right. This last quality was particularly important in that it distinguished the right of publicity from trademark rights.

The idea of using the "right of publicity" label to recognize a person's rights in commercial uses of his or her identity gained further credence as a result of the Supreme Court's decision in *Zacchini v. Scripps-Howard Broadcasting Co.*, 433 U.S. 562 (1977). A television station had videotaped and replayed Hugo Zacchini's fifteen-second "human cannonball" act. A lower court had concluded that the First Amendment immunized the television station from liability; the Supreme Court reversed. The decision focused on the scope of the First Amendment, but the opinion made references to a "right of publicity" even though it did not explore the contours of that right.

For some, the right of publicity remained an outgrowth of the right of privacy, a view that may still be seen in the common law in some jurisdictions. *See, e.g., Cheatham v. Paisano Pubs.*, 891 F. Supp. 381 (W.D. Ky. 1995). The Restatement (Second) of Torts (1976) defined the right of privacy as incorporating four rights: "The right of privacy is invaded by (a) unreasonable intrusion upon the seclusion of another . . . ; or (b) appropriation of the other's name or likeness . . . ; or (c) unreasonable publicity given to the other's private life; or (d) publicity that unreasonably places the other in a false light before the public . . . ." RESTATEMENT (SECOND) OF TORTS § 652A(2) (1976). Part (b), appropriation of the other's name and likeness, expresses the right of publicity.

By contrast, in many states, the right of publicity is recognized as an intellectual property right independent of the rights of privacy. Similarly, the Restatement (Third) of Unfair Competition (1995) expressly recognizes the right of publicity in §§ 46–49.

Proponents of the right of publicity have invoked some traditional economic interests as well as some less traditional interests in support of recognizing the right. As to the former, some have argued that the right of publicity provides incentives to encourage individuals to engage in valuable work, or that it secures to individuals the rewards of their labors. It may also protect consumers from misleading advertising, although it should be noted that no deceptiveness element need be proven in order to make out a right of publicity claim. Some have also argued that the right of publicity exists to give individuals autonomy over the commercial use of their images, avoiding the psychic harm that might result from unconsented uses.

2. OVERVIEW OF ELEMENTS; IN-GROSS PROPERTY RIGHT; RELATIONSHIP WITH COPYRIGHT AND TRADEMARK

The cause of action for violations of the right of publicity, as articulated in many jurisdictions, has five elements: defendant has (1) appropriated the value (2) of another's identity (3) without consent (4) during a prescribed time period (5) for commercial purposes. *See, e.g.*, RESTATEMENT (THIRD) OF UNFAIR COMPETITION § 46 (1995) (providing a similar list of elements without a prescribed time period); compare Indiana IC § 32–36–1–8(2) (similar list of elements including a time period). The following sections discuss several of these elements.

The right of publicity differs from the trademark right in that the right of publicity is an in-gross property right as normally conceptualized. The right of publicity cause of action does not require a showing of likelihood of confusion. The right of publicity is also freely alienable, at least in jurisdictions where the in-gross nature of the right has been fully elaborated. For example, the Indiana statute explicitly denominates rights of publicity as "property rights" which are "freely transferable and descendible" by ordinary means, such as contract, testamentary document, or intestate succession. Indiana IC 32–36–1–16.

The right of publicity also differs from rights under copyright law, but here the relationship is arguably more complex, because the copyright statute includes a preemption provision that displaces state law rights that are equivalent to the rights under copyright law. 17 U.S.C. § 301. The copyright preemption inquiry under Section 301 of the Copyright Act has two major prongs: (1) whether the subject matter that is allegedly preempted is fixed in tangible form and comes within the subject matter of copyright as specified in Sections 102 and 103 of the Copyright Act; and (2) whether the rights asserted in the subject matter are equivalent to at least one of the rights specified in Section 106 of the Copyright Act. Courts have split on the application of both prongs. The Eighth and Ninth Circuits have held that copyright law preempts certain right of publicity claims. *Maloney v. T3 Media*, 853 F.3d 1004 (9th Cir. 2017) (right of publicity claim under California law relating to depictions of college athletes in photographs in NCAA Photo Library); *Jules Jordan Video, Inc. v. 144942 Canada Inc.*, 617 F.3d 1146 (9th Cir. 2010) (right of publicity claim under California law relating to use of name and persona in allegedly counterfeited copies of motion picture); *Laws v. Sony Music Entertainment, Inc.*, 448 F.3d 1134 (9th Cir. 2006) (right of publicity claim under California law relating to use of voice in sound recording). *See also Dryer v. National Football League,* 814 F.3d 938 (8th Cir. 2016) (right of publicity claims under various state laws relating to the depiction of retired NFL football players in video footage of games). In *Maloney*, for example, the court reasoned that whereas copyright law should not preempt a publicity claim based on the use of a person's name or likeness on merchandise or advertising, it should preempt a publicity claim where the person's likeness has been captured in a copyrighted work and the publicity claim seeks to prevent the dissemination of the work.

Other courts have declined to find preemption. *See, e.g., Facenda v. N.F.L. Films, Inc.*, 542 F.3d 1007 (3d Cir. 2008) (right of publicity claim under Pennsylvania law relating to use of name and likeness in television production); *Toney v. L'Oreal USA, Inc.*, 406 F.3d 905 (7th Cir. 2005) (right of publicity claim under Illinois law relating to use of photograph in advertisement). These latter courts have found that rights in a person's identity are not fixed in the form of an individual copy—distinguishing, for example, between a person's appearance (the subject of the right of publicity) and a photograph of the person (the subject of copyright). They have also found that the right of publicity claim includes an extra element beyond that required by the copyright claim. For example, in *Facenda*, the court found that the right of publicity claim required a showing that the protected identity had commercial value.

3. PROTECTABLE ASPECTS OF IDENTITY

As we have noted, the right of publicity provides a property right in personal identity. Necessarily, this requires a court to identify (1) whether the plaintiff is entitled to any rights in his or her identity; and (2) whether the particular aspects of the plaintiff's identity that have been appropriated in the case are protectable.

As to the first element, right of publicity laws generally confer rights of publicity on all natural persons whose personal identities have commercial value. *See, e.g.*, Indiana IC 32–36–1–6 (defining "personality"). Celebrity status is probably not required, but evidence that the personal identity is distinctive and widely recognized may be required. *See, e.g., Cheatham v. Paisano Publications, Inc.*, 891 F. Supp. 381 (W.D. Ky. 1995) (applying Kentucky common law). Some jurisdictions appear to require some evidence that the person intended to profit from the commercial value of his or her image, while others do not require any showing that the person has authorized the exploitation of his or her identity for commercial purposes. *See, e.g.*, Indiana IC 32–36–1–6 (no requirement that the person "uses or authorizes the use of the person's rights of publicity for a commercial purpose during the person's lifetime").

As to the second element, many cases involve straightforward claims of uncontroversial aspects of persona—such as a person's name or likeness. Other cases have found a right of publicity violation for the unauthorized use of a catchphrase ("Here's Johnny") associated with a particular person, *Carson v. Here's Johnny Portable Toilets, Inc.*, 698 F.2d 831 (6th Cir. 1983), and for the unauthorized use of a photograph of a race car recognized as the car of a well-known driver. *Motschenbacher v. R.J. Reynolds Tobacco Co.*, 498 F.2d 821 (9th Cir. 1974). In these more difficult cases, the critical question is identifiability—whether the defendant has appropriated an aspect of the plaintiff's persona that is reasonably identifiable.

In *Midler v. Ford Motor Co.*, 849 F.2d 460 (9th Cir. 1988), the court determined that Bette Midler had a claim against Ford when Ford used a vocal impersonator of Bette Midler in the soundtrack for a television commercial. Midler could not prevail under California Civil Code § 3344, protecting against the unauthorized use of a person's "name, voice, signature, photograph or likeness," because no recording of Midler's actual voice had been used. However, Midler had a claim under the common law right of publicity in circumstances where "a distinctive voice of a professional singer is widely known and is deliberately imitated to sell a product . . . " Similarly, Vanna White's right of publicity claim against Samsung should not have been dismissed on summary judgment according to the Ninth Circuit in *White v. Samsung Electronics America, Inc.*, 971 F.2d 1395 (9th Cir. 1992), *cert. denied*, 508 U.S. 951 (1993). A Samsung advertisement featured a blond-wigged robot together with items evoking an association with the "Wheel of Fortune" game show, which White co-hosted. While Samsung had not appropriated White's actual physical likeness, and so had not violated California Section 3344, there was at least a triable issue as to whether White was identifiable from the advertisement.

Similar questions have arisen in cases involving the publicity rights of actors who have portrayed fictional characters, where the defendant is making use of attributes of the fictional character. In the "Dracula" case, Justice Mosk, concurring, suggested that courts consider whether the actor has played a well-defined part and whether that part has become inextricably identified with the actor's persona. *Lugosi v. Universal Pictures*, 603 P.2d 425 (Cal. 1979) (Mosk, J., concurring). He also took the view that "[a]n original creation of a fictional figure played exclusively by its creator" may generate publicity rights in the actor. The court in *McFarland v. Miller*, 14 F.3d 912 (3d Cir. 1994) placed less stress on originality, emphasizing instead the inextricable link or association between actor and character: "[w]here an actor's screen persona becomes so associated with him that it becomes inseparable from the actor's own public image," the actor obtains rights of publicity in the screen persona. This required more than merely a showing that an actor has become known for a single role. Instead, it required a showing that the actor's identity merged into and became indistinguishable from that of the portrayed character. We find these tests to be useful as far as they go, but they do not go particularly far. Indeed, it seems to us that they restate the question without giving much guidance as to the answer. We expect that these cases will continue to call for subtle determinations on a case-specific basis.

4. COMMERCIAL PURPOSES; LIMITATIONS

The right of publicity must be cabined to ensure that it does not intrude on protected speech interests. *Zacchini v. Scripps-Howard Broadcasting Co.*, 433 U.S. 562 (1977); *Cardtoons, L.C. v. Major League Baseball Players Ass'n*, 95 F.3d 959 (10th Cir. 1996). This basic concept is well-understood, but implementing it has proven to be difficult and controversial.

One standard limitation on the right of publicity is that the defendant's unauthorized use will only trigger liability if the use is for a commercial purpose. *See, e.g.*, Indiana IC 32–26–1–8(2) (under the Indiana right of publicity, "[a] person may not use an aspect of a personality's right of publicity for a commercial purpose . . . without having obtained previous written consent . . . ") Under the Indiana statute, a use is for a "commercial purpose" if it is a use "(1) on or in connection with a product, merchandise, goods, services, or commercial activities; (2) for advertising or soliciting purchases of products, merchandise, goods, services, or for promoting commercial activities; (3) for the purpose of fundraising." Indiana IC 32–26–1–2.

The Indiana statute limits the publicity right further by including a list of express exclusions that appear to be intended to anticipate the types of uses that would typically have implications for speech interests. For example, uses "in literary works" and other specified creative works are statutorily excluded from the scope of the right of publicity, as are uses in materials having "political or newsworthy value." Indiana IC 32–36–1–1(c)(1)(A)–(B). In addition, uses "in connection with the broadcast or reporting of an event or a topic of general or public interest" are expressly excluded, Indiana IC 32–36–1–1(c)(3), and the statute includes other targeted exclusions. Whether these exclusions collectively will pass muster under a First Amendment challenge has yet to be litigated. A case that may be illustrative, although it does not arise under the Indiana statute, is *Montana v. San Jose Mercury News, Inc.*, 40

Cal.Rptr.2d 639, 34 Cal.App.4th 790 (1995). The defendant newspaper publisher sold posters that were exact reproductions of the newspaper's various front-page stories about the San Francisco 49ers' Super Bowl championship. The posters featured photographs and sketches of Joe Montana, the 49ers' quarterback. Montana sued, invoking the right of publicity. The court found that the First Amendment protected the newspaper's sale of the posters because the posters depicted a newsworthy event—though the court did admit that it had been unable to find any cases "directly on point."

In *Jordan v. Jewel Food Stores, Inc.*, 743 F.3d 509 (7th Cir. 2014), the court explored the commercial/non-commercial distinction to decide a right of publicity claim brought by basketball star Michael Jordan against a grocery store chain, Jewel. Jewel had circulated an advertisement that saluted Jordan's selection to the NBA Hall of Fame, while also prominently featuring the Jewel logo. The court concluded that Jewel's ad qualified as commercial speech in the First Amendment sense, because the ad was, in fact, in the form of an advertisement (not in the form editorial content), it promoted patronage at Jewel stores generally (even though it was not directed towards some specific product), and it served Jewel's economic interests. Accordingly, Jewel could not claim the benefit of the higher standard of scrutiny accorded to restrictions on non-commercial speech.

In common law jurisdictions, courts have developed tests that attempt to balance the right of publicity against First Amendment interests on a case-by-case basis. The California Supreme Court developed a "transformative" test, borrowing from copyright fair use jurisprudence. *Comedy III Productions, Inc. v. Saderup*, 21 P.3d 797 (Cal. 2001). Under this test, if the defendant's use adds "transformative elements" of expression, rather than merely appropriating aspects of a protected persona, then the defendant's use is more likely to fall outside the permissible scope of protection for publicity rights. Put another way, courts are to engage in the following inquiry: "whether a product containing a celebrity's likeness is so transformed that it has become primarily the defendant's own expression rather than the celebrity's likeness." The Court also identified a second inquiry: "does the marketability and economic value of the challenged work derive primarily from the fame of the celebrity depicted?" If not, according to the Court, the challenged work is presumptively transformative and does not violate the right of publicity. Thus, the "transformative" test actually has two independent elements: the defendant may show that the challenged work contains transformative expression, or that the challenged work does not derive its value primarily from the fame of the depicted personality. The Court in *Comedy III* reasoned that its test balanced competing interests in protecting expression from government interference and in protecting the fruits of a personality's "artistic labors." As applied in *Comedy III*, the Court concluded that the defendant's drawing of the Three Stooges did not contain significant transformative expression (it was instead a "literal, conventional" depiction of the Three Stooges), and the marketability of the drawing *did* derive primarily from the fame of the depicted actors. Hence, the challenged work violated the right of publicity. In a subsequent case involving comic book characters that allegedly bore some resemblance to musicians Johnny and Edgar Winters, the California Supreme Court found that the defendant's use satisfied the transformative test. *Winter v. DC Comics*, 69 P.3d 473 (Cal. 2003). In *ETW v. Jireh Pub., Inc.*, 332 F.3d 915 (6th Cir. 2003), the court decided that a painting featuring Tiger Woods contained "significant transformative elements" and accordingly the First Amendment precluded right of publicity liability. By contrast, in litigation brought by retired NFL players against EA Sports over video games depicting historic NFL teams, the Ninth Circuit concluded that the video games did not contain sufficient transformative elements to avoid liability. *Davis v. Electronic Arts Inc.*, 775 F.3d 1172 (9th Cir. 2015)

The Missouri Supreme Court rejected the "transformative" test on the ground that it gives too little consideration to the likelihood that any given use will contain both commercial and expressive (and potentially transformative) elements. *Doe v. TCI Cablevision*, 67 U.S.P.Q.2d 1604 (Mo. 2003), *cert. denied* 540 U.S. 1106 (2004). The Court in *TCI* advocated the use of a "predominant use" test in which a use that predominantly exploits the commercial value of the personality's likeness would trigger liability even if the use has some expressive components. Applying its test, the Court held that the defendant's speech interests must give way because the defendant's use of the plaintiff's name and identity was predominantly "a ploy to sell [defendant's] comic books and related products rather than an artistic or literary expression." The Court's predominant use test does not appear to have gained much traction in other jurisdictions.

Yet another test, advocated in the Restatement of Unfair Competition, has sometimes been called the "relatedness" test. Under this test, there is no right of publicity liability for the use of a person's identity in a work that is "related" to the person (such as a news story about the person, an unauthorized biography, or a fictional work). RESTATEMENT (THIRD) OF UNFAIR COMPETITION § 47 cmt. c (1995).

In *C.B.C. Distrib. & Mktg., Inc. v. Major League Baseball Advanced Media*, 505 F.3d 818 (8th Cir. 2007), in which the court was bound to apply Missouri law, the court did not invoke the predominant use test, nor did it expressly endorse any of the other tests that we have discussed. Instead, the court simply balanced what it perceived to be the competing First Amendment and right of publicity interests. The case involved CBC's use of major league baseball player names and performance statistics in fantasy baseball products. On the side of First Amendment interests, the court concluded that the names and statistics constituted expressive speech and were of public value. As for right-of-publicity interests, the court found that these interests were barely implicated. Players were already being well-compensated for their appearances in games (and in advertisements), there was no real prospect of psychic injury to the players, and, given the manner in which the names and information were presented in the fantasy games, there was little likelihood that consumers would be deceived into believing that particular players endorsed the defendant's product.

5. JURISDICTION; CHOICE OF LAW

Because the right of publicity is a matter of state law, right of publicity litigation can present procedural issues that would not arise in a unified regime of federal rights. Jurisdiction and choice of law issues are both likely to arise with some frequency.

As to jurisdiction, subject matter jurisdiction will be determined based on the situs of the tort. One approach is to declare that the situs of the tort is the location where the allegedly infringing acts occur. The Indiana statute takes this approach, asserting jurisdiction over any "act or event that occurs within Indiana, regardless of a personality's domicile, residence, or citizenship." Indiana IC 32–36–1–1; *see also* 32–36–1–9(1), (2). The statute also purports to assert jurisdiction over transporting, or causing to be transported, allegedly infringing merchandise into Indiana (IC 32–36–1–9(3)), or knowingly causing allegedly infringing advertising material to be disseminated in Indiana. IC 32–36–1–9(4).

6. REMEDIES; DURATION

The full range of civil remedies should be available to redress violations of the right of publicity. Plaintiffs may be expected to seek permanent injunctive relief, and compensatory damages for past infringing acts. The Indiana statute provides for actual or statutory damages, and trebling for willful violations. Indiana IC 32–36–1–10. The statute also provides that the prevailing party is entitled to attorney's fees. Indiana IC 32–36–1–12.

Important questions have been raised about the appropriate duration for a right of publicity. If the right is a personal right, it might seem that the right should terminate upon the person's death. In some jurisdictions, such as California, that indeed appeared to be the rule, although Section 3344.1 of the California statute was amended in 2007 to extend the right post-mortem. In other jurisdictions, post-mortem rights have been recognized. Under the Indiana statute, for example, the right of publicity endures "during the personality's lifetime or for one hundred (100) years after the date of the personality's death." Indiana IC 32–36–1–8(2). In New Jersey, a common law jurisdiction, the court recognized a post-mortem right of publicity in *McFarland v. Miller*, 14 F.3d 912 (3d Cir. 1994), reasoning that the right of publicity was analogous to a civil trespass action, and noting that under New Jersey law, civil actions for trespass survive the property owner's death.

CHAPTER 12
REMEDIES

This chapter addresses civil remedies for Lanham Act violations. The available civil remedies may be grouped into two categories. First, and most importantly, prevailing plaintiffs in Lanham Act actions may seek injunctive relief. (*See* Part A.) Prohibitory injunctive relief is usually critical in Lanham Act cases to prevent against ongoing injury to goodwill. Plaintiffs may seek other equitable remedies in some circumstances, such as seizure and destruction of infringing goods. Second, plaintiffs may seek compensatory damages for past violations. (*See* Part B.) An award of actual damages is the norm, although statutory damages may be available in special cases, such as counterfeiting.

A. EQUITABLE REMEDIES AND LIMITATIONS: INJUNCTIVE RELIEF; LACHES

Section 34 of the Lanham Act provides that the courts "shall have the power to grant injunctions, according to the principles of equity and upon such terms as the court may deem reasonable," as a remedy in Lanham Act cases. The statute specifies that injunctive relief may be sought in order to prevent "the violation of any right of the registrant" (typically Section 32 trademark infringement actions), or a violation of Section 43(a) (encompassing actions to enforce unregistered marks and false advertising actions), Section 43(c) (actions against dilution), or Section 43(d) (actions against cybersquatting). Although the decision to grant injunctive relief in a Lanham Act case is a matter of the court's equitable discretion, the grant of such relief is typical, because damages are normally regarded as inadequate to compensate for reputational injury of the type that the Lanham Act seeks to prohibit. *See* RESTATEMENT (THIRD) OF UNFAIR COMPETITION § 35, cmts. b, h (1995).

1. PRELIMINARY INJUNCTIONS

Tests for preliminary injunctions. Although preliminary injunctive relief is sometimes characterized as an extraordinary remedy to be applied when there is an urgent need for judicial intervention to preserve the status quo, it is not uncommon for plaintiffs in Lanham Act cases to seek preliminary injunctive relief, and the grant of such relief to prevailing plaintiffs is probably more routine than the standard characterizations imply. Tests for the grant of preliminary injunctive relief vary among the circuits, but courts have begun to incorporate the four-factor test espoused by the Supreme Court in *eBay Inc. v. MercExchange, L.L.C.*, 547 U.S. 388 (2006) (a patent case involving permanent injunctive relief). In *Voice of the Arab World v. MDTV Medical News Now, Inc.*, 645 F.3d 26 (1st Cir. 2011), the court observed that the *eBay* test was thought to be based on "traditional equitable principles," and Lanham Act Section 34 required courts to abide by those principles when deciding whether to grant injunctive relief in Lanham Act cases, just as the Patent Act required courts to do when fashioning injunctive relief in patent cases. Moreover, the First Circuit found no obvious distinction between preliminary and permanent injunctions that would suggest confining the *eBay* test to the latter.

The *eBay* test calls for the plaintiff to demonstrate "(1) that it has suffered an irreparable injury; (2) that remedies available at law, such as monetary damages, are inadequate to compensate for that injury; (3) that, considering the balance of hardships between the plaintiff and defendant, a remedy in equity is warranted; and (4) that the public interest would not be disserved by a permanent injunction." In earlier cases, courts had elaborated slightly different tests. For example, in *GoTo.com, Inc. v. Walt Disney Co.*, 202 F.3d 1199 (9th Cir. 2000), the Ninth Circuit held that a plaintiff is entitled to a preliminary injunction in a trademark case when it demonstrates either (1) a combination of "probable success on the merits" and "the possibility of irreparable injury" or (2) the existence of "serious questions going to the merits" and that "the balance of hardships tips sharply in his favor." Some courts also had explicitly considered "the effect on the public interest." *See, e.g., American Greetings Corp. v. Dan-Dee Imports, Inc.*, 807 F.2d 1136 (3d Cir. 1986). In light of the *eBay* decision, it seems probable that courts will revisit and revise these standards when appropriate cases arise.

The analysis of the irreparable injury prong of the test has proven to be controversial in the wake of the *eBay* decision. Prior to *eBay*, courts in intellectual property cases had routinely held that if the plaintiff could show a likelihood of success on the merits of the case, the court would presume that there was an irreparable injury. After *eBay*, courts began to question whether such a rule was consistent with the *eBay* Court's approach, which seemed to eschew bright-line rules as being inconsistent with the practice of equity. In addition, in another case outside the intellectual property field, the Supreme Court had emphasized the importance of the irreparable harm criterion. *See Winter v. Natural Resources Defense Council, Inc.*, 555 U.S. 7 (2008) (criticizing courts for relying on a standard of "possible" irreparable harm). The court in *Voice of the Arab World* declined to reach the question of whether *eBay* and *Winter* affected the presumption of irreparable harm in trademark cases. However, in *Herb Reed Enters., LLC v. Fla. Entm't Mgmt., Inc.*, 736 F.3d 1239 (9th Cir. 2013), the court expressly jettisoned the presumption and insisted on evidence of irreparable harm going beyond mere conclusory statements. Although the matter remains controversial, plaintiffs in Lanham Act cases may find it more difficult to secure preliminary injunctive relief in future cases.

Unexplained delay in seeking preliminary relief is likely to be fatal to any argument of irreparable harm. *Wreal, LLC v. Amazon.com, Inc.*, 840 F.3d 1244 (11th Cir. 2016). This is a likely result whether or not the court applies a presumption of irreparable harm.

Mandatory vs. prohibitory preliminary injunctions. Preliminary injunctive relief is usually "prohibitory."

In a trademark case, this means that the injunctive relief suspends Lanham Act violations to preserve the status quo. In addition to prohibitions, injunctive relief may also include affirmative mandates. For example, the infringer may be required to turn over the infringing articles during the pendency of the litigation. The Second Circuit has suggested that if the injunction alters the status quo, it will be treated as a "mandatory injunction," rather than a purely "prohibitory injunction," and granted only if the plaintiff makes a higher showing, namely either (1) a clear or substantial showing of entitlement to the relief requested, or (2) a showing that extreme or very serious damage will result from the denial of preliminary relief. *See Tom Doherty Assocs. v. Saban Entm't*, 60 F.3d 27 (2d Cir. 1995).

2. PERMANENT INJUNCTIONS

Test for permanent injunctive relief. Although definitive rulings have yet to emerge, it appears that courts will apply the *eBay* four-factor test to determine the appropriateness of permanent injunctive relief in Lanham Act cases, and that courts will discard any presumption of irreparable harm in these cases. *See Oriental Financial Group, Inc. v. Cooperativa de Ahorro y Credito Oriental*, 832 F.3d 15 (1st Cir. 2016) (endorsing the use of the *eBay* factors to assess whether to grant permanent injunctive relief in a trademark infringement case); *La Quinta Worldwide LLC v. Q.R.T.M., S.A.*, 762 F.3d 867 (9th Cir. 2014) (same).

Scope of relief—the "safe distance" rule. In fashioning orders for injunctive relief, courts are likely to take into account not only the specific behavior that triggered Lanham Act liability, but also the court's interest in avoiding fresh litigation between the same parties over very similar subject matter. In view of that interest, some courts apply a "safe distance" rule when determining the appropriate scope of injunctive relief. For example, according to the Sixth Circuit, "a competitive business, once convicted of unfair competition in a given particular, should thereafter be required to keep a safe distance from the margin line—even if that requirement involves a handicap as compared with those who have not disqualified themselves." *Taubman Co. v. Webfeats*, 319 F.3d 770 (6th Cir. 2003). An injunction that prohibits an infringer from using a particular logo "or colorable imitations thereof" is sufficiently specific to satisfy the requirements of Rule 65(d) of the Federal Rules of Civil Procedure (which prescribes the required contents of injunction orders). *Scandia Down Corp. v. Euroquilt, Inc.*, 772 F.2d 1423 (7th Cir. 1985). "The court may require the [infringer] to choose a distinctively different mark rather than to hew so close to the line that the parties must interminably return to court to haggle about every mark." *Id.* Where an injunction uses the "colorable imitation" language and a dispute arises over whether the infringer's new mark is a colorable imitation (typically in the context of a contempt proceeding), a truncated confusion analysis is appropriate. The mark owner should not be required to offer a full-fledged likelihood of confusion case with arguments going to each confusion factor. *See Wolfard Glassblowing Co. v. Vanbragt*, 118 F.3d 1320 (9th Cir. 1997).

While the safe distance concept is well-accepted as a factor in determining the scope of injunctive relief (and in assessing whether an infringer should be held in contempt of such an order), mark owners occasionally have sought to incorporate a "safe distance" concept into the standard for initial liability, particularly in a case in which the parties have clashed in previous trademark disputes that resulted in infringement findings. In *PRL USA Holdings, Inc. v. United States Polo Ass'n Inc.*, 520 F.3d 109, 118–119 (2d Cir. 2008), the court rejected the mark owner's argument. The argument advanced the view that in light of the outcome of the prior litigation, the alleged infringer should be held to a "higher standard of conduct" than that which would have applied initially. This was problematic, according to the court, because it seemed to encourage a finding of liability even in the absence of a proper showing of likelihood of confusion. Similarly, in *John Allan Co. v. Craig Allen Co.*, 540 F.3d 1133 (10th Cir. 2008), the court stressed that the safe distance rule does not impose some legal duty on the trial court that forces the trial court to craft an injunction that covers some activities that do not even give rise to a likelihood of confusion. Instead, the safe distance rule is meant to guide the trial court in how carefully it should scrutinize the new mark of a prior infringer.

Affirmative mandates in permanent injunctions. Prohibitory permanent injunctions are perhaps the most common in trademark litigation, but, as with preliminary injunctions, permanent injunction orders may include other elements requiring the defendant to undertake various actions. For example, the defendant may be required to turn over infringing articles for destruction, or add labels or disclaimers to the defendant's products. Especially in false advertising cases, the injunctive relief may include a requirement for the defendant to distribute corrective advertising.

3. LACHES

The equitable doctrine of laches is accepted in U.S. trademark law as a limitation on Lanham Act remedies. The test for laches has two elements: (1) the plaintiff's delay in bringing suit must be unreasonable; and (2) the defendant was prejudiced by the delay. *See, e.g., Au-Tomotive Gold, Inc. v. Volkswagen of Am.*, 603 F.3d 1133 (9th Cir. 2010). To analyze whether delay is unreasonable, courts have tended to consider the most closely analogous state law statute of limitations. *Tandy Corp. v. Malone & Hyde*, 769 F.2d 362 (6th Cir. 1985), *cert. denied* 476 U.S. 1158 (1986). For example, in *Au-Tomotive Gold*, the court concluded that a three-year delay was unreasonable because it exceeded the relevant state statute of limitations. The court ruled that the delay triggered a presumption of laches.

As for the prejudice element of the laches test, courts may distinguish between a defendant's mere expenditures in promoting the infringing mark, and valuable investments that build up the mark as the identity of the defendant's business. The former is insufficient to establish prejudice; evidence of the latter is required. Where a defendant relied primarily on pay-per-click online advertisements that typically did not include the mark at issue, the court concluded that the defendant had not invested in building up brand recognition in its mark and thus had not suffered prejudice even though the plaintiff had delayed unreasonably in asserting its rights. *Internet Specialties West v. Milon-Digiorgio Enters., Inc.*, 559 F.3d 985 (9th Cir. 2009).

When a court finds that a defendant has satisfied the laches test, the court must then determine how laches should limit the plaintiff's remedies. In some early cases, the U.S. Supreme Court seemed to say that laches would eliminate claims for past monetary damages but would not necessarily preclude an injunction. *See, e.g., McLean v. Fleming*, 96 U.S. 245 (1878). Subsequent cases appear to stand for the proposition that laches could preclude the mark owner from receiving any relief, including an injunction against future infringement, if the equities run strongly against the mark owner. *See, e.g., Ancient Egyptian Arabic Order v. Michaux*, 279 U.S. 737 (1929) (laches precluded injunctive relief in a case involving lengthy delay and behavior by the plaintiff that could be construed as reflecting racial bias). Mere delay alone will not necessarily suffice to preclude injunctive relief. RESTATEMENT 3D OF UNFAIR COMPETITION § 30 cmt. e (1995). It appears that the effect of a laches finding will vary depending upon the circumstances. This is consistent with the equitable nature of the doctrine.

Laches is available in litigated matters, as the above discussion indicates. Indeed, effective in 1989, laches became available even as to incontestable registrations, when Congress added Section 33(b)(8) (now 33(b)(9)) to the list of statutory exceptions to incontestability.

Laches may also be available in *inter partes* proceedings, particularly in cancellation proceedings. Recall from the discussion in Chapter 5 that cancellation petitions generally must be brought within five years of registration, but that Section 14(3) provides that some grounds of cancellation can serve as the basis for a petition at any time—for example, genericness, or scandalousness/disparagement under Section 2(a). In cancellations based on these grounds, the owner of the mark that is targeted for cancellation might attempt to invoke laches against the cancellation petitioner, asserting that the petitioner delayed unreasonably in initiating the cancellation, causing the mark owner to suffer prejudice. Courts are split on whether laches should apply, with some courts taking the position that Section 14(3)'s authorization to cancel on the specified grounds "at any time" overrides the equitable doctrine of laches. *See Marshak v. Treadwell*, 240 F.3d 184 (3d Cir. 2001) (taking this view); *but see Bridgestone/Firestone Research Inc. v. Automobile Club de l'Ouest de la France*, 245 F.3d 1359 (Fed. Cir. 2001) (concluding that the laches argument should be available). The laches doctrine has been the subject of protracted litigation in the cancellation petitions brought by Native American petitioners against the National Football League's Washington Redskins. *See, e.g., Pro-Football, Inc. v. Harjo*, 567 F. Supp. 2d 46 (D.D.C. 2008) (granting the football team's motion for summary judgment invoking laches against the petitioners), *aff'd* 565 F.3d 880 (D.C. Cir. 2009), *cert. denied* 130 S.Ct. 631 (2009).

Some courts distinguish between laches and acquiescence. Whereas laches is associated with negligent or unintentional failures to protect one's trademark rights, acquiescence connotes intent. Acquiescence is "an equitable doctrine that permits the court to deny relief in an action for trademark infringement if the evidence shows that the owner of the mark has, through his words or conduct, conveyed his consent to the defendant's use of the mark." *Hyson USA, Inc. v. Hyson 2U, Ltd.*, 821 F.3d 935, 940 (7th Cir. 2016). Courts have sometimes articulated a three-part test for acquiescence: (1) the senior user actively represented that it would not assert its trademark rights; (2) the senior user's delay between this representation and assertion of its trademark rights was not excusable; and (3) the delay caused the defendant undue prejudice. *See, e.g., SunAmerica Corp. v. Sun Life Assurance Co.*, 77 F.3d 1325 (11th Cir. 1996).

The Lanham Act includes no statute of limitations or time limitation on damages. Thus, conflicts that have arisen in patent and copyright law between the equitable doctrine of laches and statutory limitations on damages will not carry over to trademark infringement cases. SCA Hygiene Prods. Aktiebolag v. First Quality Baby Prods., LLC, 137 S.Ct. 954 (2017) (patent); Petrella v. Metro-Goldwyn-Mayer, Inc., 134 S.Ct. 1962 (2014) (copyright).

B. MONETARY RELIEF

Although equitable relief is perhaps the most critical form of relief in typical Lanham Act cases, some cases do involve significant amounts of monetary damages to the mark owner. Lanham Act Section 35 provides several avenues for compensatory monetary awards in such circumstances.

A few threshold considerations must be satisfied in order for a mark owner to be entitled to claim monetary relief. First, if the requested relief is for actual damages, the mark owner must prove that there has been actual confusion or deception resulting from the Lanham Act violation at issue, as we have discussed in Chapter 7. *See, e.g., PPX Enterprises, Inc. v. Audiofidelity Enterprises, Inc.*, 818 F.2d 266 (2d Cir. 1987). Second, the mark owner must have complied with the marking requirements in Lanham Act Section 29 (or, alternatively, must show that the infringer had actual notice of the mark owner's claim of rights, as Section 29 specifies). Third, the case must not be one in which the defendant qualifies for one of the damages exemptions specified in Lanham Act Section 32— such as the damages exemption for innocent printers, for example. Fourth, the case must not be one in which the equitable doctrine of laches limits the damages recovery. Lanham Act § 35(a) (specifying that the damages award is made "subject to the principles of equity").

Subject to those caveats, a mark owner may claim actual damages under Lanham Act Section 35(a). That provision permits the award of monetary remedies in the form of (1) an award of defendant's profits; (2) any damages sustained by the plaintiff; and (3) the costs of the action. Some courts have articulated multi-factor tests to guide the process of awarding damages. For example, the Third, Fourth, and Fifth Circuits use the following factors:

> (1) whether the defendant had the intent to confuse or deceive, (2) whether sales have been diverted, (3) the adequacy of other remedies, (4) any unreasonable delay by the plaintiff in asserting his rights, (5) the public interest in making the misconduct unprofitable, and (6) whether it is a case of palming off.

See Synergistic Int'l LLC v. Korman, 470 F.3d 162 (4th Cir. 2006); *Banjo Buddies, Inc. v. Renosky*, 399 F.3d 168 (3d Cir. 2005); *Quick Techs., Inc. v. Sage Group PLC*, 313 F.3d 338 (5th Cir. 2002). This is a curious list that blends notions of compensation together with notions of deterrence, and also incorporates equitable considerations that would ordinarily be associated with the award of injunctive relief and the assessment of laches.

Where the plaintiff seeks to measure damages by way of the second category specified in Section

35(a)—the "damages sustained by the plaintiff"—the rules are relatively straightforward. The plaintiff must attempt to quantify its direct injury, perhaps by showing the amount of lost profits that it would have earned but for the defendant's infringement. *Lindy Pen Co., Inc. v. Bic Pen Corp.*, 982 F.2d 1400 (9th Cir. 1993).

Where proof of direct injury is difficult, plaintiff might instead opt to have damages measured by reference to *defendant's* profits, as authorized in the first category of damages set forth in Section 35(a). The plaintiff must establish the amount of defendant's gross sales attributable to the infringement with reasonable certainty, and the burden is then on the defendant to prove "all elements of cost or deduction claimed." Lanham Act § 35(a).

Although the statute does not explicitly impose a willfulness requirement, some appellate courts have imposed such a requirement for an award of infringer's profits. *See Fifty-Six Hope Rd. Music, Ltd. v. A.V.E.L.A., Inc.*, 778 F.3d 1059 (9th Cir. 2015); *Merck Eprova AG v. Gnosis S.p.A.*, 760 F.3d 247 (2d Cir. 2014). Other courts decline to apply such a requirement. *See Synergistic Int'l, LLC v. Korman*, 470 F.3d 162 (4th Cir. 2006); *Quick Techs., Inc. v. Sage Group PLC*, 313 F.3d 338 (5th Cir. 2002). Courts in the former group appear to be concerned with preventing windfalls to plaintiffs, particularly in cases in which the parties do not compete directly. Courts in the latter group tend to rely on the absence of an explicit willfulness requirement in Section

35(a), and the fact that Congress imposed an express willfulness requirement for awards damages for dilution violations. It appears that the willfulness requirement will remain controversial until the Supreme Court or Congress intervenes.

In *George Basch Co., Inc. v. Blue Coral, Inc.*, 968 F.2d 1532 (2d Cir. 1992), the court pointed out that even where willful deceptiveness is shown, the award of an accounting of defendant's profits would not be automatic. Instead, the statute instructs courts to act in accordance with the principles of equity. According to the court in *George Basch*, there were several factors to be taken into account in this exercise of equitable discretion: "(1) the degree of certainty that the defendant benefited from the unlawful conduct; (2) availability and adequacy of other remedies; (3) the role of a particular defendant in effectuating the infringement; (4) plaintiff's laches; and (5) plaintiff's unclean hands." Courts were to assess the relative importance of these factors in a given case and then determine whether, as a whole, the equities favored an award of an accounting.

Section 35(a) also provides for various enhancements to civil damages awards. The provision authorizes courts to increase damages up to three times actual damages "according to the circumstances of the case." In addition, the provision permits the court to award "reasonable attorney fees" to the prevailing party if the case is deemed exceptional.

The patent law includes an identical attorney fee provision, codified at 35 U.S.C. § 285. In *Octane*

Fitness, LLC v. Icon Health & Fitness, Inc., 134 S.Ct. 1749 (2014), the Supreme Court ruled that under that provision, "an 'exceptional' case is simply one that stands out from others with respect to the substantive strength of a party's litigating position (considering both the governing law and the facts of the case) or the unreasonable manner in which the case was litigated." *Id.* at 1756. The Court overruled the Federal Circuit's test, which had required a showing that a party acted in subjective bad faith in addition to bringing an objectively baseless claim. *Id.* A number of appellate courts have applied *Octane* in cases involving claims for attorney fees under Lanham Act Section 35(a). For example, in *SunEarth, Inc. v. Sun Earth Solar Power Co., Ltd.*, 839 F.3d 1179 (9th Cir. 2016) (en banc), the Ninth Circuit held that district courts analyzing request for attorney fees should "examine 'totality of the circumstances' to determine if case was exceptional, exercising equitable discretion in light of the nonexclusive factors, and using a preponderance of the evidence standard." *See also Baker v. DeShong*, 821 F.3d 620 (5th Cir. 2016); *Fair Wind Sailing, Inc. v. Dempster*, 764 F.3d 303 (3d Cir. 2014).

In an action involving "the use of a counterfeit mark [as defined elsewhere in the Lanham Act] in connection with the sale, offering for sale, or distribution of goods or services," the mark owner may elect an award of statutory damages in lieu of profits and actual damages. Lanham Act § 35(c). Permissible statutory damages range from $1,000 to $200,000, or, in cases of willful use of the counterfeit mark, up to $2 million, in both instances measured "per counterfeit mark per type of goods or services sold, offered for sale, or distributed, as the court considers just." Lanham Act § 35(c)(1), (2).

INDEX

References are to Pages

CAUSES OF ACTION
Lanham Act, 14–16

CONFUSION-BASED TRADEMARK LIABILITY THEORIES
Generally, 209
Actionable Use, 213
Actual Confusion, 239
Factors Analysis, 220
Factors Analysis as Applied, 230
Initial Interest Confusion, 248
Intent, 245
Mark Strength, 237
Post-Sale Confusion, 255
Reasonably Prudent Purchaser, 245
Relatedness of Goods, 243
Reverse Confusion, 259
Similarity of Marks, 231
Standard of Review, 229

COPYRIGHT
Interface with Trademark, 50–56
Right of Publicity, 383

COUNTERFEITING
Generally, 302
Civil Liability, 302–306
Criminal Liability, 306–308
Protection Against Counterfeit Imports, 309–310

CYBERSQUATTING
Generally, 293
Anticybersquatting Consumer Protection Agency (ACPA), 294–299

ICANN Uniform Domain Name Dispute Resolution Policy (UDRP), 299–300
Relationship Between UDRP and ACPA, 301–302

DILUTION
Generally, 273
Actual Association, 286
By Blurring, 281
By Tarnishment, 288
Elements, 276
Exclusions, 290
Fame Requirement, 279
Federal Registration as Bar, 292
Intent, 285
Nature of Defendant's Use, 281
Registration Context, 292
Remedies, 291
Similarity, 283
Strength, 285

DISTINCTIVENESS
Genericness, 30–39
Nonverbal Identifiers, 39–50
Secondary Meaning, 26–30
Spectrum, 21–26

FALSE ADVERTISING
Generally, 353
Causation and Injury, 369
Commercial Advertising or Promotion, 360
Elements of the Section 43(a)(1)(B) False Advertising Claim, 362
Evolution of Section 43(a) False Advertising Claims, 353
Falsity and Deception, 363
Materiality, 368
Remedies, 371
Standing, 357

FALSE AFFILIATION
Generally, 376
False Over-Attribution, 377
False Under-Attribution, 379

Section 43(a) False Affiliation Theories, 376

FUNCTIONALITY
  Generally, 57–59
Aesthetic Functionality Test as Applied, 80–85
Categories, 59
  Aesthetic, 60–61
Evidence from Utility Patents, 71–74
Evidence of Alternative Designs, 74–78
Modern Approach, 65–71
Predecessors to Modern Approach, 61–65
Utilitarian/Mechanical, 59–60
Utilitarian/Mechanical Functionality Test as Applied, 78–80

GEOGRAPHIC LIMITS ON TRADEMARK RIGHTS
  Generally, 167
Concurrent User Registration, 183
Extraterritorial Enforcement of U.S. Trademark Rights, 201
Junior Registrant vs. Senior User, 180
Limitations on Common Law Rights: *Tea Rose* Doctrine, 168
Limitations on Registered Rights: *Dawn Donut* Rule, 176
Senior Registrant v. Intermediate Junior User, 182
Territorial Nature of U.S. Trademarks Rights, 185
Well-Known Marks, 190

INDIRECT LIABILITY
  Generally, 264
Contributory Infringement, 265

NON-CONFUSION-BASED CLAIMS
  Generally, 273
Counterfeiting, 302
Cybersquatting, 293
Dilution, 273

NON-VERBAL IDENTIFIERS
  Generally, 39
Color, 42–43
Logos, 40–42
Scent, 49–50
Sound, 49–50
Trade Dress, 43–49

PERMISSIBLE USES OF ANOTHER'S TRADEMARK
Generally, 311
Descriptive Fair Use, 313
Good Faith, 321
Grey Market Goods, 338
In Dilution Actions, 328
Nominative Fair Use, 322
Parody, Art, or Speech 344
Reconditioned Goods, 335
Repackaged New Goods, 333

POST-REGISTRATION PROCESS
Generally, 139
Cancellation, 141
Incontestability and the Time Limit on Cancellation, 142
Renewal, 140

PRIORITY
Analogous Use, 106
Foreign Priority, 108
Tacking, 104
Unlawful Use as a Basis for Priority, 107

PURPOSE
Nature of Trademark Right, 1–6
Nature of Unfair Competition Law, 6–8
Overview, 9–17

REGISTRATION
Generally, 129
Application: Bases for Registration, 130
Examination, 134
Foreign Application, 131
Fraudulent Procurement, 134
Incontestability, 142
Madrid Protocol, 133
Opposition, 138
Procedural Aspects of Registration, 130
Publication, 138
Section 2 Bars to Registration, 145

REMEDIES
Generally, 401
Enhancements to Civil Damages Awards, 415
Equitable Remedies and Limitations, 401
False Advertising Cases, 371
Genericness Cases, 37
Innocent Printers or Publishers, 412
Laches, 408
Monetary Relief, 412
Permanent Injunction, 405
Preliminary Injunctions, 402
Right of Publicity Cases, 399
The Safe Distance Rule, 406

RIGHT OF PUBLICITY
Generally, 383
Commercial Purpose, 392
Common Law Jurisdictions, 394
Duration, 399
Jurisdiction, 398
Limitations, 392
Origin, 384
Overview of Elements, 387
Relationship with Copyright Law, 387
Remedies, 399

SECTION 2 BARS TO REGISTRATION
Generally, 145
Confusion, 163
Deceptiveness, 149
Descriptiveness, 165
Dilution, 166
Functionality, 165
Geographic Indications, 157
Geographically Descriptive Marks, 151
Government Insignia, 165
Name Marks, 158
Primarily Geographically Deceptively Misdescriptive Marks, 155
Scandalous/Disparaging Marks in Light of *Matal v. Tam*, 146

UNFAIR COMPETITION LAW
Relationship to Trademarks, 6–8

USE
Generally, 87
Actionable Use, 213
Actual Use, 90
Constructive Use, 99
Failure to Control Uses, 119
Foreign Use, 108
Identifying the User, 110
Non-Use, 116
Tacking, 104
Use as a Jurisdictional Prerequisite, 87
Use as a Prerequisite for Establishing Rights, 89
Use for the Benefit of Another, 110

VICARIOUS LIABILITY
Generally, 271